Acinemas

Acinemas

Lyotard's Philosophy of Film

Edited by Graham Jones and Ashley Woodward

EDINBURGH
University Press

Edinburgh University Press is one of the leading university presses in the UK. We publish academic books and journals in our selected subject areas across the humanities and social sciences, combining cutting-edge scholarship with high editorial and production values to produce academic works of lasting importance. For more information visit our website: edinburghuniversitypress.com

© editorial matter and organisation Graham Jones and Ashley Woodward, 2017
© the chapters their several authors, 2017

Edinburgh University Press Ltd
The Tun – Holyrood Road,
12(2f) Jackson's Entry,
Edinburgh EH8 8PJ

Typeset in 11/13 Adobe Garamond by
IDSUK (DataConnection) Ltd

A CIP record for this book is available from the British Library

ISBN 978 1 4744 1893 5 (hardback)
ISBN 978 1 4744 1895 9 (webready PDF)
ISBN 978 1 4744 1894 2 (paperback)
ISBN 978 1 4744 1896 6 (epub)

The right of Graham Jones and Ashley Woodward to be identified as the editors of this work has been asserted in accordance with the Copyright, Designs and Patents Act 1988, and the Copyright and Related Rights Regulations 2003 (SI No. 2498).

Contents

Acknowledgements — vii
Abbreviations — ix
Translators' Note — xi

I. Openings

1. Setting the Scene — 3
   Graham Jones and Ashley Woodward
2. Why Lyotard and Film? — 10
   Susana Viegas and James Williams
3. Cinema Lyotard: An Introduction — 17
   Jean-Michel Durafour

II. Lyotard's Essays on Film

4. Acinema — 33
   Jean-François Lyotard
5. The Unconscious as Mise-en-scène — 43
   Jean-François Lyotard
6. Two Metamorphoses of the Seductive in Cinema — 55
   Jean-François Lyotard
7. The Idea of a Sovereign Film — 62
   Jean-François Lyotard

III. Approaches and Interpretations

8. Imaginary Constructs? A Libidinal Economy of the Cinematographic Medium — 73
   Julie Gaillard

9. Lyotard and the Art of Seduction 87
   Keith Crome

10. Authorisation: Lyotard's Sovereign Image 102
    Peter W. Milne

IV. Applications and Extensions

11. Discourse, Figure, Suture: Lyotard and Cinematic Space 119
    Jon Hackett

12. On Dialogue as Performative Art Criticism 136
    Vlad Ionescu

13. Give Me a Sign: An Anxious Exploration of Performance on Film, Under Lyotard's Shadow 150
    Kiff Bamford

14. How Desire Works: A Lyotardian Lynch 163
    Graham Jones and Ashley Woodward

15. Aberrant Movement and Somatography in the Hysterical Comedies of Roméo Bosetti 180
    Lisa Trahair

Appendices

1. Lyotard's Film Work 197
   Claudine Eizykman and Guy Fihman

2. *Memorial Immemorial* 207

3. Filmography 214

4. Bibliography 215

Notes on Contributors 219
Index 222

Acknowledgements

This book began as a research project centred around a two-day conference, Acinemas: Aesthetics and Film in the Philosophy of Jean-François Lyotard, held at the University of Dundee, 7–8 May 2014. We would like to thank everyone who participated in the conference, and the Scots Philosophical Association and the School of Humanities at the University of Dundee for supporting it. Particular thanks are due to Peter W. Milne, who has not only contributed to the translations, written a chapter, and provided the basis for the Bibliography, but who suggested the initial idea from which this book has developed. Thanks are due to Amélie Berger Soraruff for many helpful suggestions on the translations. Thanks also to Jon Roffe. And of course, we would like to thank everyone who contributed to this book.

Specific thanks are due to the following people and organisations for permission to include the indicated material:

Jean-Michel Durafour and Toni d'Angel, editor of *La Furia Umana*, for 'Cinema Lyotard: An Introduction'. Dolores Lyotard for 'Acinema', 'The Unconscious as Mise-en-scène', 'Two Metamorphoses of the Seductive in Cinema', 'The Idea of a Sovereign Film' and '*Memorial Immemorial*'. Paisley N. Livingston for permission to include, as well as to modify, his translation of 'Acinema'. The Center for 21st Century Studies at the University of Wisconsin-Milwaukee for 'The Unconscious as Mise-en-scène'. Claudine Eizykman and Guy Fihman for 'Lyotard's Film Work'. Jean-Louis Deotté for '*Memorial Immemorial*'. Ken McMullen for the still from *Ghost Dance*. The National Film Board of Canada for the image from *The Metamorphosis of Mr Samsa* and Warner Bros. for the still from *Inception*. And finally, Cinédoc Paris Films Coop for the images from *L'Autre scène* and *Mao Gillette*.

Grateful acknowledgement is made for permission to reproduce material previously published elsewhere. Every effort has been made to trace the copyright holders, but if any have been inadvertently overlooked, the publisher will be pleased to make the necessary arrangements at the first opportunity.

Abbreviations

Abbreviations used to refer to works by Jean-François Lyotard

Ac   'Acinema', this volume.
CA   *The Confession of Augustine*, trans. Richard Beardsworth, Stanford: Stanford University Press, 2000.
D   *The Differend: Phrases in Dispute*, trans. Georges Van Den Abbeele, Manchester: Manchester University Press, 1988.
DF   *Discourse, Figure*, Minneapolis: University of Minnesota Press, 2011.
DP   *Des Dispositifs pulsionnels*, Paris: Union Général d'Editions, 1973.
DT   *Duchamp's TRANS/formers*, trans. Ian McLeod, Venice, CA: Lapis Press, 1990.
DW   *Driftworks*, ed. Roger McKeon, New York: Semiotext(e), 1984.
HJ   *Heidegger and 'the jews'*, trans. Andreas Michel and Mark S. Roberts, Minneapolis: University of Minnesota Press, 1990.
IN   *The Inhuman: Reflections on Time*, trans. Geoffrey Bennington and Rachel Bowlby, Cambridge: Polity Press, 1991.
ISF   'The Idea of a Sovereign Film', this volume.
KA   *Karel Appel: A Gesture of Colour*, trans. Vlad Ionescu and Peter W. Milne, Leuven: Leuven University Press, 2009.
LAS   *Lessons on the Analytic of the Sublime*, trans. Elizabeth Rottenberg, Stanford: Stanford University Press, 1994.
LE   *Libidinal Economy*, trans. Iain Hamilton Grant, London: Athlone, 1993.
LR   *The Lyotard Reader*, ed. Andrew Benjamin, Oxford: Basil Blackwell, 1989.
LRG   *The Lyotard Reader and Guide*, ed. Keith Crome and James Williams, Edinburgh: Edinburgh University Press, 2006.
MP   *Misère de la philosophie*, Paris: Galilée, 2000.

MT1   *Miscellaneous Texts I: Aesthetics and Theory of Art*, ed. Herman Parret, Leuven: Leuven University Press, 2012.
MT2   *Miscellaneous Texts II: Contemporary Artists*, ed. Herman Parret, Leuven: Leuven University Press, 2012.
P   *Peregrinations: Law, Form, Event*, New York: Columbia University Press, 1988.
PC   *The Postmodern Condition: A Report on Knowledge*, trans. Geoff Bennington and Brian Massumi, Manchester: Manchester University Press, 1984.
PF   *Postmodern Fables*, trans. Georges Van Den Abbeele, Minneapolis: University of Minnesota Press, 1997.
PW   *Jean-François Lyotard: Political Writings*, trans. Bill Readings and Kevin Paul, Minneapolis: University of Minnesota Press, 1993.
RP   *Rudiments païens: genre dissertatif*, Paris: Unions générale d'éditions, 1977.
TM   'Two Metamorphoses of the Seductive in Cinema', this volume.
TP   *Toward the Postmodern*, ed. Robert Harvey and Mark S. Roberts, Atlantic Highlands, NJ: Humanities Press, 1993.
UM   'The Unconscious as Mise-en-scène', this volume.
WP   *What to Paint?*, ed. Herman Parret, Leuven: Leuven University Press, 2012.
WPh   *Why Philosophize?*, trans. Andrew Brown, Cambridge: Polity, 2013.

Translators' Note

As far as possible we have tried to maintain a consistency of terminology in the translations of the four essays by Lyotard on film. The following are brief explanations of some of our terminological choices.

Cinéaste. See *Metteur en scène*.

Découpage. 'Editing' is a common but misleading translation. In his original translation of 'Acinema', Paisley Livingston translates it as 'the final script and the spatio-temporal synthesis of the narration'. This captures something of the complexity of the term as it is used in French film theory, but for the sake of parsimony we have preferred 'scene organisation'. For a detailed discussion of the various meanings of this word and its history and uses in French film theory, see Timothy Barnard's extensive note in his translation of André Bazin, *What is Cinema?* (Montreal: Caboose, 2009).

Déroulement. We have translated this as 'progression', and have marked the French in brackets. When 'The Unconscious as Mise-en-scène' at one point uses terms such as 'unroll' and 'rolling along', it is presumably translating variations of *déroulement*. We have chosen 'progression' because it suggests a teleology at work in the narrative structure, which is sometimes at stake when this term is used. Nonetheless, it should be borne in mind that *déroulement* also implies an 'unfolding' in the way that in English we describe a plot as unfolding, as well as what is sometimes called 'continuity' in the context of film. In such a context, it also connotes the way a movie reel or the spools of a video cassette 'unroll'. This variety of meanings is difficult to capture in any one English term.

Dispositif. While this term has typically been translated in Lyotard's writings as 'set-up' or (less often) 'apparatus' or 'device', we have chosen to leave it untranslated to reflect the familiarity it has now attained in English-language scholarship, for example in relation to the works of philosophers such as Michel Foucault, Gilles Deleuze and Giorgio Agamben. On the relevance of this term for contemporary film theory, see Adrian Martin, 'Turn the Page: From *Mise en scène* to *Dispositif*', *Screening the Past* 31 (2011), http://www.screeningthepast.com/2011/07/turn-the-page-from-mise-en-scene-to-dispositif.

Étrange. In 'The Idea of a Sovereign Film' we have translated this as 'uncanny', since this seems to capture the sense of the *unheimlich* that seems to be in play better than the more mundane 'strange'. However, it should be borne in mind that Lyotard is not using this term in the technical sense of Freud's uncanny, at least not in any straightforward way, and his specific comments about psychoanalysis in the essay would need to be taken into account in any interpretation.

Metteur en scène. We have translated this as 'director', in distinction to *réalisateur* and *cinéaste*, both of which we have translated as 'filmmaker'.

Mise-en-scène. While Paisley Livingston had 'film direction', we have chosen to leave this well-known term untranslated, in order to maintain consistency with 'The Unconscious as Mise-en-scène'. It also removes some of the strangeness and potentially misleading nature of phrases such as 'film direction is not an artistic activity' in Livingston's original version.

Mise hors scène. This acts as a section title of 'Acinema', which Livingston translated as 'Direction: putting in, and out of, scene'. We have substituted the more parsimonious 'putting out of scene' for this term.

Réalisateur. See *Metteur en scène*.

Récit, raconter, narratif, narration. These terms can all be translated by variations of the English 'narration'. We have marked the difference in parentheses at key points.

Peter W. Milne and Ashley Woodward

PART I

Openings

CHAPTER 1

Setting the Scene

Graham Jones and Ashley Woodward

> I adore films, and just about any kind of films.
> Jean-François Lyotard (1985)

We are pleased to present here a collection of resources for working on Lyotard and film. Jean-François Lyotard was the most significant aesthetician and philosopher of art of the poststructuralist generation. As Susana Viegas and James Williams point out in the next chapter, while his explicit contributions to film-philosophy are small in comparison to Gilles Deleuze's magisterial two-volume study, they nevertheless take on greater significance when understood in the context of a much vaster and wider-ranging meditation on the arts available in his other writings. In French, Lyotard's contributions to film have been explored in Jean-Michel Durafour's *Jean-François Lyotard: questions au cinéma* (2009), the most significant study to have appeared so far. We are pleased to present a translation of this most important author's work as an introduction to the themes of this volume. In addition, Lyotard's approach to cinema is distinguished by his own practical experiments with the medium, largely unknown outside of France. Durafour introduces this dimension of Lyotard's work, and it is further explained here (in Appendix 1) by those most qualified to do so: Claudine Eizykman and Guy Fihman, two filmmakers with whom Lyotard worked.

Lyotard has already received some significant interest in Anglophone scholarship for his work on film, but so far this has been restricted in two ways: it has almost exclusively considered only two of his four essays on film (the two previously available in English translation), and it has generally proposed the significance of his work only for limited areas: experimental film in particular, but also comedy (Trahair 2005; 2008), spectacle (Knox 2013) and horror (Mee 2016). This volume makes available for the first time the full range of Lyotard's main writings on film to Anglophone scholars. It also presents a collection of essays which explore the potential of these writings for a deep and broad impact on the philosophy and theory of film.[1]

Many of the contributions in this volume serve very well to introduce Lyotard's philosophy of film, to situate it in relation to film-philosophy and criticism more generally, and to explain the context in which Lyotard wrote about and made several of his own experimental films. Instead of repeating such ground, we will limit this initial chapter to explaining the architectonic of the volume, so that the reader may better orient him or herself to its reading, and to giving some background to Lyotard's philosophy for those approaching his work for the first time.

The texts in this book are grouped into five sections. The first contains essays that are all introductory in nature, and provide an orientation to what follows. The second section, which in some senses constitutes the 'core' of the book, collects Lyotard's four main essays on film. Two of these – 'Two Metamorphoses of the Seductive in Cinema' and 'The Idea of a Sovereign Film' – are published here for the first time in English translation. The most well-known of the four essays, 'Acinema', has been slightly modified from its original translation in the interests of imposing a degree of continuity regarding technical terms and expressions. Unfortunately it was not possible for us to do this with the remaining essay, 'The Unconscious as Mise-en-scène', as we were not able to locate a French original. (Its first and only publication was in an English translation by Joseph Maier, which we reproduce here.)

Lyotard was the antithesis of the philosopher who establishes a position and then spends a career defending it. He wrote like a thinker 'on the run', his views rapidly changing. Moreover, he consciously multiplied the genres in which he wrote. Together, these features make his work both difficult to approach and richly rewarding for those who take the time and care to do so. Since the four main essays on film collected here span a number of changes in Lyotard's theoretical outlook, some introductory comments will be helpful in orienting the reader.

Lyotard's first theoretical interventions were in the Marxist vein: in the 1950s and '60s he was a member of the radical leftist movements Socialisme ou Barbarie (Socialism or Barbarism) and Pouvoir Ouvrir (Workers' Power). After losing faith in revolutionary politics, Lyotard began to see the art world as the barometer of social reality and a site of political activism. His doctoral dissertation *Discourse, Figure* (1971) staged a confrontation between three of the major trends in aesthetics and art criticism in France in this period: phenomenology, structuralism and psychoanalysis. He conceived the book – an exploration of the nature of the visual image and the aesthetic effect more generally – as a prolegomena to a critique of ideology. This critique was never forthcoming in a fully developed way, but we see it emerge in the early work in experimental film described by Eizykman and Fihman in their contribution to this volume.

Moreover, Lyotard gives a good indication of this approach in the following passages from a 1970 text, 'Notes on the Critical Function of the Work of Art', where he makes explicit reference to film. These passages are worth quoting as an invaluable insight into this early approach to film, and as a supplement to the more developed essays presented here. First, Lyotard explains how film can serve an ideological function:

> It is obvious that the image – notably in cinema – most often does not function as an image, i.e. as something that belongs to this sort of intermediary scene and sense that are not the real scene or the actual sense of reality, but that it begins to function as a scene in which my desire is caught and comes to fulfillment. This can happen, for example, in the form of a projection into the characters or the situations staged by cinema or, in the case of so-called erotic images, to the extent that the roles presented can directly find a place in my own fantasizing or yet again, more subtly, when the film's cutting and editing as well catch my desire in their net, also fulfilling it, no longer from the point of view of the image itself, but through the organization of the narrative. (DW 71)

Lyotard then indicates how cinema can, on the other hand, act as a critique of ideology:

> Take the example of a widely distributed film: *Je t'aime, je t'aime* [dir. Alain Resnais, 1968]. A film of fiction. The subject: a man, who attempted suicide, is taken in hand by a group of scientists who think they can make man go back into the past. The film was very well received. What is truly astonishing is the articulation of the flash-backs. A real deconstruction of normal editing, which respects the spatio-temporal frameworks that are those of the secondary process, of reality-testing, is operated. What one is dealing with here is a total deconstruction of sequence. The subject finds himself in different time periods, and even the recurrence of the same scene from the past serves to deconstruct it. By inserting the whole thing in a very connoted science fiction context, Resnais succeeds in making it acceptable to a public that, in general, goes to the cinema to 'forget,' in effect to find itself again, that is to say, not to look at the pictures, but to fulfill its own desires through them. I believe that Resnais obliges the public to stop fantasizing. The spectator finds himself in the reversing, critical function of the work and his desire collides with the screen, because the screen is treated as a screen and not as a window. In the case of this film, the critical reversal is brought about by its cutting and editing. The work is the most difficult to do as far as the cinema, mass medium par excellence, is concerned. The cinema belongs to 'culture,' and three-fourths of

its function consists in stirring up and in recovering phantasy by having it find fulfillment through the screen, by putting people in a situation of day-dreaming. The cinema – place of contact with the proletariat – is where certain things can be done: turning the spectator's attention around by reversing the space of representation and obliging him to unfulfill his desire is a revolutionary function. (DW 75–6)

The first of Lyotard's essays on film, 'Acinema' – while evolving from this early experimental work and published alongside essays by others involved in this filmic work of ideology critique – is already guided by his next theoretical phase, most fully expressed in his second major book, *Libidinal Economy*. In this phase Lyotard may be seen as a representative of that French amalgamation of Nietzsche, Freud and Marx typified by Deleuze and Guattari's *Anti-Oedipus*. This book much influenced Lyotard and arguably galvanised his drift away from revolutionary Marxism towards the analysis of the social economy of desire and the affirmation of libidinal intensities as a political alternative. Now, the idea of ideology is rejected on Nietzschean grounds: it suggests that there is a truth of social relations behind the distortions imposed by the capitalist mode of production. 'Acinema' proposes a view of film as continuous with society, where what is at stake is not the 'truth' of images, but their relative intensity in an economy of representations and affects. While the popular film *Joe* (dir. John G. Avildsen, 1970) provides one of the most striking examples here, the essay is predominantly critical of mainstream, commercial cinema, and celebrates underground, experimental film, citing filmmakers such as Hans Richter, Gianfranco Baruchello and Viking Eggeling.

After *Libidinal Economy*, Lyotard underwent what was probably his most surprising and dramatic shift of theoretical perspective and style, from the unrestrained delirium of libidinal intensities to the spare, formal analysis of the pragmatics of language (from Nietzsche, Freud and Marx to the sophists, Kant and Wittgenstein). His next essay on film, 'The Unconscious as Mise-en-scène', is perhaps one of the most transitional in his entire oeuvre, spanning as it does a brief reiteration of some of the themes from *Discourse, Figure* (especially the chapter 'Fiscourse Digure: The Utopia Behind the Scenes of the Phantasy') regarding the nature of the unconscious and desire in relation to art, to his first invocation of the term 'postmodern'. Notably, this essay was presented for the forum on 'Performance in Postmodern Culture' at the Center for 20th Century Studies, University of Wisconsin-Milwaukee, in 1976, and the literary and cultural critic Ihab Hassan – who also presented a paper – is referenced as a source for this term. Lyotard develops it in his own way, however, suggesting that postmodernism in the arts concerns the multiplication of perspectives, rather than the revealing or concealing of a truth. The film discussed to elaborate this theme is a classic of underground cinema, Michael Snow's *La Région centrale* (1971).

Perspectivism is a Nietzschean theme, and Lyotard had devoted a lecture course to Nietzsche and the sophists in 1975, exploring the idea of perspectivism in the Ancient Greek teachers of rhetoric who were so much reviled by the philosophers. The analysis of the pragmatics of language which Lyotard studied with the sophists, with the Ancient Greek philosophers, and with recent philosophers such as Wittgenstein explicitly becomes the theoretical framework for his next essay on film, 'Two Metamorphoses of the Seductive in Cinema'. He announces this perspective quite clearly: 'We no longer scan the depths of desire and pleasure. We stick to the categories of linguistic pragmatics' (TM 56). Notably, this essay is roughly contemporaneous with what remains Lyotard's best-known (though arguably unrepresentative) book, *The Postmodern Condition*. The theme, seduction – and how it might be avoided in filmic effects – resonates with the earlier concerns with ideology critique, though elaborated in different terms. The films discussed are primarily Francis Ford Coppola's *Apocalypse Now* (1979) and, quite briefly, the works of Hans-Jürgen Syberberg.

The last of Lyotard's essays devoted to film, 'The Idea of a Sovereign Film', dates from 1995, and the last decade of his life and work. His work in this period is not so easily categorised, and has in general received less critical attention. Neither psychoanalysis nor linguistic pragmatics are primary theoretical references here. Instead, there is the invocation of Kant (though not of the aesthetic of the sublime), typical of Lyotard from the 1980s; of Bataille, to whose works Lyotard returned during this period; and to a critical reconsideration of Merleau-Ponty, an intermittent concern throughout his writings in aesthetics, but one also particularly characteristic of this late period. Perhaps the most notable fact about this essay is that it marks a clear departure from the focus on experimental cinema which dominates the aesthetics of the earlier essays, and further develops familiar thematic concerns in order to encompass realist, narrative, mainstream cinema. As such, it constitutes a very significant extension of Lyotard's philosophy of film, and one which deserves to be finally available in English.

The third section of this book, 'Approaches and Interpretations', collects essays which are primarily exegetical, and which help us to understand in more depth and detail Lyotard's often dense, sometimes obscure, yet always rich writings. The chapters in the fourth section, 'Applications and Extensions', are more exploratory, and range beyond Lyotard's writings themselves to connect their themes with a variety of topics, applying them to films and directors Lyotard doesn't himself write about, comparing his views with those of others, and examining his philosophy of film from alternative angles.

The last section, the Appendices, aims to provide information about Lyotard and film not presented in thorough detail elsewhere. The first section presents a translation of an essay by Claudine Eizykman and Guy Fihman which provides an overview of the practical dimension of Lyotard's engagements with film, along with valuable explanations of the themes and techniques that characterised the experimental films Lyotard was involved in making. Appendix 2 supplements this essay with the synopsis for a later film project which they do not mention, *Memorial Immemorial*, which Lyotard proposed but which was not produced. The third appendix gives a concise summary of Lyotard's filmography, while the fourth gives a bibliography of writings by and on Lyotard and film.

While it has taken quite some time for Lyotard's philosophy of film to be made available in the English-speaking world, we believe its current presentation with this volume is in fact very timely. The last decade has seen an exponential growth of interest in what has become known as 'film-philosophy', developing from a popular interest in Deleuze's *Cinema* books, and centring on the journal and conference of the same name. This signals a current appetite for the intersection of philosophy and film. Moreover, the specific approach of Deleuze's colleague at Vincennes to these themes resonates with a number of currently prevailing interests in the arts and humanities. While Lyotard's work was of course first taken up in the Anglophone world under the banner of postmodernism, much of it is in fact strongly opposed to the 'culturalism' with which that term was typically associated. Instead, Lyotard's concerns are often closer to several key themes on which the accent has begun to fall in much contemporary research. These include affect, matter, and a concern with 'the real' (which is not common sense or empirical 'reality'). Jean-Michel Durafour's chapter indicates ways that Lyotard's work on film can, for example, contribute to current developments in materialist aesthetics. Demonstrating the timeliness of Lyotard's work from a different angle, Jon Hackett's application of his notion of the figural to digital film and animation in his chapter demonstrates the usefulness of Lyotardian concepts for newer modes of filmmaking. We hope, then, that this introduction of the full range of Lyotard's work in philosophy of film will contribute to the current context and spur new work in cinema studies, in film-philosophy, and indeed perhaps also in the practice of film.

NOTE

1. A similar project has previously been undertaken in Italian: 'L'acinema di Lyotard', a special issue of the journal *Aut Aut* 338 (2008), ed. Antonio Costa and Raoul Kirchmayr. See Appendix 4 for details of specific papers.

REFERENCES

Durafour, Jean-Michel (2009), *Jean-François Lyotard: questions au cinéma. Ce que le cinéma se figure*, Paris: PUF.
Knox, Simone (2013), 'Eye Candy for the Blind: Re-introducing Lyotard's Acinema into Discourses on Excess, Motion, and Spectacle in Contemporary Hollywood', *New Review of Film and Television Studies* 11:3, pp. 1–16.

Lyotard, Jean-François (1985), 'A Conversation with Jean-François Lyotard'. Interview with Bernard Blistène, *Flash Art*, 121, pp. 32–9.

Mee, Sharon Jane (2016), 'A Terrifying Spectatorship: Jean-François Lyotard's Dispositif and the Expenditure of Intensities in Steven Kastrissios's *The Horseman*', *Philament* 21, pp. 19–44.

Trahair, Lisa (2005), 'Figural Vision: Freud, Lyotard, and Early Cinematic Comedy', *Screen* 46:2, pp. 175–94.

Trahair, Lisa (2008), *The Comedy of Philosophy: Sense and Nonsense in Early Cinematic Slapstick*, Albany: SUNY Press.

CHAPTER 2

Why Lyotard and Film?

Susana Viegas and James Williams

Does Lyotard have a significant place in the philosophy of film? He has written intriguing short pieces on film, but they are only a small sample among many more important essays on other subjects. The cinema pieces show neither particularly acute interpretations of film, nor great conceptual invention. None of his books are on film and none of them include a sustained discussion of cinema. Yet, he is one of the foremost writers on art and aesthetics of the twentieth century, renewing important concepts such as the postmodern and the sublime, while coining new ones like the figural and the *differend*. Influential writers on film, such as D. N. Rodowick, Jean-Michel Durafour and Jacques Rancière have written at length on Lyotard, critically demonstrating the value of his philosophical and political ideas. To take their works further, this volume brings together Lyotard's writings on film, and critical assessments by film and art theorists and philosophers. Their studies allow us to ask and begin to answer the sceptical question: why Lyotard and film?

Lyotard is not alone in having skimmed over cinema. Despite its newfound passion for film, philosophy has not always been in love with moving images. It is quite a recent relationship. Philosophy of film requires an interest in the moving image, something that Lyotard broaches in his early essay 'Acinema'. Traditionally, philosophy has shown greater interest in the image that does not move: the image that represents something else, that tells truths and sometimes misreports, rather than the image that flickers fleetingly only to disappear in favour of the next. Many twentieth-century philosophers (Wittgenstein in particular[1]) have been interested in cinema as form of life and as entertainment, using it as an imaginative exercise, more easily associated with a dream-like experience or practical experiment than pure philosophical effort. In 1936, Sartre published a book devoted to the systematic, historical and philosophical study of images and thought (Sartre 2012), but, regrettably, he 'takes into account every type of image except the cinematic image' (Deleuze 1995: 47). In the early part of the twentieth century, although there was undoubtedly a curiosity about this new art form, there was also a general philosophical devaluation of film, matched by the lack of a consistent philosophical study of the moving image. During the 1970s and 1980s, however, Cavell and Deleuze undertook the systematic study of the philosophical significance of films. Importantly, they would not confine themselves to producing a mere philosophy of art – in the sense that a movie would be used to illustrate a certain philosophical idea or a certain argument, say ethical or political. Instead, they allowed film to have a strong effect on philosophical praxis.

The classic works of these film-philosophers, most notably Cavell's *The World Viewed* and Deleuze's *Cinema 1* and *Cinema 2*, have no parallel in recent philosophical film studies, film theory, or aesthetics. But what about Lyotard's writing? What could be considered Lyotard's major philosophical work on cinema? It is strange to give importance to the relationship between Lyotard and moving images when, in his writings on the arts, his comments about cinema (or about audio-visual images in general) are scarce compared to his deep and influential studies of other arts (painting and theatre foremost among them). In the case of cinema, however, the echoes of his thoughts greatly surpass the number of comments directly addressing cinematic art (as well as sporadic references to films). Nonetheless, his name is absent from the majority of anthologies and introductory books published on film and philosophy. When mentioned he is reduced to brief references.[2] To fill this gap, it is important to understand the nature of this echo, of how Lyotard's philosophy and aesthetics resonate with cinema without spending much time discussing film directly.

In answer to questions about Lyotard's influence, his four main essays on the moving image (including his last conference paper on cinema[3]), collected in this volume, are key to a better understanding of how his ideas on modern philosophy of art might inspire an aesthetics of film. Lyotard's concepts such as 'acinema', 'the figural' and 'the sublime' have had a resilient impact on recent continental film-philosophers and aesthetic theories. In this vein, we would argue that the figural, far more than acinema, is the stronger concept to have drifted from the other arts into his philosophical analysis of the cinema (see, for example, Brenez's (2011) figural analysis of the difference between seeing and saying). The idea of the figural, taken from *Discourse, Figure*, should be seen as ancestor to the idea of acinema. The event of a figural interruption to discourse is the model for acinema's rupture with the conventions of film. This argument is about conceptual influence. But what about influence over the full scene of film theory? And is this influence mutual? More precisely, in light of the contributions collected here, how should we delineate and define Jean-François Lyotard's place in aesthetics and philosophy of art, and more specifically in philosophy of film? Where should film be placed in his thought? Is it central, or marginal?

The first work by Lyotard addressing moving images appears in the 1970s, a decade dominated by film theories based on Lacanian psychoanalysis, structuralism, semiotics and Marxist film theory. More than reading films within these theoretical paradigms, philosophy of film is concerned with general questions of scepticism, of knowing and doubting the world through cinema. It is concerned with the philosophical interest of film as thinking. It seeks to define the role and nature of cinema in relation to other forms of art, most often around its ontological and temporal paradoxes. Rather than revealing the truth hidden beneath each image, read from within the paradigm of psychoanalytic film theory, today's cinematic analyses prefer to follow a network of many different 'circles' within a post-continental-post-analytic philosophical approach. Following the path of Lyotard's own philosophical interests, film theory has entered into post-Kantian philosophical debate, not only as regards artistic and aesthetic experience, but also in terms of ethical and socio-political pragmatism, as a self-transformative experience that engages the viewer in a perceptual, intellectual and philosophical activity. This explains in part why Lyotard's work is rich in references for reflection on film. He has given a conceptual and sense-based vocabulary to this post-Kantian moment; notably in shifting the sublime, the event, the ethical, and ideas of political hiatus and interruption, to centre stage. It is not the organised flow of movement and its conditions that matter, but rather the breaks in flow and resistances to ordered conditions. This is exactly what Lyotard saw in avant-garde cinema.

Recently, philosophers of film such as Badiou, Rancière and Agamben have renewed the ethical and political engagement of contemporary film studies. Although film is not discussed in his 1974 *Libidinal Economy*, we find a sketch for a libidinal economy of cinema in 'Acinema', in which Lyotard presents a distinction between cinema (mainstream films) and acinema (experimental and avant-garde films). We would also argue that *Libidinal Economy* is itself in many of its most emblematic moments unusually cinematic for a work of philosophy; notably, in its initial lingering on the unwrapping of a body, in the various dramatic scenes of discombobulation by labyrinth, and perhaps also in its picturing of sexual exchange, money and desire chiming surprisingly with post-crisis Hollywood high-finance films. By considering the division between cinema and acinema as time-based, he divides the latter into two distinct *dispositifs* that he borrows from his philosophy of art, especially from the aesthetic divide between representation and anti-representation, between narrative and figural anti-discourse. Lyotard distinguishes the 'tableau vivant' (extreme immobility) and 'abstraction' (extreme mobility) as the two opposite ways of analysing acinema. This aesthetics of film, concerned with the gesture of the work, differentiates cinema from acinema by taking into account the temporal economy of images and sound, as well as sensuous and affective qualities of films, rather than an intellectualised system of moving images, or an analysis of the images' representational content, or a study of the processes of filmmaking. The turn towards affect and stasis against narrative turns out to have been one of the longest-running themes of his philosophy. He teaches us to be aware, but also wary, of the apparatus hidden behind the apparent naturalness of narrative. Lyotard enjoins us to fight against the results – the lessons – of resolutions in plot and drama so essential to the propaganda of everyday normality and consensus.

Running in parallel to Lyotard's own philosophical and political development, the aesthetics of film dates back to the peak of Marxist theory and the proliferation of debates between narrative and non-narrative experimental films. Narrative films were considered pre-eminently political, in the sense that the filmmaking process had to deal with representation and the critique of economics and politics on grand and personal scales over periods of social conflict and contradiction. In order to undo the hegemony of the plotline and lesson, of the flow of film, Lyotard argues that all moving elements in a film (both audio and visual) are submitted to a consideration of selection and elimination, without which the final cinematographic object would be an assemblage of perfect and clear images along with imperfect and unclear ones. According to the practice of filmmaking, surrounding mess should be effaced in favour of the purity, the noiselessness, of clean image flow. Lyotard is concerned with the manner and reasons behind the question of which moving elements are selected and which ones eliminated. More radically, he asks why such a choice should take place at all. As ever in his philosophical work, where the underlying motive is always political and ethical, the driving concern is to reveal the political and to render it ethical. By proposing the concept of acinema, he is struggling against a political economy of production-consumption (the law of value that rules the 'which' and the 'why' of the productive process). His claim is for a paradoxical *jouissance* of sterile moments, which he compares to the evanescence of pyrotechnic displays. It is important that the image should go up in smoke after capturing our senses, rather than flow into a reassuring result, tamed, and remaining to be exchanged in markets of ideas and values. In contrast with Žižek's Hegelianism, for example, Lyotard always resisted investment in a combination of interpretation, resolution and judgement. Like the later sublime event, the image of acinema is the last ethical call to resist capitalist exchange and surplus value and to re-intensify the arts without subjecting them to another metanarrative of salvation and redemptive truth over time. The interesting question is not whether this ethical turn is possible, since there is plenty of evidence from avant-garde film that it is. The deep question is whether film is any different, any worse or better, than the other arts at this ethical work of resistance.

Again, consistent with Lyotard's wider philosophical interests and the development of his thought around *The Differend*, perhaps part of the answer can be drawn from a study of time where, following Deleuze (and Guattari) – as Lyotard often does when he works on film – cinema takes on the role of the art of temporality *par excellence*. In a temporal economic reading of the process of economic exchange and consumption in cinema, we might say that in the sterile moments of acinema there is neither a 'before' (production) nor an 'after' (consumption). Instead, there is only the 'presenting present' (IN 59), the 'not yet' or 'no longer' present. The flow of film is halted in a present that renounces its past and foregoes its future. This is the paradoxical value of sterility for Lyotard. It is the moment that expresses the inexpressible, that presents the unpresentable, and that creates a sense for timelessness. If mainstream narrative and representational cinema aim at ordering time and movements, within an economic perspective of the film industry and production (the minimum resources for the highest effects, leaving no waste behind), in acinema we find the power of those films that synthesise both spatial and temporal ordering in the present as abyss, rather than over time as formative narrative and medium of exchange. Acinema therefore responds to the need to create sounds and images just for the sake of '*il y a*' or 'it is', for the sake of an event outside of time and of sensations for themselves rather than for judgement and exchange. In acinema, sterile movements are not eliminated or avoided. They therefore escape the dominance of mise-en-scène techniques that outline narrative linearity. Drawing from his long-standing interest in hyperrealism in painting (in Jacques Monory for example), Lyotard cites the example of the hyperrealistic helicopter scene in Coppola's *Apocalypse Now* (1979), which breaks with realism and with 'seduction' (TM). The tableaux vivants of the scene interfere with our conditioning towards the real and hence interrupt two flows of realism: the flow of the film as realist representation and the flow of the real as smooth and well-ordered unfolding over time. We become caught in the tableaux, unable to move on and unable to resolve them as real and manageable – exchangeable – events.

However, hyperreal tableaux vivants are still representative and figurative forms of art. We are familiar with them in classical paintings by Caravaggio and contemporary video art by Bill Viola. They stand in opposition to abstract cinematic forms, which are closer to abstract expressionism and non-objective art, and which could be considered as truly figural acinema, not representing a reality and not being recognisable as one: beyond even the hyperreal. Later, therefore, Lyotard will critically rethink acinema and its libidinal economy, as well as its psychoanalytical and ideological analysis anchored in the stark conflicts of the 1970s. He does this by developing his approach to experimental films and with the apparently contradictory introduction, following Bazin, of some of the most representative of post-Second World War neo-realist filmmakers (De Sica, Rossellini and Antonioni). It is only an apparent contradiction, because the move back to realism is designed to take us within the tableau, within the image, to take it apart rather than inflate it. Where hyperrealism creates an effect of interruption by suspending our trust in the real through full-frame intensification, the realist image has stronger resources for breaking our conditioning to the flow of the real and to the consistency of the image through frame breakdown.

As interesting as Lyotard's sparse comments on the dominant narrative cinema are, his thoughts on experimental and avant-garde filmmakers such as Eggeling, Thompson and Baruchello are more so. They derive from his studies of Pollock, Rothko, Francis, Richter, among other abstract painters, and point to a more radical direction for film theory and practice. These avant-garde pieces are self-referential film works that become both subject and object. They involve a performative instantiation of questions regarding the supposedly simple functions attributed to the cinematic apparatus designed to select and register reality in its spatial consistency and temporal linearity (if we follow Aristotelian narrative structure), thereby creating an artwork with minimum waste and dead moments. However, by privileging formal self-reflexivity, these self-referential and non-narrative films risk lacking any possible political content, inviting the criticism of nihilism and apathy, thereby negating Lyotard's passion for the political. From a Marxist analysis of cinema's paradigmatic function, we might argue that all 'acinematic' artwork is a waste of time (wasted sterile movements, wasted money, unrewarding experience, and so on). Acinema would lead to unproductive time in its lack of narrative purpose and in its failure to fit into Aristotelian and post-Hegelian narrative structures.

Lyotard's answer to this critique is that the aim of avant-garde moving images is not to record reality, but to film the unpresentable. Experimental and avant-garde films free themselves from cinema's photographic, representational and realistic nature in order to bear witness to the voices silenced by realist flow, organisation and narrative. But how should one derive pleasure from works of art such as Thompson's kaleidoscopic *N.Y., N.Y.* (1957) or Snow's frameless *La Région centrale* (1971)? Lyotard's work seeks to elide such questions by slipping from pleasure to *jouissance*, and from the beautiful to the sublime. The completion of pleasure and purposiveness without purpose of the Kantian beautiful are to be replaced by the vibratory tension of *jouissance* and the contradictory co-presence of pleasure and pain, attraction and repulsion, in the incomplete sublime event. The paradoxical fruition of avant-garde films is spatial and temporal fracture. It defies the possibility of suspending the tension between objective time (narrative and intra-diegetic temporality) and subjective time (the completed act of having seen and having heard). As a result, spectators experience timelessness – the event of no result at all.

Lyotard argues that neo-realist filmmakers 'write' extreme acinematic immobility; these are Ozu's 'cases of stasis' or 'still lives' that Deleuze synthetised as the direct time-image.[4] But the 'written' movement may also be saturated with excessive audio-visual speed. From slow cinema to fast editing, images can tell us 'another story', independent of the official plot. The hegemony of sovereign powers can be resisted by the danger of sovereign moments. Welles' *The Magnificent Ambersons* (1942) is one of Deleuze's examples of the crystal-image, not only in the sense that Welles' film fits the concept, but also and more importantly, that this philosophical concept was created for Welles' films. This is where a distinction can be drawn between the two French thinkers. The crystal allows for other stories in ways that seem impossible for Lyotard's events. For Lyotard, the Welles movie involves a coexistence of narrative and chronological time, which characterises mainstream films, with punctuations by descriptive time, thereby introducing a certain type of arrhythmia into time.

In contrast to Deleuze's long plot and mise-en-scène descriptions (consistent with auteur theory), Lyotard's method is erratic and unsystematic. His work with painting or with theatre is a dialogue, a shared journey, but cinema comes after a philosophical inquiry which, most of the time, is about something other than the seventh art. He never analyses a whole movie, preferring instead to choose a particular sequence of a specific film to exemplify what he has in mind; he might well have an entire oeuvre in purview, but it still remains an exemplification rather than a provocation to philosophy. So, finally, why is there no systematic film theory by Lyotard? Maybe it is because there ought not to be systematic theory (for anything) (see Durafour 2009). The event resists the system, as avant-garde acinema shows us, in its paradoxical and ethical moments of suspension.

NOTES

1. See Read and Goodenough 2005 and Szabados and Stojanova 2011.
2. Two important exceptions: Rodowick 2001 and Trahair 2009.
3. Lyotard, 'The Idea of a Sovereign Film', this volume.
4. Deleuze quotes respectively Schrader, Burch and Richie's ideas in *Cinema 2* (2008: 15–16).

REFERENCES

Brenez, Nicole (2011), 'Recycling, Visual Study, Expanded Theory: Ken Jacobs, Theorist, or the Long Song of the Sons', trans. Adrian Martin, in *Optic Antics: The Cinema of Ken Jacobs*, ed. Michele Pierson, David E. James and Paul Arthur, New York: Oxford University Press.
Deleuze, Gilles (1995), *Negotiations 1972–1990*, trans. Martin Joughin, New York: Columbia University Press.
Deleuze, Gilles (2008), *Cinema 2: The Time-Image*, trans. Hugh Tomlinson and Robert Galeta, London and New York: Continuum.
Durafour, Jean-Michel (2009), *Jean-François Lyotard: questions au cinema. Ce que le cinéma se figure*, Paris: PUF.
Read, Rupert and Jerry Goodenough (eds) (2005), *Film as Philosophy: Essays on Cinema after Wittgenstein and Cavell*, Basingstoke: Palgrave Macmillan.
Rodowick, D. N. (2001), *Reading the Figural: Or, Philosophy After the New Media*, Durham: Duke University Press.
Sartre, Jean-Paul (2012), *The Imagination: A Psychological Critique*, trans. Kenneth Williford and David Rudrauf, New York: Routledge.
Szabados, Bella and Christina Stojanova (eds) (2011), *Wittgenstein at the Movies: Cinematic Investigations*, Lanham: Lexington Books.
Trahair, Lisa (2009), 'Jean-François Lyotard', in *Film, Theory and Philosophy: The Key Thinkers*, ed. Felicity Coleman, Chesham: Acumen.

CHAPTER 3

Cinema Lyotard: An Introduction

Jean-Michel Durafour

Let us dispel a persistent injustice. For reasons I will come back to later, it has taken several decades for the name of Jean-François Lyotard to be able to appear, without a feeling of arbitrary unfairness or of audacious anomaly, alongside those of Gilles Deleuze, André Bazin or Serge Daney in a dossier dedicated to French cinema theory (as much as Lyotard detested this word 'theory', which reeks of monotheism and accounting. . .).[1] Looking a little more closely at the facts, which are all equally as stubborn as the theoreticians, we find it hard to understand how such an ostracism – there is no other word for it – has been able to impose itself in the discourse on cinema, despite the fact (we will see this later also) that numerous theoreticians, sometimes those very ones who keep obstinately quiet about it, have openly stolen Lyotard's whole box of methodological and operative tools (the figural), with more or less good fortune. (That is said in passing.)

Certainly, one will not find in Lyotard anything comparable to the enterprise later conducted by Deleuze with his two *Cinema* volumes; and unlike his friend, the author of *Discourse, Figure* has not inspired a whole critical disciplinary trend, nor given, *coram populi*, a new face to cinema studies. But like Deleuze, Lyotard has in his own right extended a metamorphic gesture that could be traced back to Maurice Merleau-Ponty, and in particular to his celebrated 1945 conference on 'The Film and the New Psychology'. It was there that Merleau-Ponty posed the fundamentals, common to cinema and the philosophy of perception, of what he called 'a certain way of being, a certain view of the world which belongs to a generation' (1964: 59), and thereby established a programme for more than sixty years of philosophy and reflection on cinema. Merleau-Ponty himself only offered a catch-phrase or slogan for this programme – and his predecessors had never done any more on this virgin territory – since he never supported his proposition about the *cinematic* (perceptive) *process* with even the slightest, most idiosyncratic analysis of *filmic* (aesthetic) *facts*.

ON THE COMMON SAYING: IT MAY BE TRUE IN THEORY, BUT IT DOESN'T APPLY IN PRACTICE . . .

One can reasonably affirm that the Lyotardian gesture signals itself first, and perhaps foremost, by two specificities, as follows. At least for the second, our philosopher is the only one (among thinkers of calibre) of his generation.

1. *The inscription of a reflection on cinema in a broad and general aesthetic project which, far from obscuring it, gives cinema a central and select value.* When in 1973 Lyotard wrote his first important text on cinema, 'Acinema', this aesthetic had just been put in place in *Discourse, Figure* (1971), notably around an operator destined to become famous: the 'figural'. It is not my intention here to analyse in detail a work as dense and complex as *Discourse, Figure*. But we can grasp several points. The *figural* is distinguished from the *figurative* (even if the figurative is the figural 'cooled down'). While the figurative designates 'a property that applies to the plastic object's relation to what it *represents*' (DF 205), the figural names that which in the *presentation* of the plastic event is always singular and disruptive. The figural escapes from predictability (otherwise it would be pre-figured), from recognisability, identifiability and referentiality; it escapes from codification, from forms, and from isotopic and pre-established structures. In the figural, the event is welcomed *for itself,* in its *sensible symptomatic* expression. It thereby differs from the regimes of signification and designation, as well as from the *mimesis* of the figurative tradition, in which the plastic event is taken as no more than an (abstract, separate) sign which is *referred to an other* (thing, model). The figural is the vacant space left by *desire*, that is to say by sense, in the visible, and in the sensible in general. Harrowing, turbulent, it is that which makes difference; that is to say, that by which the donation of the sensible, in its constitutive difference, is possible – while words crush all intensities on the homogeneous spatiality of language and the generality of concepts.[2] Words are incapable of safekeeping the sensible event we task them with representing: 'one can say that the tree is green, but saying so does not put color in the sentence' (DF 50).

It is consequently, *stricto sensu*, impossible *to say* the figural (and still less to define it). And in fact Lyotard tells us that *Discourse, Figure* is a 'bad' book, a failed book, because it misses the singularity of its subject. But it also poses an ideal of the book on art that Lyotard sought all his life to write, or not to write; in any case a book which would be badly written, badly constructed, even badly thought (since the concept is not in its proper place in images). Such a book would be the opposite of the argumentative essay approved by the philosophical tradition, a book more *to be seen than to be read*. Needless to say, therein lies the major difficulty for all verbal (written, spoken) aesthetics subject to the non-verbal and non-dianoetic thought of works of art. And Lyotard did not cease, under one form or another, to encounter this difficulty. The whole problem is announced right away in *Discourse, Figure*: how can we express that which, in art and in particular in visual art (painting, literature), escapes the readable and the sayable ('[r]eading is understanding, not seeing' (DF 211))?

How can we express that which takes place behind language – since at the same time one cannot situate oneself in complete exteriority to articulated language? One sees because one speaks (did the Argentinian writer Jorge Luis Borges not ask himself in which language he would die?) since at the same time one cannot but resort to concepts in order to account for the otherness of aesthetic experience. Is not philosophy still needed in order to express what escapes philosophy? How can we express the symptom which dazzles, uncodable, uncharacterisable, on this side of language and figures, with words that the image leaves us with, and which replay in the present something of the prepredicative and originary experience of the world, of the time before the distinction between subject and object, before knowledge and reflection?[3] But if it is true that, on the one hand, sense is 'muddled, inaudible, as if inexistent', 'until the military front of the words – so to speak – has contacted it' (WPh 75), the fact remains that, on the other hand, speech 'is already inarticulately present to what is not yet said' (WPh 82), just as the word, the *muttum*, always keeps a vestige – the sounds impish, treacherous – of the *muttus* which structures it; that there is a 'colloquy prior to all articulated dialogue' (WPh 93). Elsewhere: 'One needn't be immersed in language [*langage*] in order to be able to speak. . . . What speaks is something that must remain outside of language as system and must continue to remain there even when it speaks' (DF 8). How then to keep fidelity to the fact that 'one does not paint in order to speak, but in order to keep silent' (Lyotard 2015: 38)?

2. *The extension of the theoretical gesture in a certain practice of film. But this practice also precedes the theoretical gesture, and gives weight to it, in a creative process.* Lyotard did in fact make several films on celluloid or video, from an essentially experimental perspective. From the end of the 1960s, within a collective composed equally with Dominique Avron, Claudine Eizykman and Guy Fihman, he participated in the creation of the video *L'Autre scène*, a six-minute short film on the analogy between the work of the dream and the work of film, intended as the extension of a seminar on Freud. A first, silent version dates from 1969, but the film in its definitive form, with sound, was not completed until 1972. Two years later, Lyotard made on his own an experimental three-minute short film on 16mm, *Mao Gillette* (1974). The 1970s drew to a close with *Tribune sans tribun* (1978), an appropriation by Lyotard of a report for French television, for the programme *Tribune Libre*. He chose to turn it into an experimental video whose title indicates its subject: the absence of legitimation of the speakers on the televised stage, who speak of anything and everything. Thus ended a decade of experimentation with images, certainly on one level modest, but which, for

a philosopher, is an event sufficiently rare for it to be appreciated for its proper value. A last film, from 1982, *À blanc*, breaks with the experimental gesture in that it presents itself first and foremost as an exegetical essay in images, on someone else's aesthetic expression (which is why I excluded it from my survey in the little book that I scribbled on the question of cinema in Lyotard (Durafour 2009)): it's a brief video dedicated to a series of canvases by the painter René Guiffrey.

Lyotard's entry into cinema theory is hence made by a double path: the aesthetic of the figural, and the practice of experimental cinema. The latter appears to put the former to work in a filmic figural aesthetic: that is to say, a *pulsional* aesthetic, subject to desire, to difference, through which the cinema would escape from industry (capital, revenue, the same, *mimesis*), and clearly would be an art. We will come back to this shortly. First, however, we can conclude this second point by noting that the Lyotardian concept of acinema directly inspired for several years the work of Guy Fihman and Claudine Eizykman (*V.W. Vitesses Women, Ultrarouge-Infraviolet*). Moreover, the experimental filmic moment played an essential role for Lyotard in the passage from the aesthetic paradigm of modern art (Cézanne, Klee) – which for the most part, even if not uniquely, characterises *Discourse, Figure*, and which is primarily a legacy of the phenomenology of Merleau-Ponty – to the great dialogues with contemporaries (Jacques Monory, Valerio Adami, Sam Francis, Karel Appel) which began thereafter.

1973

Everything on the theoretical plane begins then with the initial text 'Acinema'. It first appeared in 1973 in the special issue of *Revue d'esthétique* edited by Dominique Noguez, 'Cinéma: Théorie, Lectures', and was subsequently collected, the same year, in *Des Dispositifs pulsionnels*. In this text, Lyotard appears to apply the principles of figural aesthetics developed in *Discourse, Figure* to cinema.

Experimental cinema is a cinema of irreverence and 'irreference', as Dominique Noguez (1979: 42) said; it refuses the conventions and the analogical imprint indexed on dominant *mainstream* cinema. It is a cinema of apparition more than of appearances; appearing, in effect, to comply with all the characteristics of the figural: a cinema which refuses *mimesis*, representation, narration (which the recognition of figures implies: what do they go on to become?). Lyotard calls it *acinema*: being the negation (a-) of the majoritarian (industrial, commercial) cinema, that is to say of the cinema norm, where the movement (*kinêma*) and the image are neutralised in a middle range acceptable to the largest number of viewers. Acinema is experimental cinema. But not all experimental cinema is acinema. Or, more precisely, Lyotard restricted the concept and excluded all cinema which still, *despite everything*, rests on the narrative and the figuration (surrealist cinema, for example) – that is to say all cinema in which the indexical analogism still plays the role of a *signifying* centre. Acinema is cinema which accepts 'what is fortuitous, dirty, confused, unsteady, unclear, poorly framed, overexposed' (Ac 33): intensities, timbres, nuances, colours, drips, bursts, breaks, scratches, cuts, openings. In a word, the *energetic*: the tenuous, the unstable and shifting, which always escapes the deterministic and reductive constructions of the well-formed.

In this text Lyotard proposes, on either side of the 'normal' movements of *mainstream* cinema, a distinction between a cinema of extreme mobility, or 'lyric abstraction' (Ac 40) (for example, Hans Richter, Viking Eggeling), and a cinema of extreme immobilisation, or 'tableau vivant' (Ac 40) (he doesn't give any examples, but such a gesture characterises, among others, a filmmaker like Andy Warhol. . .). In my book *Jean-François Lyotard: questions au cinéma. Ce que le cinéma se figure*, I spoke of '*exo-cinema*' and '*endo-cinema*' (Durafour 2009: 35–8). Exo-cinema corresponds to the cinema of agitation and makes representational figuration *explode* by attacking it from the exterior: it's the cinema of the *avant-gardes* (notice the original military sense of the expression). Endo-cinema corresponds to the cinema of immobility and makes the figuration *implode* by drilling it from its interior: it's the cinema called *underground*, literally 'of the sub-soil' (even if historically, we know, the term responded to other imperatives).

Lyotard paid dearly for his fondness for experimental cinema, which did no more at the time than develop the underground movement theoretically,[4] and which had to remain in purgatory for a long time. (And incidentally, when he became interested in a completely different cinema later, people didn't really take it into account.) Pascal Bonitzer – characteristic of the attitude that we recalled in opening, and in his typically virulent style – has not hesitated to qualify acinema purely and simply as 'puke' (1976: 70). Various commentators continued to be frequently discomforted by it. Thus Dominique Chateau, in *Cinéma et philosophie*, after having recalled, almost as an excuse, that '[Lyotard's] contribution to the philosophy of cinema is, if not contradictory, at least relatively disparate' (2003: 126), situates the essence of this contribution (incidentally he is not the only one to do so) in the figural (the word first encountered in a working note of the late Merleau-Ponty). Yet without doubt we owe the recourse to the terminology of the figural in the filmic regime less to Lyotard himself than to those who are – more or less directly – influenced by him. In *Discourse, Figure*, cinema is mentioned only in a footnote concerning Méliès (yet it is to this foundational text that most of the figural analyses of cinema refer). And in 'Acinema', there is not the slightest mention of the word 'figural', even though it was readily available (and was still brand new). . . All this is, to say the least, curious, and opens up some complex questions that it is not possible to deal with here (among which the principal one is surely this: is cinema a plastic art?).

This last point, which accounts for the ambiguous status of *underground* cinema, which is lodged *in figurative representation*, then makes possible another reading: a more accurate reading of this text which is usually poorly understood, and certainly very poorly liked (but perhaps because poorly understood?) – but also liked, when it is, for the wrong reasons.

TAKING INTO ACCOUNT THE FIGURATIVE

Lyotard always displayed a great suspicion of the critical gesture, which consists in wanting to take hold of an exteriority, but which only perpetuates *in another sense* what it rejects. To this posture he always preferred clandestine infiltration, undercover work.[5] I recalled this earlier here, apropos of language. One can say the same for representation: *it is impossible to position oneself in complete exteriority to it.*[6] With language, we must situate ourselves *in language outside of language*, in the eye of the cyclone (the pivotal zone where everything is very calm), as it exists as a 'well of discourse' (DF 7). We affirm that there exists in the same way a *wellspring of figuration* in which the figure is secreted from representation; that is to say, from what is always already figurative. And years later, Lyotard will end up somewhere else by detaching himself from the figural. In *What to Paint?* (1988), he did not hesitate to write that *Discourse, Figure* is 'a book which makes a screen to the anamnesis of the visible' (WP 96).[7]

For Lyotard produced more than one text on cinema (even if we silently pass over the multiple examples taken from cinema in the framework of his philosophical writings). While these writings are 'disparate' (Chateau's word is appropriate), this does not however permit the conclusion that they lack coherence or unity, or that they remain minor or imperfect thoughts. Lyotard simply never felt the necessity or the desire to collect them or to develop them into a book. There is no need to ask why: it is a fact. We just have to live with it.

What are these texts? It is not my project to make a catalogue or some kind of taxonomy. If I leave aside – in addition to 'Acinema', which I have just spoken about – pages here or there where mention is made of such and such a film, such as interviews mentioning the films presented during the exhibition *Les Immatériaux* at Beaubourg in 1985 (which require a proper perspective), we can propose as the most important the following texts, generally put in the garbage of cinema theory:

1. An article in English, 'The Unconscious as Mise-en-Scène' (1977), which appeared in the collection edited by Michel Benamou and Charles Caramello from the University of Wisconsin Press, *Performance in Postmodern Culture*. It presents, in the entire final section, an analysis of Michael Snow's *La Région central*, starting from the work of the unconscious.

2. 'Deux métamorphoses du séduisant au cinema' [Two Metamorphoses of the Seductive in Cinema] (1980), a contribution to the book edited by Maurice Olender and Jacques Sojcher, *La Séduction*, which appeared from the publisher Aubier-Montaigne. Here the principal focus is Francis Ford Coppola's *Apocalypse Now* (1979), and just at the end, very rapidly, some films of Hans-Jürgen Syberberg (*Hitler, ein Film aus Deustchland, Winifred Wagner und die Geschichte des Hauses Wahnfried von 1914–1975*).

3. Finally, the posthumous publication of the manuscript of a conference paper delivered in Munich in 1995, 'Idée d'un film souverain' [The Idea of a Sovereign Film], included by Dolorès Lyotard in *Misère de la philosophie* in 2000. The subject of this crucial paper is filmic invention in the so-called 'modern' cinema (in Yasujirō Ozu, Orson Welles, etc.).

If the first of these texts still inscribes itself in the continuity of the acinematographic libidinal theses, it is not at all the same with the other two. These two texts do not break purely and simply with acinema, but oblige us to reconsider its nature. Starting by coming back to the seminal article of 1973 and proposing a slightly different reading, we are clearly enabled, in my opinion, to grasp an important stake of this text which has so far escaped us. We can understand what it was about Lyotard's writings that made the cinema theorists uncomfortable: their refusal to constitute a system (system is closure, capitalisation, hoarding, theorisation), to offer a fully delivered, established global theory; their 'drift' (a Lyotardian word), that one could take for disorder, or see as superficiality. The necessity which is ours, to which they oblige us, is that of needing to *present and represent* them in order to 'squeeze the juice out of them', so to speak. But in this lies what in Lyotard's eyes always counted the most (and this was also the basis of his interest in experimental cinema): a fondness for differences, a fidelity to singularities, a passion for dissensus.

'Two Metamorphoses of the Seductive in Cinema' and 'The Idea of a Sovereign Film' do not then fully satisfy the model of acinema. Let us move forward from this observation. It is difficult, in effect, to see *Apocalypse Now* or *The Magnificent Ambersons* as experimental films. That being so, they include some *acinematographic moments* (the helicopter attack with all its smoke and pyrotechnics in the first, for example). This is what Lyotard calls, in the second of these texts, '*filmic facts* [*faits*]' (ISF 68; my emphasis). In this regard, if one reads a little quickly, one could see a *conservative* weakening of the orthodox acinematographic position, particularly in 'The Idea of a Sovereign Film'. This text was undertaken after the publication of the two volumes of *Cinema* by Deleuze, from whom Lyotard acknowledges, in the note sent to the journal *Libération* on the occasion of his death, having appropriated several ideas (MP 193). Had

Deleuze not presented a philosophy of the event and of singularity able to think *all cinema*, including when it is figurative and narrative (which it is never either straightforwardly; if such were the case, as Eugène Green (2003: 35) said, there would be no difference between a cinematic film and a tourist film[8]), and even if the figurative and narrative axis is not the one retained by the author of *The Movement-Image*?[9] In this conference paper, Lyotard in fact displaces the acinematographic marker taken as filmic *totality* towards the 'filmic fact', which alone guarantees the *sovereignty* of film. What does this mean? It means that sovereignty excludes totality.[10]

Do we witness a frightful rupture?

1. One can first of all say that the 'filmic fact' *makes a difference, visually or auditorily*, in relation to a globally maintained 'narrative-representative form' (ISF 64, 68). In this sense, it maintains fidelity to the difference of the event because such a difference can only be perceived on a homo-audio-visual ground from which it is detached (Merleau-Ponty, in his *Phenomenology of Perception*, called it the 'phenomenal field'). When there is only difference, when difference is all there is, when difference makes a *totality*, it cancels itself as difference. When everything is different, nothing is different. It is therefore appropriate to keep the figurative ground, at least in this capacity. But there's more. In addition, the filmic fact is a 'faded' reality; it consists in 'moments [which correspond to] outcrops of the visual or the vocal in the surface of the visible and the audible' (ISF 69).

2. Next, this gesture permits us at once to widen the scope to Deleuzian proportions,[11] to make a case for the application of the acinematographic criterion, without abandoning it, to a cinema *more expanded* and less restrictive than acinema strictly speaking. To be given henceforth by examples of acinematographic moments, of 'filmic facts', of 'intense instants, temporal spasms, which are only transcendents because they *emanate from immanence*, that is to say from a realist experience and existence – one says in filmography: neo-realist' (ISF 62; my emphasis). Moreover, was acinema really as restrictive as it appeared to be? One will remember what we recalled earlier: that despite superficial appearances, the profound originality of the acinematographic thesis of 'Acinema' *bore principally on the figurative and representative image* (which begins to explain the absence of the explicit terminology of the figural. . .). This was precisely the *underground* cinema: attacking representation *from the interior of representation* (the under-ground), and not with any putative and deceptive exteriority, like the eye of the cyclone (one will recall the image from *Discourse, Figure*) where it is neutralised at its centre. Thus, in 'Acinema', it is clearly *underground* cinema which Lyotard prefers, for reasons, one could say, of a 'general philosophical' nature (total exteriority is an illusion). Now what does he say of this cinema? This: 'the paradox of

immobilisation is seen to be clearly distributed along the *representational* axis' (Ac 40; my emphasis). This is the only sentence in the article where Lyotard addresses himself directly to his reader, which would suffice to underline its importance, or at least its difference. Moreover, in placing the accent on the representation of the perceptive reality in the image, such a formula appears to be a counter-current to the figural perspective. Without doubt that's why this exclusively disruptive perspective will never really have existed (as will be said differently in later texts).

FILMIC MATTER (PRESENT POTENTIAL)

In the philosophical and aesthetic canon, matter, in contrast to form (which informs), has generally been taken to be purely passive. The source is above all Platonic – the *Timaeus* (50c) describes matter as 'the stuff from which everything is moulded', the principal 'wax' (*ekmageîon*), 'modified and moulded by the things that enter it, with the result that it *appears* different at different times' (Plato 2008: 42). Matter is only the '*that in which*' of the thing, whose form is the '*that for which*'. It is, before all information, unlimited, therefore imperfect, tending towards non-being, since it is form which has definition and completion (form is closed).

Nevertheless we can say right away that such an opposition – to which materialism only takes the opposite stance, which means it fails to put it in question – is problematic. Henri Focillon, in *The Life of Forms in Art* (1934), had already attracted attention to this apparently extravagant proposition: matter determines form, *matter is the form (the determination) of form*. And he proposed to speak of *matters* rather than of matter, in order to designate the plural and complex 'formal vocation' (Focillon 1989: 97) of matter: grains, waves, notches. Such matters – marble, metal, wood, graphite, charcoal, voice, etc. – are not anodyne for an artistic project, nor are they equivalent to each other; they differ according to their flexibility or the effects aimed at. '[A] charcoal drawing copied in wash . . . at once assumes totally unexpected properties; it becomes, indeed, a new work' (1989: 100). In the same way, the tool in its materiality, and not in the gesture which manipulates it (which is form, the design of the artist), contributes to making the final form of the work: 'Certain plates reek of the tool and conserve a metallic aspect [from it]' (1989: 114). Moreover the term 'form', in an expression such as 'matter imposes its form on the form', need not be heard univocally in both occurrences: the 'form' of the matter is not the 'form' of the form. The formative power of the matter has its proper principles, which must not be confused with those of form.

Lyotard will go a lot further than Focillon (who in the end remains rather conventional, especially from the point of view of 'well written' language) by inscribing himself ardently in this opening. From the Greeks – as we know – matter is opposed to *logos*. We cannot *say* matter, even with the scholastic (originally Aristotelean) title of the *materia prima*, pure potentiality, of perceptive experience, because it gives us nothing to grasp. Lyotard responds: no discourse, which is always putting-in-form, putting-in-signs, can *signify* matter. Matter can only be *expressed*.

Lyotard thinks matter in a first period through the figural, and the privilege of the visual over the visible and the readable: *the event of the image*. (This period culminates in *Discourse, Figure*, still in some regards very much a conventional book in its format and organisation.) That being so, the pulsional energy of desire makes established figures burst like a saxifrage plant; it breaks the decorum of the monotone, of the predictable, of that which is set in stone. There is a transgression of codes and writing by the irruption of the primary processes (intensities, desires) in the secondary processes (language, actions) by virtue of what Freud called, apropos of the formation of dream images from unconscious thoughts, the *Rücksicht auf Darstellbarkeit* ('the taking into account of figurability'). It's this figural matter which, in reflection on cinema (Philippe Dubois, Raymond Bellour) or art in general (see the work of Georges Didi-Huberman), has dominated and still largely dominates the field of analysis.

But we have seen that the figural does not constitute the whole of the Lyotardian thought of the image, and that cinema breaks with it. And it's without doubt here that Lyotard's reflections are more fascinating for both *theoretical research* and *an actual aesthetic* of cinema. In the last decade of his philosophical activity, Lyotard spoke of '*an energetics or . . . a general dynamics*' (MT1 199; my emphasis).[12] This 'energetics' envisages matter, no longer from the figural point of view, but *from the side of figurative invention*. What is the difference between the two? In a word: the figural concerns the presentable, not the representable (that is to say it concerns the event, not the thing, the *res*). The 'general energetics' is the fact that *there is*, in the representation, the unpresentable. What is unpresentable is presence itself. The presence of sound is not sonorous, as the presence of blue is not blue, as the presence of a rock is not mineral. This amounts in the end to the grandeur of art, when it opens onto the originary opening of our rapport with the world: the presentation of unpresentable matter – which fixes itself as objective (in the various social, professional, etc., uses that we make of matter, which *present* everything quite well) – is in fact always aporetic. The question of painting: how does the colour perceive itself in itself? The question of music: how does sound perceive itself in itself?

> The presence of the sensible world that cannot be taught, that is anterior to any symbolism and accomplished anew in art through its initial chromatic stridency, has always persistently overtaken pale discourse and its wan digressions . . . Beyond the spirit that meditates and the eye that reads, vision is already in the process of seeing. (MT2 659)

From this then comes the exigency of a new aesthetic orientation, which Lyotard here and there calls '*anaesthetic*' (in opposition to the traditional aesthetic of forms). This aesthetic is concerned not with presented forms, but with matter; and a matter not only stolen, pilfered from between forms, but a matter which it is all the more possible to welcome in its unpresentability because it is itself unformed. Since the aesthetic subject, which here no longer recognises itself (recognition is form), is numb, groggy, precisely *anaesthetised*. One cannot see matter (one sees forms); one can only eye it up. In the sense not of objectification (this is still form: constraint), but of the French verb *mater*, understood as eyeing up furtively *as if one had not clearly seen*. As if one could not get over having seen that one had not seen.

This matter finds a fertile ground for expression in the cinematic image. We must not let ourselves be misled by its photorealism. I have argued in my book already cited (it is impossible for me to repeat here the long demonstration) that, through a relationship with pictorial hyperrealism, which plays itself out in cinema, including in its more figurative and narrative aspects, there is an explosion of the criteriology of traditional, analogical *mimesis* (resemblance). In cinema, one has little business with an image which resembles, better than another image, the thing which it models. Rather, cinema is concerned with the fact that, for the eye habituated to old images, the thing resembles *itself* in a way never before seen (black-and-white changes nothing here: for decades, this has been the norm of the realism of the photographic image, and colour in cinema only started to increase the exoticism, the fantasy, the dream. . .). It's not a question of saying that cinema gives us the 'things themselves': how would we know what they are? But the thing, as Lyotard said apropos the hyperrealism that I am drawing out here for cinema, comes half-way to meet us, and stumbles; it becomes '*a bit too much* before the eyes' (MT2 485;[13] my emphasis). It is not only abstraction which gives a skewed image of the world: '*showing* reality' (MT2 471[14]) can do this just as much. In this 'excess of presence' a certain conventional image of the world *dematerialises* itself, under the cover of its minute and scrupulous renewal, and *materialises* what can only be eyed up [*être maté*]: a donation of presence-matter contravening established forms so that the classic aesthetic subject (with its coded certitudes, its mastery) feels itself threatened through and through by being touched by nullity. The form is that by which the figure *exists*, the matter that by which it *insists*. And this insistence is, at the same time, my private concern, my business, but also a demand which intimidates me intimately.

I will give, in conclusion, a very short filmic example of an analysis according to anaesthesic matter. John Cassavetes' *Faces* (1968) is celebrated in the history of cinema for its big shots exacerbating the grain of the skin of the body; an operation intensified in various ways by the Éclair NPR, Kodak 4x16mm film, and powerful lighting by quartz lamps. One can do a figural reading of this film by paying attention to the jump cuts, the broken speeches, the over-the-shoulder shots, the variations of focus, and so on and so forth; in short, by paying attention to the vicissitudes of the form. But the 'general energetic or dynamic' makes sense of it in another way: a way of *insisting*, and not of *rerouting* (the figural) with regard to images, *including those more figurative, more coded*. It's a question of a phobic matter, which places the spectator before the anxiety of his or her proper aesthetic condition: that of perception. Better: it performs here, in these various images, an affection – what I have called above a commanded and intimidating intimacy, coming from *the unpresentable presence of matter (the unrepresentable in representation)*. This announces: that in virtue of which we are beings of sensation is not anything. In the face of these skins visible to the pores, in the face of *these prominent holes*, with all their doors and all their windows (Leibnizian language), it's not only the form of the skin that we see [*voyons*]; we see [*matons*] the anxiety of being penetrated ourselves because if we see, if we feel, *it's because we are penetrated*. Matter reveals sensation to us as anxiety by connecting us to the unpresentable condition of presentational perception. Like Klein bottles, we do not have a (full) body because we are only gaps, voids, atomic bonds. And this is because we have neither interior nor exterior (the film then asks: where are feelings, emotions, held? Between bodies?. . .). Matter is 'the suffering of a body visually bewildered' (PF 231); in effect, unpresentable matter, inasmuch as Lyotard defined the artistic power of cinema in this way: 'I think that a filmmaker, if he or she is not a commercial trader of images, carries in him or herself the idea of a sovereign film where from time to time the realist plot allows the presence of the ontological real to pass . . . to which [idea] no object, here no film, can correspond in experience . . .' (ISF 69).

Translated by Ashley Woodward[15]

NOTES

1. This chapter was first published in *La Furia Umana*, Paper #3 (2013), pp. 121–36.
2. 'Every word immediately becomes a concept, inasmuch as it is not intended to serve as a reminder of the unique and wholly individualized original experience to which it owes its birth, but must at the same time fit innumerable, more or less similar cases – which means, strictly speaking, never equal – in other words, a lot of unequal cases. Every concept originates through our equating what is unequal' (Nietzsche 1976: 46).
3. The *topos* of phenomenology since Husserl. On the notion of *Lebenswelt*, see in particular Husserl 1970: 103–13.
4. See, in addition to the academic work of Noguez from the end of the 1960s (on North American underground cinema), from the other side of the Atlantic: Parker Tyler's *Underground Film* (1969), the articles by Annette Michelson and Manny

Farber in the journal *Artforum*, Jonas Mekas's *Ciné-journal* (1971), P. Adams Sitney's *Visionary Film* (1974), etc.

5. Once again, permit me to refer you to my book – Durafour 2009: 69.
6. The reading of Lyotard for cinema that I propose here distinguishes itself from this complementary work by Jean-Louis Déotte. Déotte is less interested, in Lyotard, in what is thought of cinema or what can aid us *by first beginning from reflections on cinema*, than to what, in his philosophy of language (*The Differend*), can serve the purpose of an understanding of the phenomenon of montage: namely, montage as the expression of a *differend* between frames thought of as analogues of linguistic phrases, as irreducible 'universes' (each phrase presents a type of universe), between which it is necessary, despite everything, *to link* (one will have recognised the axiomatisation of *The Differend*). See in particular Déotte 2004.
7. I do not have the liberty, in the context of the present introductory article, to develop the arguments advanced by Lyotard in this extremely rich book. We can just note a difficulty attendant to the figural: at what time can we identify it? Because to identify is to recognise, and we can only recognise what is repeated, what reproduces itself a number of times. But is this then still the figural?
8. In Deleuze's two books, incidentally, experimental cinema occupies a restrained and marginal place (gaseous perception), while the central paradigm for thinking cinematic perception is *liquid* (equivalence of all spatial points, a-centric, immanence. . .) in opposition to ordinary human perception of the *terrestrial* type (differentiation and hierarchisation of points, centric, transcendence).
9. Deleuze repeats it in several places: 'In art, and in painting as in music, it is not a matter of reproducing or of inventing forms, but of capturing forces. For this reason no art is figurative' (2003: 56).
10. The argument is primarily political: totality aims at unity under a dominating 'grand narrative', and is therefore the enemy of singularities, feelings, events; of all others, all dissenters. In fact, where there is totality, the sovereignty of 'little narratives', of differences, is neutralised by homogenising and generalising reason.
11. The 'filmic facts' are described by Lyotard in terms which are manifestly very Deleuzian: for example, 'vacuoles, or blocks of time, in the realist-narrative progression' (ISF 64).
12. I develop this question of the place and role of matter in Lyotard's aesthetics in further detail in the epilogue to MT1.
13. TN: Translation modified.
14. TN: Translation modified.
15. TN: Thanks are due to Véronique Malcolm for generously taking the time to provide helpful comments on this translation.

REFERENCES

Bonitzer, Pascal (1976), *Le Regard et la Voix*, Paris: UGE.
Chateau, Dominique (2003), *Cinéma et philosophie*, Paris: Nathan.
Deleuze, Gilles (2003), *Francis Bacon: The Logic of Sensation*, trans. Daniel W. Smith, London and New York: Continuum.

Déotte, Jean-Louis (2004), *L'Époque des appareils*, Paris: Lignes-Léo Scheer.
Durafour, Jean-Michel (2009), *Jean-François Lyotard: questions au cinéma. Ce que le cinéma se figure*, Paris: PUF.
Focillon, Henri (1989), *The Life of Forms in Art*, trans. Charles Beecher Hogan, New York: Zone Books.
Green, Eugène (2003), *Présences. Essais sur la Nature du cinéma*, Paris: Desclée de Brouwer.
Husserl, Edmund (1970), *The Crisis of European Sciences and Phenomenology*, trans. David Carr, Evanston: Northwestern University Press.
Lyotard, Jean-François (2015), 'Freud According to Cézanne', trans. Ashley Woodward and Jon Roffe, *Parrhesia* 23, pp. 24–40.
Merleau-Ponty, Maurice (1964), *Sense and Nonsense*, trans. Hubert L. Dreyfus and Patricia Allen Dreyfus, Evanston: Northwestern University Press.
Nietzsche, Friedrich (1976), 'On Truth and Lie in an Extra-moral Sense', trans. Walter Kaufmann, in *The Portable Nietzsche*, ed. Kaufmann, New York: Viking.
Noguez, Dominique (1979), *Éloge du cinéma experimental*, Paris: Centre Georges-Pompidou.
Plato (2008), *Timaeus and Critias*, trans. R. Waterfield, Oxford: Oxford University Press.

PART II

Lyotard's Essays on Film

CHAPTER 4

Acinema

Jean-François Lyotard

THE NIHILISM OF CONVENTIONAL MOVEMENTS

Cinematography is the inscription of movement, a writing with movement, a writing with movements – all kinds of movements: for example, in the film shot, those of the actors and other moving objects, those of lights, colours, frame and lens; in the film sequence, all of these again plus the cuts and splices of editing; for the film as a whole, those of scene organisation [*découpage*]. And over or through all these movements are those of the sound and words coming together with them.

Thus there is a crowd (nonetheless a countable crowd) of elements in motion, a throng of possible moving bodies which are candidates for inscription on film. Learning the techniques of filmmaking involves knowing how to eliminate a large number of these possible movements. It seems that image, sequence and film must be constituted at the price of these exclusions.

Here arise two questions that are really quite naive considering the deliberations of contemporary cine-critics: *which* movements and moving bodies are these? Why is it necessary to select, sort out and exclude them?

If no movements are picked out we will accept what is fortuitous, dirty, confused, unsteady, unclear, poorly framed, overexposed. . . For example, suppose you are working on a shot in video, a shot, say, of a gorgeous head of hair à la Renoir; upon viewing it you find that something has come undone: all of a sudden, swamps, outlines of incongruous islands and cliff edges appear, lurching forth before your startled eyes. A scene from elsewhere, representing nothing identifiable, has been added, a scene not related to the logic of your shot, an undecidable scene, worthless even as an insertion because it will not be repeated and taken up again later. So you cut it out.

We are not demanding a raw cinema, like Dubuffet demanded an *art brut*. We are hardly about to form a club dedicated to the saving of rushes and the rehabilitation of clipped footage. And yet... We observe that if the mistake is eliminated it is because of its incongruity, and in order to protect the order of the whole (shot and/or sequence and/or film) while banning the intensity it carries. And the order of the whole has its sole object in the functioning of the cinema: that there be order in the movements, that the movements be made in order, that they make order. Writing with movements – cinematography – is thus conceived and practised as an incessant organising of movements following the rules of representation for spatial localisation, those of narration for the instantiation of language, and those of the form 'film music' for the soundtrack. The so-called impression of reality is a real oppression of orders.

This oppression consists of the enforcement of a nihilism of movements. No movement, arising from any field, is given to the eye-ear of the spectator for what it is: a simple *sterile difference* in an audio-visual field. Instead, every movement put forward *sends back* to something else, is inscribed as a plus or minus on the ledger book which is the film, *is valuable* because it *returns* to something else, because it is thus potential return and profit. The only genuine movement with which the cinema is written is that of value. The law of value (in so-called 'political' economy) states that the *object*, in this case the movement, is valuable only in so far as it is exchangeable against other objects and in terms of equal quantities of a definable unity (for example, in quantities of money). Therefore, to be valuable the object must move: proceed from other objects ('production' in the narrow sense) and disappear, but on the condition that its disappearance *makes room for still other objects* (consumption). Such a process is not sterile, but productive; it is production in the widest sense.

PYROTECHNICS

Let us be certain to distinguish this process from sterile motion. A match once struck is consumed. If you use the match to light the gas that heats the water for the coffee which keeps you alert on your way to work, the consumption is not sterile, for it is a movement belonging to the circuit of capital: merchandise-match → merchandise-labour power → money-wages → merchandise-match. But when a child strikes the match-head *to see* what happens – just for the fun of it – he enjoys the movement itself, the changing colours, the light flashing at the height of the blaze, the death of the tiny piece of wood, the hissing of the tiny flame. He enjoys these sterile differences leading nowhere, these uncompensated losses; what the physicist calls the dissipation of energy.

Intense enjoyment and sexual pleasure [*la jouissance*], in so far as they give rise to perversion and not solely to propagation, are distinguished by this sterility. At the end of *Beyond the Pleasure Principle* Freud cites them as an example of the combination of the life and death instincts. But he is thinking of pleasure obtained through the channels of 'normal' genital sexuality: all *jouissance*, including that giving rise to a hysterical attack or, contrariwise, to a perverse scenario, contains the lethal component, but normal pleasure hides it in a movement of return, genital sexuality. Normal genital sexuality leads to childbirth, and the child is the *return* of, or on, its movement. But the motion of pleasure as such, split from the motion of the propagation of the species, would be (whether genital or sexual or neither) that motion which in going beyond the point of no return spills the libidinal forces outside the whole, at the expense of the whole (at the price of the ruin and disintegration of this whole).

In lighting the match the child enjoys this diversion [*détournement*] (a word dear to Klossowski) that misspends energy. He produces, in his own movement, a simulacrum of pleasure in its so-called 'death instinct' component. Thus if he is assuredly an artist by producing a simulacrum, he is one most of all because this simulacrum is not an object of worth valued for another object. It is not composed with these other objects, compensated for by them, enclosed in a whole ordered by constitutive laws (in a structured group, for example). On the contrary, it is essential that the entire erotic force invested in the simulacrum be promoted, raised, displayed and burned in vain. It is thus that Adorno said the only truly great art is the making of fireworks: pyrotechnics would simulate perfectly the sterile consumption of energies in *jouissance*. Joyce grants this privileged position to fireworks in the beach sequence in *Ulysses*. A simulacrum, understood in the sense Klossowski gives it, should not be conceived primarily as belonging to the category of representation, like the representations which imitate pleasure; rather, it is to be conceived as a kinetic problematic, as the paradoxical product of the disorder of the drives, as a composite of decompositions.

The discussion of cinema and representational-narrative art in general begins at this point. Two directions are open to the conception (and production) of an object, and in particular, a cinematographic object, conforming to the pyrotechnical imperative. These two seemingly contradictory currents appear to be those attracting whatever is intense in painting today. It is possible that they are also at work in the truly active forms of experimental and underground cinema.

These two poles are immobility and excessive movement. In letting itself be drawn towards these antipodes the cinema insensibly ceases to be an ordering force; it produces true, that is, vain, simulacrums, blissful intensities, instead of productive/consumable objects.

THE MOVEMENT OF RETURN

Let us back up a bit. What do these movements of return or returned movements have to do with the representational and narrative form of the commercial cinema? We emphasise just how wretched it is to answer this question in terms of a simple superstructural function of an industry, the cinema, the products of which, films, would lull the public consciousness by means of doses of ideology. If mise-en-scène is a directing and ordering [*mise en ordre*] of movements it is not so by being propaganda (benefiting the bourgeoisie some would say, and the bureaucracy, others would add), but by being a propagation. Just as the libido must renounce its perverse overflow to propagate the species through a normal genital sexuality allowing the constitution of a 'sexual body' having that sole end, so the film produced by an artist working in capitalist industry (and all known industry is now capitalist) springs from the effort to eliminate aberrant movements, useless expenditures, differences of pure consumption. This film is composed like a unified and propagating body, a fecund and assembled whole transmitting instead of losing what it carries. The diegesis locks together the synthesis of movements in the temporal order; perspectivist representation does so in the spatial order.

Now, what are these syntheses but the arranging of the cinematographic material following the figure of *return?* We are not only speaking of the requirement of profitability imposed upon the artist by the producer, but also of the formal requirements that the artist weighs upon his material. All so-called good form implies the return of sameness, the folding back of diversity upon an identical unity. In painting this may be a plastic rhyme or an equilibrium of colours; in music, the resolution of dissonance by the dominant chord; in architecture, a proportion. Repetition, the principle of not only the metric but even of the rhythmic, if taken in the narrow sense as the repetition of the same (same colour, line, angle, chord), is the work of Eros and Apollo disciplining the movements, limiting them to the norms of tolerance characteristic of the system or whole in consideration.

It was an error to accredit Freud with the discovery of the very motion of the drives. Because Freud, in *Beyond the Pleasure Principle*, takes great care to dissociate the repetition of the same, which signals the regime of the life instincts, from the repetition of the other, which can only be other to the first-named repetition. These death drives are just outside the regime delimited by the body or whole considered, and therefore it is impossible to discern *what* is returning, when returning with these drives is the intensity of extreme *jouissance* and danger that they carry. To the point that it must be asked if indeed any repetition is involved at all, if on the contrary something different returns at each instance, if the *eternal return* of these sterile explosions of libidinal discharge should not be conceived in a wholly different time-space than that of the repetition of the same, as their impossible copresence. Assuredly we find here the insufficiency of *thought*, which must necessarily pass through that sameness which is the concept.

Cinematic movements generally follow the figure of return, that is, of the repetition and propagation of sameness. The scenario or plot, an intrigue and its solution, achieves the same resolution of dissonance as the sonata form in music; its movement of return organises the affective charges linked to the filmic 'signifieds', both connotative and denotative, as Metz would say. In this regard all endings are happy endings, just by being endings, for even if a film finishes with a murder, this too can serve as a final resolution of dissonance. The affective charges carried by every type of cinematographic and filmic 'signifier' (lens, framing, cuts, lighting, shooting, etc.) are submitted to the same law of a return of the same after a semblance of difference; a difference that is nothing, in fact, but a detour.

THE INSTANCE OF IDENTIFICATION

This rule, where it applies, operates principally, we have said, in the form of exclusions and effacements. The exclusion of certain movements is such that the professional filmmakers are not even aware of them; effacements, on the other hand, cannot fail to be noticed by them because a large part of their activity consists of them. Now these effacements and exclusions form the very operation of mise-en-scène. In eliminating, before and/or after the shooting, any extreme glare, for example, the director and cameraman condemn the image of film to the sacred task of making itself recognisable to the eye. The image must cast the object or set of objects as the double of a situation that from then on will be supposed real. The image is representational because recognisable, because it addresses itself to the eye's *memory*, to fixed references or identification, references known, but in the sense of 'well known', that is, familiar and established. These references are identity measuring the returning and return of movements. They form the instance or group of instances connecting and making them take the form of cycles. Thus all sorts of gaps, jolts, postponements, losses and confusions can occur, but they no longer act as real diversions or wasteful drifts; when the final count is made they turn out to be nothing but beneficial detours. It is precisely through the return to the ends of identification that cinematographic form, understood as the synthesis of good movement, is articulated following the cyclical organisation of capital.

One example chosen from among thousands: in *Joe* (a film built entirely upon the impression of reality) the movement is drastically altered twice: the first time when the father beats to death the hippie who lives with his daughter; the second when, 'mopping up' a hippie commune, he unwittingly guns down his own daughter. This last sequence ends with a freeze-frame shot of the bust and face of the daughter who is struck down in full movement. In the first murder we see a hail of fists falling upon the face of the defenceless hippie who quickly loses consciousness. These two effects, the one an immobilisation, the other an excess of mobility, are obtained by waiving the rules of representation which demand real motion recorded and projected at 24 frames per second. As a result we could expect a strong affective charge to accompany them, since this greater or lesser perversion of the realistic rhythm responds to the organic rhythm of the intense emotions evoked. And it is indeed produced, but to the benefit, nevertheless, of the filmic totality, and thus, all told, to the benefit of order; both arrhythmies are produced not in some aberrant fashion but at the culminating points in the tragedy of the impossible father/daughter incest underlying the scenario. So while they may upset representational order, clouding for a few seconds the celluloid's necessary transparency (which is that order's condition), these two affective charges do not fail to suit the narrative order. On the contrary, they mark it with a beautiful melodic curve, the first accelerated murder finding its resolution in the second immobilised murder.

Thus the memory to which films address themselves is *nothing* in itself, just as capital is nothing but an instance of capitalisation; it is an instance, a set of empty instances which in no way operate through their content; *good* form, *good* lighting, *good* editing, *good* sound mixing are not good because they conform to perceptual or social reality, but because they are a priori scenographic *operators* which on the contrary determine the objects to be recorded on the screen and in 'reality'.

PUTTING OUT OF SCENE [*LA MISE HORS SCÈNE*]

Mise-en-scène is not an artistic activity; it is a general process touching all fields of activity, a profoundly unconscious process of separation, exclusion and effacement. In other words, direction is simultaneously executed on two planes, with this being its most enigmatic aspect. On the one hand, this task consists of separating reality on one side and a play space on the other (a 'real' or an 'unreal' – that which is in the camera's lens): to direct [*mettre en scène*] is to institute this limit, this frame, to circumscribe the region of de-responsibility at the heart of a whole which *ideo facto* is posed as responsible (we will call it *nature*, for example, or *society* or *final instance*). Thus is established between the two regions a relation of representation or doubling accompanied necessarily by a relative devaluation of the scene's realities, now only representative of the realities of reality. But on the other hand, and inseparably, in order for the function of representation to be fulfilled, the activity of mise-en-scène (a placing in and out of scene, as we have just said) must also be an activity which unifies all the movements, those on *both sides* of the frame's limit, imposing here *and* there, in 'reality' just as in the real [*réel*], the *same norms*, the same ordering of all drives, excluding obliterating, effacing them *no less off* the scene than on. The references imposed on the filmic object are imposed just as necessarily on all objects outside the film. Direction first divides – along the axis of representation, and due to the theatrical limit – a reality and its double, and this disjunction constitutes an obvious repression. But also, beyond this representational disjunction and in a 'pre-theatrical' economic order, it eliminates *all impulsional movement, real or unreal, which will not lend itself to reduplication,* all movement which would escape identification, recognition and the mnesic fixation. Considered from the angle of this primordial function of an exclusion spreading to the exterior as well as to the interior of the cinematographic playground, mise-en-scène acts always as a factor of *libidinal normalisation,* and does so independently of all 'content' be it as 'violent' as might seem. This normalisation consists of the exclusion from the scene of whatever cannot be folded back upon the body of the film, and outside the scene, upon the social body.

The *film*, strange formation reputed to be normal, is no more normal than the *society* or the *organism*. All of these so-called objects are the result of the imposition and hope for an accomplished totality. They are supposed to realise the reasonable goal *par excellence*, the subordination of all partial drives, all sterile and divergent movements to the unity of an organic body. The film is the organic body of cinematographic movements. It is the *ecclesia* of images: just as politics is that of the partial social organs. This is why mise-en-scène, a technique of exclusions and effacements, a political activity *par excellence*, and political activity, which is mise-en-scène *par excellence*, are the religion of the modern irreligion, the ecclesiastic of the secular. The central problem for both is not the representational arrangement and its accompanying question, that of knowing how and what to represent and the definition of good or true representation; the fundamental problem is the exclusion and foreclosure of all that is judged unrepresentable because non-recurrent.

Thus film acts as the orthopaedic mirror analysed by Lacan in 1949 as constitutive of the imaginary subject of *objet a*; that we are dealing with the social body in no way alters its function. But the real problem, missed by Lacan due to his Hegelianism, is to know why the drives spread about the polymorphous body *must have* an object where they can unite. That the imperative of unification is given as hypothesis in a philosophy of 'consciousness' is betrayed by the very term 'consciousness', but for a 'thought' of the unconscious (of which the form related most to pyrotechnics would be the economy sketched here and there in Freud's writings), the question of the production of unity, even an imaginary unity, can no longer fail to be posed in all its opacity. We will no longer have to pretend to understand how the subject's unity is constituted from his image in the mirror. We will have to ask ourselves how and why the *specular wall* in general, and thus the cinema screen in particular, can become a privileged place for the libidinal cathexis; why and how the drives come to take their place on the film [*pellicule*, or *petite peau*], opposing it to themselves as the place of their inscription, and what is more, as the support that the filmic operation in all its aspects will efface. A libidinal economy of the cinema should theoretically construct the operators which exclude aberrations from the social and organic bodies and channel the drives into this *dispositif*. It is not clear that narcissism or masochism are the proper operators: they carry a tone of subjectivity (of the theory of the Ego) that is probably still much too strong.

THE TABLEAU VIVANT

The acinema, we have said, would be situated at the two poles of the cinema taken as a writing of movements: thus, extreme immobilisation and extreme mobilisation. It is only for *thought* that these two modes are incompatible. In a libidinal economy they are, on the contrary, necessarily associated; stupefaction, terror, anger, hate, pleasure – all the intensities – are always displacements in place. We should read the term *emotion* as a *motion* moving towards its own exhaustion, an immobilising motion, an immobilised mobilisation. The representational arts offer two symmetrical examples of these intensities, one where immobility appears: the tableau vivant; another where agitation appears: lyric abstraction.

Presently there exists in Sweden an institution called the *posering*, a name derived from the *pose* solicited by portrait photographers: young girls rent their services to these special houses, services which consist of assuming, clothed or unclothed, the poses desired by the client. It is against the rules of these houses (which are not houses of prostitution) for the clients to touch the models in any way. We would say that this institution is made to order for the phantasmatic of Klossowski, knowing as we do the importance he accords to the tableau vivant as the near perfect simulacrum of fantasy in all its paradoxical intensity. But it must be seen how the paradox is distributed in this case: the immobilisation seems to touch only the erotic object while the subject is found overtaken by the liveliest agitation.

But things are probably not as simple as they might seem. Rather, we must understand this *dispositif* as a demarcation on both sides, that of model and client, of the regions of extreme erotic intensification, a demarcation performed by one of them, the client whose integrity reputedly remains intact. We see the proximity such a formulation has to the Sadean problematic of *jouissance*. We must note, given what concerns us here, that the tableau vivant in general, if it holds a certain libidinal potential, does so because it brings the theatrical and economic orders into communication; because it uses 'whole persons' as detached erotic regions to which the spectator's impulses are connected. (We must be suspicious of summing this up too quickly as a simple voyeurism.) We must sense the price, beyond price, as Klossowski admirably explains, that the organic body, the pretended unity of the pretended subject, must pay so that the pleasure will burst forth in its irreversible sterility. This is the same price that the cinema should pay if it goes to the first of its extremes, immobilisation: because this latter (which is not simple immobility) means that it would be necessary to endlessly undo the conventional syntheses that normally all cinematographic movements proliferate. Instead of good, unifying and reasonable forms proposed for identification, the image would give rise to the most intense agitation through its fascinating paralysis. We could already find many underground and experimental films illustrating this direction of immobilisation.

Here we should begin the discussion of a matter of singular importance: if you read Sade or Klossowski, the paradox of immobilisation is seen to be clearly distributed along the representational axis. The object, the victim, the prostitute, takes the pose, offering his or her self as a detached region, but *at the same time giving way and humiliating this whole person.* The allusion to this latter is an indispensable factor in the intensification since it indicates the inestimable price of diverting the drives in order to achieve perverse pleasure. Thus representation is essential to this fantasmatic; that is, it is essential that the spectator be offered instances of identification, recognisable forms, all in all, matter for the memory: for it is at the price, we repeat, of going beyond this and disfiguring the order of propagation that the intense emotion is felt. It follows that the simulacrum's support, be it in the writer's descriptive syntax, the film of Pierre Zucca whose photographs illustrate (?) Klossowski's *La Monnaie Vivante*, the paper on which Klossowski himself sketches – it follows that the support itself must not submit to any noticeable perversion in order that the perversion attack only what is supported, the representation of the victim: the support is held in insensibility or unconsciousness. From here springs Klossowski's active militancy in favour of representational plastics and his anathema for abstract painting.

ABSTRACTION

But what occurs if, on the contrary, it is the support itself that is touched by perverse hands? Then the film, movements, lightings and focus refuse to produce the recognisable image of a victim or immobile model, taking on themselves the price of agitation and libidinal expense and leaving it no longer to the fantasised body. All lyric abstraction in painting maintains such a shift. It implies a polarisation no longer towards the immobility of the model but towards the mobility of the support. This mobility is quite the contrary of cinematographic movement; it arises from any process which undoes the beautiful forms suggested by this latter, from any process which to a greater or lesser degree works on and distorts these forms. It blocks the synthesis of identification and thwarts the mnesic instances. It can thus go far towards achieving an *ataxy* of the iconic constituents, but this is still to be understood as a mobilisation of the support. This way of frustrating the beautiful movement *by means of the support* must not be confused with that working through a paralysing attack on the victim who serves as motif. The model is no longer needed, for the relation to the body of the client-spectator is completely displaced.

How is *jouissance* instantiated by a large canvas by Pollock or Rothko or by a study by Richter, Baruchello or Eggeling? If there is no longer a reference to the loss of the unified body due to the model's immobilisation and its diversion to the ends of partial discharge, just how inestimable must be the disposition the client-spectator can have; the represented ceases to be the libidinal object while the screen itself, in all its most formal aspects, takes its place. The film strip is no longer abolished (made transparent) for the benefit of this or that flesh, for it offers itself as the flesh posing itself. But from what unified body is it torn so that the spectator may enjoy, so that it seems to him to be beyond all price? Before the minute thrills which hem the contact regions adjoining the chromatic sands of a Rothko canvas, or before the almost imperceptible movements of the little objects or organs of Pol Bury, it is at the price of renouncing his own bodily totality and the synthesis of movements making it exist that the spectator experiences intense pleasure: these objects demand the paralysis not of the object-model but of the 'subject'-client, the decomposition of his own organism. The channels of passage and libidinal discharge are restricted to very small partial regions (eye–cortex), and almost the whole body is neutralised in a tension blocking all escape of drives from passages other than those necessary to the detection of very fine differences. It is the same, although following other modalities, with the effects of the excess of movement in Pollock's paintings or with Thompson's manipulation of the lens. Abstract cinema, like abstract painting, in rendering the support opaque reverses the *dispositif,* making the client a victim. It is the same again though differently in the almost imperceptible movements of the Nô Theatre.

The question, which must be recognised as being crucial to our time because it is that of the mise-en-scène and therefore of the staging of society [*la mise en société*] (outside scene), is the following: is it necessary for the victim to be in the scene for the *jouissance* to be intense? If the victim is the client, if there is in the scene only the film, the screen, the canvas, the support, do we lose to this *dispositif* all the intensity of the sterile discharge? And if so, must we then renounce the hope of finishing with the illusion, not only the cinematographic illusion but also the social and political illusions? Are they not really illusions then? Or is believing so the illusion? Must the return of extreme intensities be founded on at least this empty permanence, on the phantom of the organic body or subject which is the proper noun, and at the same time that they cannot really accomplish this unity? This foundation, this love, how does it differ from that anchorage in nothing which founds capital?[1]

Translated by Paisley N. Livingston
(Modified by Peter W. Milne and Ashley Woodward)

NOTE

1. These reflections would not have been possible without the practical and theoretical work accomplished for several years by and with Dominique Avron, Claudine Eizykman and Guy Fihman.

CHAPTER 5

The Unconscious as Mise-en-scène

Jean-François Lyotard

First of all, I should make clear what I mean by the word 'mise-en-scène'. 'Mettre en scène' (to stage) is to transmit signifiers from a 'primary' space to another space, which is the auditorium of a theatre, cinema, or any related art. I offer a classic example: one evening, at the Paris Opera, we are listening to *Der Rosenkavalier*, by Richard Strauss. This is a 'performance'; of what is it made? Singer-actors on stage, musicians in the orchestra pit, stage-hands and light crew in the wings, all are following a large number of prescriptions. Some of these are inscribed in certain documents: the libretto by Hoffmanstahl, the score by Richard Strauss. Others can be solely oral, from the director Rudolf Steinbock – as in stage directions for the actors or directions for the lighting and scenery. This simplified example enables us to distinguish three different phases of the staged work.

The final phase is the performance we are attending. It consists of a group of stimuli – colours, movements, light, sounds. This ensemble which besieges our sensory body 'tells' it a story – in this example, the story of *Der Rosenkavalier*. The performance steers us along a course composed of a series of audible intensities, timbres and pitches; of sentences and words arranged according to expert rhetoric; and of colours, intensities of light, etc.

The initial phase of the work (but is it a work at this point?) is characterised by the heterogeneity of the arts which will be used to put the performance together: a written drama, a musical score, the design of the stage and auditorium, the machinery at the disposal of the theatre, etc. We have here groups of signifiers forming so many messages, or constraints in any case, belonging to different systems: the rules of the German (or better, Austrian) language, the rules of the prevalent rhetoric, and those prevailing in Hoffmanstahl's writing on the one hand; and on the other hand, the constraints of musical composition and Strauss' own relation to those constraints, etc.; nevertheless, even in this initial phase, there is something which limits the disorder that could result from such a heterogeneity – this is the single reference imposed on all the messages which make up the work: the story of *Der Rosenkavalier* itself.

But what is this story itself, this reference, if not an effect of reality produced by a certain combination of various signifiers contributed by the different arts? It is the very function of this kind of mise-en-scène to create this effect of reality, the story, to make it the apparent motive of the work. The mise-en-scène cannot succeed unless a great number of new decisions are made, decisions not prescribed by the writer, the musician, or the designer; the mise-en-scène must specify the execution of such and such a narrative sequence in the finest detail, and that implies the detailed coordination of the orchestra's actions and those of the singer-actors, together with the lighting effects controlled by the light crew.

The intervention of the director is thus no less creative than that of the poet or the musician; but it is not on the same level as theirs. The director's intervention is a subsequent elaboration of their product. In this sense, the mise-en-scène is subordinate to the noble arts of drama, music, etc. But inversely, the mise-en-scène takes hold of the text, the score and the architectural space and it 'gives life', as they say, to these signifiers. 'Gives life' means two things: 1) the mise-en-scène turns written signifiers into speech, song and movements executed by bodies capable of moving, singing and speaking; and this transcription is intended for other living bodies – the spectators – capable of being moved by these songs, movements and words. It is this transcribing on and for bodies, considered as multi-sensory potentialities, which is the work characteristic of the mise-en-scène. Its elementary unity is polyaesthetic like the human body: capacity to see, to hear, to touch, to move . . . The idea of performance (in French: *la représentation de ce soir*, this evening's performance) even if it remains vague, seems linked to the idea of inscription on the body.

I might add that I would find the same essential characteristics were I to analyse the function of mise-en-scène in films, at least in the great Hollywood productions of the 1930s. If I have taken my example from the operas of Richard Strauss, it is only to remain in the cultural context which was Freud's. The important thing in this context is that mise-en-scène consists of a complex group of operations, each of which transcribes a message written in a given sign system (literary writing, musical notation) and turns it into a message capable of being inscribed on human bodies and transmitted by those to other bodies: a kind of somatography. Even more important, and less dependent on the classic context, is the simple fact of transcription – that is, the fact of a change in the space of inscription – call it a diagraphy, which henceforth will be the main characteristic of mise-en-scène.

Psychoanalysis is first of all an interpretative method. In any interpretative method there is the presupposition that the data to be interpreted simultaneously display and conceal a primary message which the interpreter should be able to read clearly. The interpreter unravels what the director has put together. In several studies, *The Interpretation of Dreams* (*Die Traumdeutung*) in particular, 'A Contribution to the Study of the Origins of Sexual Perversions', and at the end of the analysis of Schreber's paranoia, Freud ventures to put forward the single or various possible readings of the messages hidden in symptoms such as paranoid delusion, fantasies, and dreams. We know that for Freud desire is what gives utterance to these primary messages, whereas the unconscious is their director and gives them a disguise in order to exhibit them on the stage. The accent is on deception. In colloquial French one says to a hypocrite: '*arrête ton cinema*', 'cut the act'.

This presupposition raises a difficulty, both theoretical and technical, which comes straight from the preceding notion of mise-en-scène. If it is true that symptoms, obscure as they are, result from the mise-en-scène of transparent libidinal messages, their interpretation then requires operations closer to deciphering than translation. For translation consists, at least in principle, in transcribing linguistic signifiers into other linguistic signifiers, while referring to a signified supposedly independent of the two languages. But when we trace the symptomatic 'performance' back to the elements which, in principle, constitute its primary phase, we must shift from one register of inscription (the register of somatic symptoms in the case of conversion hysteria, for example) to an entirely different register (in the example, the register in which the desire of the patient is supposed to 'speak'), that is, a linguistic register which is clearly intelligible. This transcription encounters at least two difficulties: 1) when we say that desire 'speaks', are we using metaphor to say that desire is not nonsense? If so, it does not follow that the meaning of its expressions (the symptoms) is of a linguistic nature. If not, that is, if desire really speaks a language, then we must elaborate its grammar and vocabulary, which brings us to the second difficulty: 2) the operations that permit one to deduce the primary message from its performance do not seem to be rule-governed, as Freud himself acknowledges. The transcription of a libidinal message into symptoms seems to be achieved through irregular, unexpected devices. We may say, and Freud himself says, that the unconscious uses all means, including the most crudely fashioned puns, to stage desire. That seems likely to cut short interpretation, properly speaking.

Let us consider the case of dreams. Freud clearly distinguishes the three phases of representation we described for mise-en-scène. Dreamthoughts (*Traumgedanke*) constitute the primary data (the libretto, the score), which are supposed to be perfectly legible. Freud calls the 'performance' dream-content

(*Trauminhalt*), that is, the narrative told by the patient on the stage of the analyst's couch. The dream-work (*die Traumarbeit*), which turns dreamthoughts into dream-content, is the equivalent of mise-en-scène. According to Freud, this mise-en-scène works by means of a set of four operators: condensation, displacement, the taking into consideration of suitability for plastic representation, and secondary revision. It may be that these are universal operators for mise-en-scène. But it is certain that contrary to the hypotheses of Jacobson and Lacan they are not linguistic operators (especially those a translator would use). Even if for certain ones (condensation and displacement) we can find equivalents in language, we would not find them on the supposedly primary level of enunciation but on the very complex level of rhetorical or stylistic formulation, as Benveniste has shown. Yet that level already implies a certain mise-en-scène in the writer's or speaker's practice. Actually, these 'levels' exist only in the fiction of structuralists: the most simple utterance carries with it a primitive rhetoric. Its being uttered, its arrangements, have already made it a diminutive stage.

Still another observation on the way in which Freud, from the outset, formulates interpretation. The two basic ideas of mise-en-scène and interpretation are like the recto and verso of the same principle, which is a principle of distrust. In the presence of a dream or a symptom, in the presence of data in general, one decides to be wary: This datum, one thinks, does not say what it says; it is deceptive. This is the principle that Nietzsche identified perfectly as at the origin of the desire of knowledge. One must not be deceived just as in ethics one must not deceive. According to this principle, mise-en-scène is only the implementation of deception which in return gives rise to the counter-effect of truth on the part of the interpreter, the search for causes and errors, the correction of the data. Yet we can ask, along with Nietzsche, why is it better not to be deceived than to be deceived? And above all: aren't we surely deceived by our heeding only distrust?

Die Traumdeutung was completed in 1899. Twenty years later in 1919, Freud published the analysis of a fantasy called 'A Child is Being Beaten'. We are interested in this text for two reasons. At that time, Freud had completely revised his first typography of the psychic apparatus and was revising his libido theory (theory of instincts). It was in 1920 in *Beyond the Pleasure Principle* that he worked out the theory of death instincts and the theory of general repetition.

We are dealing with a much more sophisticated hypothesis about the messages of desire than the one developed in *The Interpretation of Dreams*. Moreover, the analysis of 'A Child is Being Beaten' is conducted in such a systematic way as to provide a veritably microscopic dissection of the unconscious as stage director.

It is a fantasy very common with women. Its appearance coincides with masturbation; and acknowledgement of the fantasy is made difficult by a strong feeling of shame. The fantasy consists in a kind of scene or tableau vivant where the patient, placed in the position of spectator, sees an adult authority figure (a school-master, a teacher) flogging some young boys. With the help of his patients' recollections, Freud 'discovers' that this scene hides another one, which he sums up with the sentence: 'The father is beating the child (that I hate).' This first phase constitutes the primary message, whereas the scene 'A child is being beaten' is similar to the final performance. In between there is the mise-en-scène.

But it is not as simple as this. Between the first and the last phase, Freud says, it is necessary to postulate an intermediate phase which he calls: 'my father is beating me'. Phase no. 2 is not related to any recollections mentioned by the patients. It results from a construction (*Konstruction*) built by the analyst. In brief, the whole process is *not* achieved in two steps but three steps to be enumerated in the following 'chronological' order: 1) the father is beating the child that I hate; 2) my father is beating me; 3) a child is being beaten.

It is impossible here to examine in detail all the transformations that succeed one another from the first phase of the fantasy to the last one. I will limit myself to two observations.

First, Freud disassociates the different components of the scene for each phase, just as we disassociated the components of the mise-en-scène that were music, libretto, lighting, etc. I mean that from one phase to the other, each component is dealt with in a specific way. He writes: 'Beating-phantasies have an historical development which is by no means simple, and in the course of which they are changed in most respects more than once – as regards their relation to the author of the phantasy, and as regards their object, their content, and their significance' (*Collected Papers*, II, 178). When Freud speaks of the *relation* of the fantasy to the patient, he refers to her position in relation to the stage: Is she on the stage or in the audience? She is a spectator in the first phase, and she seems to be so in the third; but she is an actress in the second: it is then *she* who is the child that is beaten. With the word *content* Freud refers to the clinical manifestation in which the fantasy is one symptom among others (as Jean Nassif says): phase no. 3 seems to be sadistic, like phase no. 1, and phase no. 2 masochistic. The *object* is the sex of the victim: either a boy or a girl in phase no. 1; always boys in the last phase, but in the intermediate phase, it is the patient herself as a little girl. And with *significance* Freud refers to the value in terms of affect of the act of beating: Is a person flogged through love or hatred? If my father beats the child that I – his daughter – hate, then he loves me. But if, as in phase no. 2, my father beats me, it is to punish me because he hates the incestuous love I feel for him. In the third phase the masochistic component is maintained, but enveloped in sadism: The value of the final scene in terms of affect is ambivalence.

We see that we need a great number of operations, each of them working on a particular component in phases 1 and 2, in order to arrive at the result of the final performance. And in this sense, Freud's analysis is an important contribution to the understanding of mise-en-scène, at least in the still traditional form we defined in the example of Richard Strauss. We also realise that these operations are entirely misleading. For instance, from 'the father is beating the child that I hate' to 'my father is beating me', it is necessary that the patient, who was a spectator, become an actress, that the love of the father be turned into hatred, that the hatred for the other child be changed into the hatred the little girl feels for herself, that the initial jealousy, which perhaps is not even sexualised, be replaced by a drive with a strongly anal component, that the sex of the victim be changed (from male to female), along with the position of the patient in relation to the stage. Likewise, to get from sentence no. 1 to sentence no. 3 requires linguistic transformations: the active voice in 'The father is beating the child' becomes the passive voice in 'A child is being beaten', the determinant *the* in *the child* is turned into *a*, and the part of the father is finally deleted.

After *The Interpretation of Dreams*, Freud elaborated a great number of these operations, particularly in the various studies which make up the *Metapsychology* published in 1914.

It is these operations which we find explicitly or not in the transformations undergone by the tableau of the fantasy 'A Child is Being Beaten'. Since these operations are, according to Freud, characteristic of the unconscious, it is indeed the unconscious that stages the discourse of the young girl's desire, and this mise-en-scène, far from being a translation, would be the transcription of a pictorial text of virtual bodies, with effect on the real body of the spectator (masturbation). Somatography requires both the exhibition and the concealment of the initial message.

The time has come to make a second observation on the nature of mise-en-scène in this text of Freud's compared to what it was in *The Interpretation of Dreams*. Are we able to speak here of fantasy-thoughts as Freud, in 1900, spoke of dreamthoughts? Can we identify a primary message of equally primary signification underneath the fantasmatic performance – something akin to the wish: that my father love me? Certainly not. What stands in the way is the considerably greater importance which Freud attached to the dynamics and the economy of drives. In 1900, dream-thoughts could be rather simply formulated because the conception of the desire which gave them utterance was itself rather simple: this desire was more a wish, *ein Wunsch*, than a force. The distinction could be made rather clearly between what desire 'said', even secretly, and what the unconscious mise-en-scène made it say in the dream's manifest content. But in our text of 1919, it's an entirely different matter: not only are these operations of mise-en-scène much more complex than the four operations described in *The*

Interpretation of Dreams, but desire is no longer conceived of as a wish, but as a bloc of forces, in the sense of a dynamics. These forces are called instincts, or better, drives. They are characterised by their impetus or by their aim (to love or hate, for example), by their object, that is, by whatever elements these forces lay siege to or invest. But drives are never observable in themselves; they are always represented, and by three kinds of representatives: words, images and affects.

I will not develop here the question of representing drives on the symptom-stage. The important point is that drives themselves can undergo genuine metamorphoses. Freud lists four of them in 'Drives and their Vicissitudes' (1915): 1) reversal into its opposite (love is transformed into hate, for example); 2) the turning round upon the subject's own self (for example, the love for a person who has passed away is transformed into love for oneself through griefwork; or sadism is transformed into masochism); 3) repression; and finally 4) sublimation; these last two further affecting the outcome of metamorphoses of drive-representatives.

In the case of the beaten child fantasy, we have seen that what separates phase one and phase two, for example, is not only stage work involving representatives, it is also and above all a working which affects the objects and aims of the drives themselves: the change from sadism to masochism implies the reversal of active pleasure into its opposite, passive pleasure, and the turning round of the initial object of the drives (the other child) upon the subject of the patient. Therefore it is not the director's interpretation of the libretto and the score which is modified, it is the libretto and score themselves which have changed between the two phases, to the point of expressing the opposite of what they were 'saying'. A second, entirely different mode of desire has annexed itself to the primary mode.

Will we be able to say that this second phase of the fantasy represents the first phase? That the girl's masochism is a mise-en-scène on her initial sadism? We would have to suppose that the messages of desire are not elementary but that they are already performances and that they have been worked at by a kind of pre-mise-en-scène. But this pre-mise-en-scène would then deal with nothing but the 'drive-text', if we can still go on speaking thusly, and it would be much more archaic than the mise-en-scène we have spoken of up until now, which was concerned only with drive-representatives. Finally, it would be necessary to explain why, in order to be represented, the initial sadism must be transformed into masochism.

Sometimes Freud lets himself be carried away by this vertigo of representation and causality which keeps endlessly multiplying mise-en-scène, changing representeds into representatives of other representeds. However, the properties which Freud acknowledges in the drive processes prohibit our following him along this line. They indicate the opposite direction. In numerous texts,

Freud insists on the fact that the logical, spatial and temporal properties of the 'primary processes', which are the metamorphoses of drives, do not fit into the categories of rational thought. From our perspective, this means that primary messages, subsequently staged by a set of transcriptions, do not 'speak' at all. I will give only one example of these texts; it concerns the temporality of drives and it can be applied perfectly to the case of the beaten-child fantasy. It is a passage from the 1915 article 'Drives and their Vicissitudes':

> We may split up the life of each drive into a series of 'thrusts' distinct from one another in the time of their occurrence but each homogeneous within its own period, whose relation to one another is comparable to that of successive eruptions of lava. We can then perhaps picture to ourselves that the earliest and most primitive drive-eruption persists in an unchanged form and undergoes no development at all. The next 'thrust' would then from the outset have undergone a change of form, being turned, for instance, from active to passive, and it would then, with this new characteristic, be superimposed upon the earlier layer, and so on. So that, if we take a survey of the tendency of drives from its beginning up to any given stopping-point, the succession of 'thrusts' which we have described would present the picture of a definite development of the drive.
>
> The fact that, at that later period of development, the drive in its primary form may be observed side by side with its (passive) opposite deserves to be distinguished by the highly appropriate name introduced by Bleuler: *ambivalence*.

This text, as well as those works of Freud that echo it, is of great importance for our problem. A drive-siege never lets up; the opposite or inverse investment which accompanies it does not suppress the first, does not even conceal it, but sets itself up next to it. All investments are, in this way, contemporaneous with each other: one loves and hates the same object at the same time and in the same respect, which is contrary to the rules of intelligibility and chronology.

If such are the space, time and logic of drives, then the desire of the woman who fantasises the beaten child is not a clear message; it is composed of three drive-investments that 1) are logically incompossible, 2) are simultaneous, and 3) concern the same regions of the body. Therefore we must not say that the unconscious stages the message of desire. We must at least say that desire is not a legible text, and that it need not be given a disguise by a mise-en-scène in order to be represented, since it eludes interpretation on its own, due to its dischronisms, its polytopisms and its paralogisms.

If we follow this direction which Freud indicates here and there starting in 1920, it is thus the distinction between the discourse of desire and its being disguised by the mise-en-scène of the unconscious which tends to become inoperative. For that reason, the idea of mise-en-scène tends both to expand itself inordinately and to overextend itself to the point of vanishing. And it is in this way that it becomes congruent with the theatrical, critical, artistic and perhaps political inquiries which make up what Ihab Hassan calls 'postmodernism' and which Freud's explicit and implicit aesthetics resolutely ignores.

In conclusion, to illustrate this orientation, I shall use the example of an already classic work from the visual arts Underground which permits a good approach to the problem of mise-en-scène in a contemporary context. My goal in choosing this work is to make clear *a contrario* just how much the Freudian conception of the unconscious and even desire depends on a particular aesthetic, that of official late nineteenth-century Viennese theatre and opera. If we are attentive to what is going on now, notably in the most audacious inquiries in the most recent arts, and if we bring their lessons back to Freud's discourse, not only will it seem necessary to diminish the import of his discourse but we will also better understand what are the stakes of 'postmodernism' as a whole. What is at stake is not to exhibit truth within the closure of representation but to set up *perspectives* within the return of the *will*.

La Région centrale is a 'film' by Michael Snow, shot in Canada in 1970–1. A special device designed by the filmmaker allows the axis of the camera to be positioned in all possible directions around the point where the camera is connected to the device. This device is itself attached to a mobile shaft which can also turn in every direction around a swivel joint attached to the body of the apparatus. Finally, this apparatus is fixed to the ground. The lens can thus scan every plane passing through all the points of the sphere of the shaft's movements. Because camera and shaft rotate independently of each other, the final speed resulting from their velocities can vary. The setting of the focal distance is synchronised with the motion of the lens so that the images are always legible. The apparent velocity of transition from one image to another varies with the distance of the objects. The apparatus is placed on an elevated platform which overlooks a forest skyline and a landscape with lakes on one side, but on the other side the view is limited by a rocky ridge. The zenith and the nearest patch of ground, including the base of the apparatus, appear in the shot for the same reason as do all the horizontal planes.

The film is presented as a series of continuous sequences. Each one is accorded a unit of velocity and a unit of greater complexity due to the distinctness of the respective movements of camera and shaft. The scanning thus proposed by Michael Snow lasts about three hours in all. The spectator's gaze is carried along supple and irregular trajectories explored by the lens and carried away on a both infinite and bounded voyage that opens up every perspective on sky and ground to the gaze. Not only do the angles and distances change continually but also the light and colour. No sounds assist in interpreting the images, with the exception of a weak signal which indicates changes in the program of the apparatus' movements.

It would take too long to examine the work Michael Snow has done on each of the parameters of traditional cinematographic representation. May three remarks be sufficient:

1. The stage, in its usual sense, supposes a stage-frame, a picture frame, an image-frame, that demarcates three regions with its edge: the unreal space, Freud would say fantasmatic or oneiric, where the action takes place; the real space where the spectators are; and the hidden space where the theatre machinery is concealed. Because of this framing, this kind of mise-en-scène implies a complementary unframing. Michael Snow's apparatus eliminates framing: he lets us see what traditional framing excludes from the shot, including the machinery itself. And owing to the fact that he dispenses with the wings, the orchestra pit and the idea of a meaning hidden underneath appearances, he abandons the principle of distrust.

The device which produces *La Région centrale* belongs to a paradoxical logic related to that of the sophists and Nietzsche: there is nothing but perspectives; one can invent new ones. The statement that there are only perspectives includes itself among them, just as Snow's camera aims itself at its own base. With such a logic, the function of language is no longer to signify a given object, and the function of the image is no longer to deceive by means of false recognition. Language is not made for telling the truth and film is not made to disguise truth on a fantasmatic stage. Both are inexhaustible means for experimenting with new effects, never seen, never heard before. They create their own reference, therefore their object is not identifiable; they create their own addressee, a disconcerted body, invited to stretch its sensory capacities beyond measure.

2. The closure of the movements of Snow's camera results in all the images referring to a same space, but the infinite variety of scannings results in their all being different. There we have the visual equivalent of the Freudian metaphor of drive-eruptions: many different figures, a close-up of a pebble, a lake on the horizon, a cloud, are all packed into the same region by the camera.

This region is central because all the figures smash themselves on Snow's film due to the coagulent, contripetal, materialist force of the lens' journey. But the bloc of figures thus stockpiled remains without stable identity, and that is due to the fact that the images are not actually taken from a fixed centre but by a lens whose very complex movement results from the composition of two movements, those of the camera and shaft. The accumulation of figures on the film succeeds in not constituting any identifiable geometric space, such as a stage should be so that a story may be enacted there. The centre of the region is a labyrinth.

3. The time of *La Région centrale* breaks with that of narration: the film doesn't tell any story. Not only is there no action rolling along, but any unrolling of images is at the same time their being rolled around each other because of the closure of the lens' movements. Or else, but it is still the same thing, the film tells all the tales born of all the images it shows. At every moment, the spectator has the possibility of isolating a single view and of using it to start telling a story about skylines or forests, or the stuff of the earth, or the clouds in the sky, etc.; all of these budding stories form an immense chatter in which we find all times mixed together (for example, astronomical, geological and technological time). Here again, whether the accent is placed on the atemporality of the film or on the multitemporality of these stories, we encounter an equivalent of the dischronisms of Freud's primary processes, and we understand why Michael Snow preferred the weak and, properly speaking, drive-like sound which gives a rhythm to the movements of the apparatus, to any utterance, no matter how bizarre.

Can we say that mise-en-scène has disappeared from such a spectacle? The mise-en-scène by a Rudolf Steinbock or a libretto by Hoffmanstahl and a score by Richard Strauss – yes (if at least we ignore the frame of the movie screen). But not mise-en-scène as somatography, and not as diagraphy either. For nothing prevents us from saying that here the camera is the interpreter of a text, namely, the program which Snow fed into his machine and whose written signifiers the machine transforms into movements and into emotions on the spectators' bodies.

Are Snow's instructions analogous to the discourse of desire and are the machine's operations analogous to the mise-en-scène of desire by the unconscious? This could be stretching the analogy a bit. Snow's filming machine cannot be compared to Freud's machine of the unconscious unless we underline the strange character of the operations they perform, one on drive-material, the other on visual material. And if we can say that Snow's program of movements is a result of desire, it would be on the condition of understanding desire not as a set of instructions promoted by some love- or hate-wish but as the will to create realities. This double restriction is sufficient to displace the problematic of the unconscious and mise-en-scène from Freud to Nietzsche and beyond.

When the force used to stage something has no goal other than to make manifest its potentiality, when it is the same force that produces and implements the most sophisticated programs and machines, the distinction between desire and the unconscious disappears entirely. By the same token, works must not be taken as symptoms symbolically expressing a concealed discourse, but as attempts to state perspectives of reality. Interpretation must in turn give way to descriptions of devices. As for these descriptions, they are no less prescriptive in nature than works; they continue and eventually reroute the perspective-creating potentialities these works contain. Inversely, the time has come to consider the would-be symptoms as artistic creations.

Instead of our interpreting the mise-en-scènes of the unconscious, we should use these works to set up perspectives of realities with an eye on enjoying heretofore unexperienced intensities. The machines which are drawn into play are, essentially, no longer the machines of illusion and memory, but apparati for experimentation which permit us to quarter sensibility and draw it out beyond this old body.

Translated by Joseph Maier

CHAPTER 6

Two Metamorphoses of the Seductive in Cinema

Jean-François Lyotard

1. The title is doubly deceptive. It seems assertive; it should be interrogative. The question is: whether anything escapes from seduction. It is proposed apropos of political cinema. The two cases are: the work of Syberberg, and the sequence of the attack on the Vietnamese village by the American dragoon helicopters in Coppola's *Apocalypse Now*. But I will say hardly anything about the work of Syberberg.

2. There is not a Gorgias fragment preserved which does not rest on the *peithô* (persuasion), the *goètéia* (sorcery) of language, on its deception (*apatè*), its power (*dunastès*). Tragedy is a deception, he says, and he adds: 'the deceiver is more honest than the non-deceiver, and the deceived is wiser than the non-deceived' (DK 82 B23; Freeman 1953: 201).[1] Gorgias says further that 'the power of speech over the constitution of the soul can be compared with the effect of drugs on the bodily state' (DK 82 BII, 14; Freeman 1953: 198). He wonders about this power; he says that it consists in the metastasis of the opinions of the listener: their displacement, the displacement of their foundation. In a dialogue entitled *Menexenes*, Plato's Socrates describes the efficacy of the funeral oration that an orator is charged to deliver every year to the memory of the citizens who died for Athens. It appears that this efficacy consists in the metastasis of the names on the pragmatic places of the addressee (*you*), and of the referent (*they*), according to the following *dispositif*:
 – these dead were virtuous
 – they were virtuous because they were Athenians and died for Athens
 – you are Athenians
 – you are virtuous

We have in these analyses of Ancient rhetoric the rudiments of a pragmatics of seduction by language.

3. These indications suffice to situate the manner in which it appears to me interesting to speak of seduction. I don't mean as an intentional action exercised by a seducer on a victim: Gorgias' observation on tragedy signifies that both play a single game and that it's seduction itself (deception, *apatè*) which determines the rule. We no longer scan the depths of desire and pleasure. We stick to the categories of linguistic pragmatics: a discourse with what it signifies and also with its form, an addressor, an addressee, a referent (that about which the discourse speaks). Seduction would be a case of the pragmatic efficacy of discourse.

4. The question is: in what does this efficacy consist? And the method: are there pragmatic situations in which the efficacy of the discourse owes nothing to seduction? I imagine two cases: one where the discourse engenders some pragmatic effects without 'sorcery', and one where its effect is to suspend the pragmatic relation between addressor, addressee and referent. That is to say, on the one hand the non-seductive pragmatic relation; on the other hand, the suspended pragmatic relation.

5. Let us grant that the pragmatic efficacy of the seductive discourse consists in a metastasis, as Gorgias says. How to understand this? Plato gives an indication apropos of the funeral oration. The theme of the discourse is: *They (our dead) were good.* It is a descriptive narrative utterance. And yet, it acts like a prescriptive utterance: *Be good!* Likewise, the descriptive: *You have truly clear eyes*, acts like the prescriptive: *Let you approach.* Or again, the interrogative: *Where will I find affection?*, means: *Love me.* And of course a narrative of the type: *He then came across a woman whose walk made him turn around,* this narrative addressed to a woman can count as a prescription by the narrator, to beware of his interest. And not only in the case where she considers herself to walk as the heroine. It suffices in general that the story, whatever the relation of its heroes to the addressee, be 'well told', so that it modifies the position of this latter with regard to the narrator.

6. On the basis of these examples, one could venture to say in what seduction consists, at least from the point of view of the addressee: seduction would have the effect, on the addressee, of making a discourse, even if non-prescriptive, into *an obligation*. The discourse can be descriptive, interrogative, narrative, exclamative, etc.: it always conveys a non-formulated prescription. A prescription (in general) *obliges* the addressee in the sense that it suggests that he or she carry out what it orders, demands, beseeches, implores be done. The execution (*performance*) of the prescription, if it takes place, moves the addressee onto

the scene of the referent, where he or she will play out the act prescribed: on the injunction, *Close the door*, the addressee will go to close the door. But the explicit prescription only produces the obligation: the addressee may not move on to the execution. It's only on this condition that he or she can feel obliged, and not constrained.

It is in this precise sense that a descriptive discourse *does not oblige* its addressee. If, for example, it is of a scientific nature, it does not position him or her as an actor on the stage of the referent, but as an addressor of a new utterance confirming or refuting the one for which he or she was the addressee. If the descriptive discourse works through obligation, and therefore like a prescriptive, we will say that there is seduction. It's the same thing for the other genres of discourse when they have not only their specific effect (to agree or not for the demonstrative, to reply for the interrogative, etc.), but in addition place the addressee in a position of obligation.

7. That is, a narration with a high mimetic content, like Plato says, or even a completely mimetic one, which is to say one where the pragmatic relation of the narrator with his addressee is almost completely, or is completely, effaced, to the benefit of the pragmatic relations between the heroes of the story (on the stage of the referent). This is the case of theatre, at least classical theatre: the dramaturge doesn't speak as such to the spectators, but the heroes speak between themselves. The same goes for Hollywood cinema (after the invention of the talkie, the importance of which we can guess for our subject). The same goes as well for the project of total art that Wagner meant to achieve with opera. The prescriptive relation when it is explicit, performed as such, demands an I who obliges and a You who must decide. These grand narrations can represent it on the referential stage. But they obscure the places of the addressor (the director, the dramaturge, the musician) and even of the addressee (the anonymous spectator) of the narration itself. The conditions are thus favourable to the transmission of a non-explicit prescriptive discourse. We see and we hear the history of Tristan, we register the demand: *Suffer and enjoy an impossible shared love.*

8. The term realism, in cinema, must designate a perfect occultation of the places of the narrator and the narratee, that is to say, the perfect mimesis. This occultation is only realisable if the spatial and temporal frame in which the action unfolds [*se déroule*] does not permit the intervention of a director to be divined: thus, if this frame is also as consistent as possible with the cultural norms of perception in space and time that the spectators obey. These latter can then be comfortably commuted into addressees of non-explicit prescriptions conveyed by the narration. They are seduced: that they know it and accept it, or know it and don't accept it, or don't know it, is not the question. The metastasis of the spectator when *obliged* is facilitated by realism.

9. Coppola's film *Apocalypse Now* is a realist film in this sense. We see unfold [*se déroule*] the story of a dangerous search mission in the theatre of operations of Vietnam; we register the injunction: *Live the intense epic of a pointless combat.* Nonetheless, the sequence of the attack on the village by the helicopters (with the accents of the Valkyrie broadcast to the maximum power by the PA systems of the war machines) is perhaps that of another technique; call it hyperrealist. When realism becomes hyperrealist, it engenders other effects; among others, it ceases to seduce under the conditions previously described. The question is whether it ceases to seduce tout court. My hypothesis is yes. This is no more than a hypothesis. It takes shape from my perception that this scene had a completely different quality than that of the film as a whole. I have the very great difficulty of explaining myself.

10. Hyperrealism is the name that the Europeans gave to a current of American painting at the beginning of the 1970s. It was principally a novel solution given to the problem of the relation between painting and photography, a problem posed for the former since the invention of the latter. This solution holds almost entirely in three declarations. Audrey Flack: 'The photo puts within my reach things that would be inaccessible without it'; Gerhardt Richter: 'The photo is not a means useful to painting. It is painting which is a means useful to a photo created with the means of painting'; Andy Warhol, hyperrealist at least in cinema: 'If I paint in this way, it's because I want to be a machine.' Audrey Flack meant: 'The photo makes a hyperpainting possible'; Richter: 'The painting makes a hyperphoto possible'; Warhol: 'I want to be an anonymous multiplier of images, a plural and inexpressive transformer.' Mechanical reproduction (which has become a lot more than mechanical) meant for Walter Benjamin the loss of the *aura* of works. It is here accepted for three of its effects: new experimentations in the art of painting (A. Flack); new experimentations in the industrial production of images (Richter); new experimentations for the addressor, the painter (Warhol). It remains to be said what effects there are for the addressee, which is what concerns us here.

11. This acceptance of, and even the active search for, the effects of multiple reproductions is already hinted at, in reserve, in dandy art. Benjamin described it in Baudelaire, Bataille in Manet. We find it again in a certain Jacques Monory. With the theme of the multiple it finds itself associated with those of instantaneity, immobilisation (acinema), indifference (loss of *aura*), anonymity (loss of identity). But dandyism maintains them in uncertainty: should I weep or should I laugh about this new condition? Hyperrealism disregards this hesitation. It plays whole-heartedly with reproduction.

12. Bataille said that with Manet, painting lost its 'eloquence'. It no longer refers to a meaning, it seizes the event as such, it immobilises it. Eloquence is

the possibility of inscribing the painted scene in a narration, whether the latter is mythological, religious, historical, intimist, or even simply intimate in character. And the narration which situates the scene, if the latter is realist in the sense defined above, transmits to the viewer one or several prescriptions. By further destroying eloquence, the hyperrealists empty the scene of its narrative verbiage, and with the same stroke empty it of its prescriptive whispering. A reality presents itself, but without past or future. And thus, without a task proposed to the addressee. With a sort of blinding stupidity. It gives no place to history, it only relates to time through entropy or repetition. All that can happen is that the scene spoils itself or reproduces itself. The intervention of the viewer is not solicited. He or she is in no way *obligated*. In perceiving the scene, he or she reproduces it. Just as Warhol wants, he or she forms part of the machine, is devoid of the authority to transform the scene, since he or she does not receive any implicit (or obviously explicit) prescription.

13. The sequence of the attack on the village in *Apocalypse Now* placed me in something close to this condition. The difference with hyperrealism comes from the fact that the scene is not painted or photographed, but filmed, and therefore in movement. The movement of images and of sounds lends itself in principle to narrative eloquence, and to the seductive prescription which accompanies it. But here, it becomes a moment in which the scene is saturated by sonorous and visual elements all in ultra-rapid displacement, where the eye and the ear are exceeded by what is given and where the addressee is made to suffer from an excess of reality. There is a panic on the scene. All the previously sketched little stories [*petites histoires*] concerning the principal and secondary characters are wiped out or blurred, rendered ungraspable in an instant. The scene empties itself of meaning. The eloquence, along with the implicit prescriptions that are associated with it, founder in the excess of information.

14. The spectator no longer receives from the scene the implicitly given prescriptions to act: *Do this, think that.* He is in a state of loss of obligation. We have all seen many war or political films. They are all eloquent, they all show either a positive saga, or a negative saga, or an impossible saga, or a mixture of these. *Apocalypse Now* is a complete mixture: positive saga of the hero, negative saga of the sought-after officer, impossible saga of the war. But the block of images of the attack of the village does not belong to the saga, that is, to the narration, at all. One is not thrust in the direction of a task to accomplish, even an affective one. There is nothing to do, nor to project, nor to remember, nor to sense, there is no horizon. One is stupid. The panic is that no narrative can take charge of this chaos of data and suggest an obligation to the addressee. The latter is not seduced. Gorgias would say that this is not wise, or that Coppola is not just. And indeed, if one of the rules of this cinema (as of tragedy) is to seduce, this sequence brings back madness and injustice.

15. One of my friends, a young American researcher and a Vietnam veteran, tried on two occasions to bring to my attention something which must have been this madness and this injustice. He had very great difficulty writing, and even giving a presentation. But the powerlessness to speak became overwhelming when the war was in question. One day he arrived without warning with some sandwiches and wine at Californian midday. Two years later, it was quite a night of drinking and smoking. We knew nothing, only that there was something. The sequence from Coppola allowed me to understand this difficulty. It is neither guilt nor horror. There are lots of images which are placed outside obligation. He was deauthorised; he had lost all authority to take the scenes back up into a narrative, into a theory. He was struck down with stupidity, immobilised by hyperreality. The silence of the deportees on their return from the camps must belong to the same deauthorisation.

16. I say that here we are at the limits of seduction. But perhaps it is only the disappearance of *a kind* of seduction. And perhaps the stupefaction and the deauthorisation are the effects of another game of seduction. It would not be a question of prescribing covertly, it would be a question of not prescribing, of not obligating the partner, of placing him or her outside the game. Another *seducer* (another operator of seduction) would take up this function. Perhaps. But, supposing that seduction is a game, that is to say, an exchange of moves obeying a minimum of rules, divided [*découpé*] into finite parts at the end of which it is permitted to recommence with a new deal, and in which *seducer* is the name that will be borne by the winner, *seduced* by the loser, I ask myself what a 'seduction' can be which places one of the partners outside the game.

17. The other case to examine should be that of the cinema of Syberberg. I will only say one thing. Syberberg's work is obviously a reflection on seduction by the Nazi narrative, of which the Wagnerian narrative was – not only in its romantic and mythic themes, but in its form of total spectacle – a sort of paradigm. The most obvious method that the addressor Syberberg employs in order to obtain the effect of reflection on us, his addressees, is that of reading: the predominance of text, layouts with illustrations (nearly immobile tableaux vivants, flaunting their seductive power), dividing up [*découpage*] into thematic chapters (in the interview with Winifred Wagner). The question is: do we who are his addressees place the detachment that comes through this putting-into-reading of the images, that is, of prescriptive-narrative givens, outside seduction? Does it act without 'sorcery'? Or does it still prescribe something to us non-explicitly? And if yes, what does it prescribe to us? One might think that Syberberg's method picks up from the aesthetic of Bertolt Brecht. But Brecht's detachment led to a *Struggle with the Exploited*, which opened onto the horizon of an epic, the Marxist grand narrative. So we know that Brecht remained seduced by it. And yet this 'eloquence' is not there in Syberberg. Is there nothing of it at all?

It seems to me that the addressee of *Hitler: A Film from Germany* finds him or herself in the following condition: called to reflect by the nature of images, he or she is at the same time encouraged to enter into the Nazi epic by the eloquence (if not Wagnerian, at least post-Wagnerian, let's say that of a piece like Stockhausen's *Hymnen*) of the soundtrack. The romanticism of a past monstrous epic never ceases to traverse musically the plastic meditation on it. This equivocity produces contrary effects on different addressees, and sometimes on the same one. Is it a case of suspended seduction?

Translated by Peter W. Milne and Ashley Woodward

NOTE

1. TN: We have given the original text's citation of the Diels (DK) references, followed by references to the English translation by Freeman.

REFERENCES

Diels, Hermann (1951–2), *Die Fragmente der Vorsokratiker*, 3 vols, 6th edn, rev. W. Kranz, Berlin: Weidmann.
Freeman, Kathleen (1953), *Ancilla to the Pre-Socratic Philosophers*, Cambridge, MA: Harvard University Press.

CHAPTER 7

The Idea of a Sovereign Film

Jean-François Lyotard

'Sovereign' in this pompous title is not *the* sovereign. The sovereign is the supreme authority, God, Emperor, King, People. But Georges Bataille, in *Literature and Evil* (1997) or *Inner Experience* (2014), calls sovereign an experience which is not authorised and which does not appeal to any authority; an experience or an existence which appears, happens, without relation to any law by which it could claim or demand to be 'what it is'.

A writer writes without being authorised to do so; a painter paints, a filmmaker [*cinéaste*] films like this. This is not to say that they are in rebellion against authority. The case is more serious: they expect nothing from authority, they ask nothing of it. The real offence which they can suffer (but this suffering is not necessary) is not to be in conflict with the figure of authority, but to find themselves elsewhere, to start to write, to paint or to film, to start to phrase in language, in colour or in the image – without waiting for the right to do so.

This situation would be nothing but a case, would be only marginal, if, still following Bataille, this sovereign indifference to authority could not sometimes (because nothing here is certain, guaranteed, authorised. . .) give rise to a 'communication' (the word is Bataille's), to a communion incomparable to all exchange of signs. A sort of communication between the reader of the book and the writer, or the viewer of the painting and the artist, or the spectator and the filmmaker, one that is not subject to the rules of exchange (you tell me this and I hear it and I respond that (interlocutory exchange); you give me this, I receive it and I give you that (socio-economic contractual exchange)). Sovereignty exchanges nothing. The literary, pictorial or filmic work – Kafka's or Beckett's, Staël's, Robert Flaherty's, Yasujirō Ozu's or Federico Fellini's – communicates intense instants, temporal spasms, which are only transcendents because they emanate from immanence, that is to say from a realist experience and existence – as one says in filmography: neo-realist.

I will call realist any art (literary, pictorial or filmic) which represents perceptual reality (visual, sonorous, etc.) and the human voices which belong to this reality. And also which narrates [*raconte*] the movement of reality, which renders its succession in a narrative [*récit*]: a beginning, an event that is a kind of conflict, a crisis, and the outcome that constitutes the conclusion of the narrative. In music, the sonata form, imposed by romanticism on the pieces for solo instruments, for small ensembles or large orchestras, obeyed the narrative principle. In cinema, there was likewise a representative-narrative form, obtained thanks to the respecting of quite strict technical rules bearing on the composition, the shot, the linking into sequences or montage and the overall scene organisation [*découpage*]. The great productions of Hollywood obeyed this form, the same whatever the screenplay was.

Around the Second World War, one saw the appearance of a new filmic mode, in Italy first with Rossellini, later with the New Wave in France around 1958, then in Germany around 1968. Italian cinema in general was at that time called neo-realist, even if there were evident differences of style or writing between Rossellini's *Paisà*, De Sica's *The Bicycle Thief*, Antonioni's *Story of a Love Affair* or Fellini's *La Dolce Vita*. The differences were not less between Rossellini and Orson Welles' *Citizen Kane*. Yet even the great thinker on cinema that was André Bazin did not hesitate to place them together: 'Rossellini and Welles have pursued the same basic aesthetic goal and have the same aesthetic conception of realism' (2009: 243). We must place the aesthetic of Yasujirō Ozu under the sign of an analogous intuition, even if here again the writing differs.

What is this conception or this intuition? Above all a relation to time which causes the filmic material of the movement-image to pass to the time-image, to take up the terms of Gilles Deleuze's books on cinema. In the classical form, the image is subordinated to the narrative movement, it is framed and assembled in order to follow the story that the film tells, to prepare the critical event which forms its acme and to draw its consequences. The form is that of a movement, at the same time the movement of the story recounted (and thus of the characters and settings), that of the narrative (which can distinguish itself from the first, for example when the narrator of the story is him or herself a part of the scene – but without losing his or her relation to the story), and finally that of the images themselves in the order and the rhythm according to which the film presents them. All these movements are placed under the authority of a general form, and are authorised by it.

In the neo-realism or neo-realisms of the years 1940–60, the form of the movements can maintain itself and continue to exercise its authority over the filmic narration [*narration*] in all its components. But it admits or tolerates, to various degrees, movements which do not flow to the same rhythm as the flux of the whole, blocks of temporality in suspense, whose relative arrhythmy does not necessarily signal that we find ourselves at the acme of the narrative [*récit*].

In the little essay from 1973, 'Acinema', I wrote:

> The acinema . . . would be situated at the two poles of the cinema taken as a writing of movements: thus, extreme immobilisation and extreme mobilisation. It is only for *thought* that these two modes are incompatible. In a libidinal economy they are, on the contrary, necessarily associated; stupefaction, terror, anger, hate, pleasure – all the intensities – are always displacements in place . . . The representational arts offer two symmetrical examples of these intensities, one where immobility appears: the tableau vivant; another where agitation appears: lyric abstraction.

On the one hand, Piero della Francesca's painted fresco *Visit of the Queen of Sheba to Solomon* in the choir of Arezzo, or Goya's *Third of May*, on the other hand, the great works of Pollock, or Cezanne's last watercolours, made from a few evanescent coloured brushstrokes.

I tried in the same text to show the respective implications of these two polarisations on the libidinal relation between the work and the viewer. It was a little naive: I suggested that the immobilisation of the subject leads to the extreme passionate agitation of the viewer, while the latter was struck by sensory-motor paralysis in the face of incessant and disorderly tiny movements inscribed on the support.

I did not then aim to understand neo-realism, but rather to oppose the work of the cinematic avant-garde to the great narrative-representative form of commercial cinema. Now, in the best 'experimental' films a kind of ingenuousness prevails, the good ingenuousness of the explorer: they believe that they can eliminate the realism that is linked to the narrative-representative form and make a totally sovereign film. But sovereignty is absolutely allergic to totality. It occupies vacuoles, or blocks of time, in the realist-narrative progression [*déroulement*]. These moment-blocks that occur in 'neo-realist' films can be recuperated in the general movement of the narrative form, but they cannot be it: this indifference to their fate manifests their sovereignty. As for the polarisation of the extremes of mobility/immobility, one can detect it at the heart of neo-realist works. Ozu goes rather in the direction of an immobile acinema, certain scenes of Welles in the direction of an excessive speed, of an instability of the object which defies its identification and its memory (this is the very subject of *Citizen Kane*). But in truth, the two cases are little different sensorially: an object fixed at length by the gaze conceals itself to the point of no longer being seen because it loses its bearings in the context; conversely, a very rapid movement, like a whirlpool hollowed in the surface of a body of water, can be perceived as an immobile form.

The sovereignty of such moments in the film comes in the two cases from the confluence of a shot — of a sequence-shot or a linkage that is necessary to the plot and thus 'functional' in relation to the overall project — with a space-time which is not finalised; call it, provisionally, crude [*brut*]. During these instants, one always recognises the objects and the individuals, even if the movement of the camera imposes on them an evanescence by means of fixity — as in some films by Michael Snow (*Wavelength*) or Andy Warhol (*Sleep, Eat*) — or by means of celerity — as in the studies of Richter (*Fugue 20, Rythmus 21*) or Eggeling. I deliberately cite examples drawn from experimental films because they study the respective effects of two arrhythmies, the slow and the rapid, as such. All the more so in neo-realism, where the recognition, the capacity to identify the object or the person or the situation, is rarely lost. What is altered, rendered other, is the space-time in which this situation, this object or this person, which nonetheless belong to the narrative [*récit*], are presented.

The breath deregulates itself, the breath which regularly animates the narrative. A tracking shot forwards or backwards, very slow or very quick, a zoom, a panorama, a freeze frame, a fade, a defocusing, an ellipsis in the linking of shots, and many other procedures can also produce this effect of breathlessness. I am not a professional. But as an amateur, whatever the technical manoeuvre employed, one cannot fail to be sensitive to such diversions in the progression [*déroulement*] of a narrative [*narratif*] film.

It's a little as if the depiction of an object, of a situation, of people, of a face, of a hand (in Bresson for example, it is often the depiction of a hand by the camera that takes on the *unheimlich* value that a face can have in others' works) — as if this depiction, which can also be done in the manner of a sudden and rapid flight, revealed the presence of an unfamiliar reality in ordinary reality.

Is descriptive time only a suspension of narrative time, or is it an other time? The question has been debated since the origin of rhetoric and poetics. But in the works that are subject to the rules of these disciplines of know-how or of knowing-what-to-say, it is accepted that the depiction must remain subordinated to the general intention of the narrative discourse and its economy. Descriptive time is a parenthesis, a 'rest' [*soupir*] in narrative time. The reality glimpsed by means of the depiction is no more than the magnification of an element of the narrated [*racontée*] reality.

Neo-realism changes this relation. Through the windows, the descriptive vacuoles, it discovers that reality, that is, that element which belongs to the narrated story, enjoys a kind of autonomy in relation to that story. In that instant, reality eludes the role that the narration makes it play. The pot of water that the woman prepares to put on the gas in order to make coffee suddenly takes on a special intensity. As if this simple pot, which has served every morning for years to heat the water for the coffee, with the calcium stuck to the bottom from the boiling water, with the wear and tear of its handle, with the traces of knocks that it carries on its rim, tells another story.

Or, rather than another narrative sequence, it is as if the sequence-shot suggested a network of associated images, a potential constellation of situations, people, objects. The camera can help us to deploy this network, and it is here that the arrhythmy intervenes: very fast or very slow. But the camera can also cease its activity, cease its movements, station itself senselessly in front of the object, like an absent-minded gaze. The pot then becomes an ambiguous reality which from one angle lives its life under the authority of the form of the narrative but appears from another angle in its sovereign materiality, immobile and evasive, by straining everywhere the linkages, the unexpected valences with other objects, words, situations, faces and hands that are associated with the pot, and which appear and disappear. These are not memories, they are snatches of passed realities, of hopes, of possible realities, unpredictable. At that moment, 'time does not flow'. Regarding a film biography of André Gide, André Bazin wrote: 'Time does not flow. It builds up in the image, to the point of overloading it with a tremendous potential' (1958: 74). It's the same in the kitchen scene in *The Magnificent Ambersons,* the sequence-shot allowing the emergence of relationships hidden in the interior of the block of space-time that it determines.

In *Transcendental Style in Film: Ozu, Bresson, Dreyer* (1972), Paul Schrader calls these uncanny [*étranges*] moments 'stases'. The word suggests the immobilisation of chronological time, the arrest of the flow of perceptual objects or the contents of thought in the temporal flux. But it also evokes a kind of spasm which contracts the space-time of perception. Does the pot establish itself in an a-temporality? One can indeed speak of an atemporal stasis. One can also maintain, with Gilles Deleuze, that it is time itself, not what changes and flows past in time, but the form of time, which does not change and does not flow past. According to this last meaning, Paul Schrader's 'stasis' would, so to speak, present, on the occasion of the modest pot, the transcendental condition of time. Condition taken in the sense of original a priori syntheses for the formation in experience of conceivable objects such as Kant analyses in the *Critique of Pure Reason*: if we can sense that the flux of duration brings about and takes away the objects of experience, the capacity to grasp the flux must not itself be subject to this flux. Or again: sensibility or the imagination holds present moments together, even in an instant: what has just passed and what arrives. This is an instant, this paradox: the no-longer and the not-yet are held together here, now. This paradoxical structure (the instant is also its own derivative) allows us to comprehend the indiscernibility of the movement and the repose as the two extreme instances of acinema. The stasis of the pot does not narrate [*raconte*], does not unfurl the parade of events that form the story of the pot. It is a gaze which takes together at a single stroke all the past and possible events associated with this pot, not by placing them in a succession, but by co-presenting them in a virtual simultaneity. The camera works here in the manner of the Kantian *Zusammennehmung* [synthesis].

The classical definition of space characterises it as a positioning of parts separated from one another, *partes extra partes*, but also all given at the same time, *tota simul*. These are also the properties of Paul Schrader's stasis: the elements associated with the pot are discontinuous but present all together. One could say that the Kantian *Zusammennehmung* is constitutive of the space of simultaneity necessary for time to flow as succession. This space is not that in which the objects are presented according to their distance from one another and from the eye; it is non-perceptual space, transcendental, spatialising, indispensable for the perception of the change of objects in time. It is the space of time.

One can find an analogue of this situation in the Freudian representation of the unconscious. In the article 'The Unconscious', which forms part of the *Metapsychology*, Freud writes: 'The processes of the system Ucs. are timeless; i.e. they are not ordered temporally, are not altered by the passage of time; they have no reference to time at all. Reference to time is bound up, once again, with the work of the system Cs' (Freud 1947–53, vol. XIV: 187). Can one understand the stasis of the uncanny moment as a direct emanation of the timelessness of the unconscious, in the Freudian sense? A block of stray unconscious that would rise up from the depths as a piece of lava would emerge in the open ocean and form an island: thus would the block of uncanny time interrupt the fluidity of the narrative-representative progression [*déroulement*]; as a witness to another life of the psyche.

But Freud himself is opposed to this hypothesis. In fact, he adds: 'The Ucs. processes pay just as little regard to reality. They are subject to the pleasure principle', they involve the '*replacement* of external by psychical reality' (187). I emphasise: replacement. Such is not the case with the uncanny moments in neo-realist films: the pot remains recognisable – I was about to say: reasonable, according to the habitual criteria of the reality principle, on the surface of the world. The same for the situations, objects, faces which give occasion to these moments. One cannot then retain the hypothesis of a brute emanation of the unconscious, as is the case with the dream. The dream is not realist, whereas neo-realisms remain realist. They don't seek to present the equivalent of oneiric images, like surrealist cinema does. They do not subject objects, people, situations, voices to the deformations analysed by Freud under the name of the dream-work: deformations, condensations, displacements, 'figurations', symbolisations.

Dreams, psychoanalysis explained, are fulfilments of desire. Even if the latter is conceived as ambivalent, erotic desire and desire for death at the same time, their fulfilment produces an imaginary world from the residue of perceptions and past events, and this world is in fact substituted for the world of reality that is called conscious. This world, Freud points out, does not resemble perceptual reality, but a rebus. But the neo-realist films maintain the general representative-narrative form and, with it, the reality principle. They content themselves with inserting instants in which that reality allows 'a real' to surface in its familiar components, one that seems to emerge from reality itself, and not from a reality which is only psychical. It is not 'my' unconscious (the filmmaker's or the viewer's) that manifests itself then, but the unconscious of reality.

The intensity of these moments comes from the ambiguity of the realities that they present, at the same time subject to the sensorial-motor and cultural organisation of our body and mind, and held up to another truth for which this organisation is incompetent. The same goes for certain pictures, such as a landscape or a still-life by Cézanne. The master's Mont St Victoire and fruit bowl with apples are as well-known as a provincial landscape. But the uncanny gaze discerns an entirely other existence in the rock and the fruit. In 'Cézanne's Doubt', Merleau-Ponty (1993) wrote that this existence was that of reality in the process of being born, before its achievement in normal perception: *in statu nascendi*. But this judgement is guilty of too much optimism; I mean: through the privilege or the prejudice that the great phenomenologist accords to what appears in the heart of appearances, the apparition. And thus to the infancy of the world. And yet one can also say that the uncanniness of the oils and (especially) the watercolours devoted to the mountain and the fruit proceeds as well from a deep sense of the disappearance of appearances and the waning of the visible world.

The pot, in the uncanny moment, appears and disappears at the same time. It cannot appear as apparition without disappearing as appearance. Similarly, time never appears as a constellated block in neo-realism except at the price of the eclipse or the ellipsis of chronological time. The gesture 'neo-' is necessarily double. The real is only revealed in ordinary reality if the evidence of the latter is an uncertain instant; one should say: faded. We recognise just fine the horses and the cows on the wall of Lascaux but their 'reality' is not of the perceptual order. It is futile to call it symbolic (even if they had a ritual function) since we do not know what they are the symbols of. The neo-realist moment seizes the real in reality without suggesting that it would be equal to something other than what it is.

Georges Braque wrote that the object of painting is not the simulation of a real situation, but the construction of a pictorial fact. The neo-realist pot becomes a filmic fact. Pier Paolo Pasolini called the vision involved in these uncanny moments a 'free indirect vision', in the way that the novelist can use free indirect discourse. In this last case, a confusion overtakes the reader with respect to the narrative voice: is it the author, the narrator, or the character who speaks?

Likewise in the uncanny filmic instant, the viewer asks if it is the character or the director who sees the pot. It is neither one nor the other: the pot is seen by a blind and subtle eye which is immanent to visible reality and the human gaze, just as the free indirect narrative [*récit*] lets a voice be heard which is anybody's, a capacity of voice common to the humans who speak, the author [*auteur*] and the characters. In the case of film as of narrative, these moments correspond to outcrops of the visual or the vocal on the surface of the visible and the audible.

Such is the pictorial or filmic fact, or the poetic fact, as Reverdy said. This fact, transcendental factuality immanent to sensations, is sovereign. It is not subordinated to a project of narration [*raconter*], of illustration, of making comprehensible (the only critique one must make of the films of the avant-garde is that they are didactic, and therefore subordinated to a programme). Neither is this fact produced by the author: it happens to him or her, and this event demands a sort of ascesis on the part of the writer or filmmaker [*réalisateur*] (and of the director of photography). I say ascesis because the uncanny instant in which one feels the fact of the visual or the voice pass demands that the writer or the director know how to efface his or her voice or sight in order to allow the vocal or the visual to surface. The treatises addressed to the Chinese and Japanese painter-scribes make ascesis the preliminary condition for the truth or the perception of the line traced by the brush: ascesis of effacement of the will, of the elimination of intentions, of blindness to all identification.

Sovereignty is at the antipodes of authority, or rather, is a stranger to it. It opens the world to us, a world neither permitted nor defended, neither good nor bad, neither high nor low, neither black nor white: or rather a world which is all this, indistinguishably – like at the end of *The Night of the Hunter* when the voices of Robert Mitchum and Lilian Gish, of the evil and the good, unite to sing the same tune, as Marguerite Duras observes, albeit differently (*Leaning, leaning on the everlasting arms/leaning on Jesus*). A world which is in the world but which only the camera or the pen can allow us to catch a glimpse of, on condition that nothing is disturbed and that it keep a low profile. The simplicity of Kafka's or Rossellini's writing is a model of this reserve, of a free indirect vision. It is not by chance if, in the eyes of Georges Bataille, Kafka is a sovereign writer par excellence.

I think that a filmmaker, if he or she is not a commercial trader of images, carries in him or herself the idea of a sovereign film where from time to time the realist plot allows the presence of the ontological real to pass. This idea must remain an Idea in the Kantian sense, a conception to which no object, here no film, can correspond in experience. There is no sovereign film, since sovereignty is incompatible with an objective totality. A film said to be sovereign would be, in truth, an authoritative film, which is to say, its opposite. But the Idea persists and suffices to ensure that there is sovereignty in films, and to continually call for new films.

Translated by Peter W. Milne and Ashley Woodward

REFERENCES

Bataille, Georges (1997), *Literature and Evil*, trans. Alastair Hamilton, London and New York: Marion Boyars.
Bataille, Georges (2014), *Inner Experience*, trans. Stuart Kendall, Albany: SUNY Press.
Bazin, André (1958), 'André Gide', in *Qu'est-ce que le cinéma? I. Ontologie et Langage*, Paris: Cerf, pp. 71–4 [1952].
Bazin, André (2009), *What is Cinema?*, trans. Timothy Barnard, Montreal: Caboose [1946–56].
Freud, Sigmund (1947–53), *The Standard Edition of the Complete Psychological Works of Sigmund Freud*, ed. James Strachey, London: Hogarth Press.
Merleau-Ponty, Maurice (1993), 'Cézanne's Doubt', trans. Michael B. Smith, in *The Merleau-Ponty Aesthetics Reader*, ed. Galen A. Johnson, Evanston, Illinois: Northwestern University Press.
Schrader, Paul (1972), *Transcendental Style in Film: Ozu, Bresson, Dreyer*, Berkeley: University of California Press.

PART III

Approaches and Interpretations

CHAPTER 8

Imaginary Constructs? A Libidinal Economy of the Cinematographic Medium

Julie Gaillard

'A cinema' envisions cinema as a libidinal set-up, *dispositif pulsionnel*, a notion elaborated in clear opposition to the Lacanian model of desire which relies on the negativity of a lack that is constitutive of the subject and limits desire to the movement of the signifying chain. Lyotard attempts to overcome this negativity, which opens the space of representation, by substituting for it the positivity of a desire that no longer relies on a foundational lack, but is instead thought dynamically in terms of quantities of energy. He finds such a positivity in the Freudian model of the death drive, a notion of desire as force that is repressed in Lacan by the pre-eminence of desire as wish. However, Lyotard elaborates his reflection on cinema in a narrow dialogue with Lacan. This dialogue, far from simply consisting in a rejection, entails crucial implications for a thinking of an efficacy of cinema envisioned as a libidinal set-up, and, more generally, for a thinking of the relationship of medial configurations with reality. Indeed, Lyotard goes as far as stating that '[t]he film acts like the orthopaedic mirror analysed by Lacan in 1949 as constitutive of the imaginary subject or *objet a*; that we are dealing with the social body in no ways alters its function' (Ac 39).

This claim creates an association between three poles. It posits an analogy between the workings of the psyche and the workings of the cinematographic medium, an analogy that in turn provides the framework from which it becomes possible to posit that the film has a concrete, transformative effect on society. We are faced with this incredible reversal: cinema, a technology designed to record reality, has, in a certain sense that we will try to understand, a formative power over reality itself. The purpose of this chapter is to attempt to understand the meaning, the importance and the limitations of this statement within the context of the libidinal economic aesthetics that Lyotard elaborates in the 1970s. More broadly, it aims at understanding how the critical dialogue with Lacan's view of desire in 'Acinema', but also in the 1977 essay 'The Unconscious as Mise-en-scène', allows Lyotard to formulate some claims on the efficacy that medial configurations in general, and cinema in particular, have on reality. The philosopher admits to a certain naivety as he looks back to certain claims of 'Acinema' in 'The Idea of a Sovereign Film' in 1995, long after he had abandoned the libidinal framework in favour of a pragmatic approach. However, it seems that his attempt at formulating a libidinal economy of the cinematographic medium lays the ground where some of his later concerns will come to be rooted: the effects of the film on the viewer; their possible dangers in terms of seduction; the 'apparition' of 'sovereign moments' in a film.

I will first show how the Lacanian model of the mirror stage can fit into Lyotard's reading of Freud's economic model of the psychic apparatus. This preliminary should allow for a clearer understanding of the stakes of Lyotard's thinking of cinema in terms of libidinal set-up. After considering Lyotard's engagement with Lacan's imaginary subject in 'Acinema', I will briefly consider how his attempt to rid desire and the unconscious of the Lacanian linguistic component in 'The Unconscious as Mise-en-scène' leads him to traverse the libidinal approach and shift towards a model of desire that seems to pave the way for a pragmatic approach to film.

DRIVE AND SUBJECTIVITY: FREUD VS FREUD AND LACAN

The fact that Lyotard, after *Discourse, Figure*, leans on the Freudian distinction between desire understood as *wish* and desire understood as *force* has been widely noted. In the essay 'On a Figure of Discourse', originally collected with 'Acinema' in *Des dispositifs pulsionnels*, he expressly chooses to aggravate the divergence between these two poles of desire – a divergence that is latent throughout Freud's corpus, but appears clearly in *Beyond the Pleasure Principle* (see TP 13; see also MT1 77–101).

According to the mechanical model of Freud's *Project for a Scientific Psychology*, desire is a quantity of energy. The purpose of psychic activity is to regulate the quantities of excitation, and to maintain them at a constant level, according to the principle of constancy. The psychic apparatus finds ways to abreact these intensities – be it, for instance, in reality via reaction formation or on a 'scene opened up within the [psychic] apparatus' (TP 13) in the case of the fantasy or the dream, as Lyotard writes in 'On a Figure of Discourse'. Lyotard states that this processing of energy by the psychic apparatus, which occurs without any remainder through objects or representations of objects, is still governed, even in the case of the dream or of fantasy, 'by a regulating brain, by a memory' (TP 13), that is, by a unifying instance pertaining to subjectivity, that binds the psychic energy so that it flows in a stable and controlled fashion. And we will see that it is precisely this connection of desire and subjectivity that Lyotard will reprove in Lacan, as it excludes the positivity of the death drive.

Elaborating on the distinction made by Freud in *Beyond the Pleasure Principle*, Lyotard opposes to this principle of constancy and its binding operations a desire that is a desire of intensities. There, intensities are not processed by a subjective instance in view of their regulation, but rather escape all regulation. The principle governing this desire is a 'non-principle' (TP 14); it is a 'force beyond the rules of negation, of implication, of alternation, of temporal succession; a force that works by means of elementary operations' (TP 14). Here, we can recognise the negative definition of the primary processes according to Freud, which Lyotard places fully on the side of the 'death drive'.

In the model of the death drive, Lyotard hopes to find a principle that would allow him to locate a force prior to representation and its foundational negativity (see Bennington 1988: 88), which might be able to account for it. Desire in its entirety is now understood as a libidinal force functioning according to two regimes: Eros and Thanatos (MT1 79). In summary, we see that these two continuous and complementary regimes of the drive oppose, on the one hand, constancy, secondary processes of binding, a unitary and unifying subjective instance, representation; and, on the other hand, intensities that do not obey the principle of constancy and its regulating operations of binding and abreaction, primary processes. These unbound intensities are not represented strictly speaking, but manifest themselves through their effects upon words, images, affects – a claim that will be essential for the elaboration of a libidinal economic aesthetics.

In his text on the mirror stage, what Lacan proposes is actually a theory of the formation of this psychic apparatus which Freud explains in economic terms. Lacan describes the moment of a primary identification with an *imago* as 'the symbolic matrix in which the I is precipitated in a primordial form' (2007: 76; see Nouvet 2009: 81ff.). It is the process of assumption of an image through which a fragmentary body, not yet perceived as unitary, is articulated into a total form, an organism. It is not itself that the child sees in the mirror. The human child, who does not yet have full mastery of the coordination of its movements, has to be held by some human or artificial support and perceives this image that holds itself standing and fixed 'in opposition with the turbulent movements with which the subject feels [they] animat[e] [this image]' (Lacan 2007: 76). The child does not recognise itself, but a *Gestalt* that it identifies as belonging to the human species. It envisions this image as a total form, and then retrojects this image onto itself, assuming it. The *imago* is thus 'a form orthopedic of [the child's] totality' (2007: 78): it is the *imago* that allows for the collection of the child's fragmented body into a total form. The child only attains the organic unity of its body through the mediation of an exterior image, this *Gestalt* that captures it and allows for its body to become articulated. Lacan calls this image an Ideal-I, to connote the admiration that the child invests in this image that it sees. This means that I can be 'myself' only in so far as I identify with this image of myself that is also an image of another.

This 'primordial form' is not yet the subject, but it 'establish[es] a relation between an organism and its reality' (Lacan 2007: 78); it opens up space and time. At the moment when the mirror stage reaches an end, the whole relation to reality, which is moulded upon this symbolic matrix of the image, 'is being mediated by the other's desire' (2007: 79). And to Lacan, the libidinal cathexis of this constitutive exteriority is ambivalent. This is also the moment when the defence mechanisms analysed by Anna Freud as constitutive of the ego come into play, as the mirror stage 'turns the I into this apparatus to which every instinctual pressure constitutes a danger' (2007: 79). Thus, the subject is inherently imaginary and therefore constructed upon what Lacan calls 'an existential negativity' (2007: 79), which is related to the identification with the image, an alienation which represses everything that could have preceded the crystallisation of the I beyond the edges of the Id, forever irreducible and unattainable. And, leaping forward in time, Lyotard associates this imaginary subject of the mirror stage to the *objet a*, which is the forever-absent cause of all desire, the fundamental lack that is foreclosed from the signifying chain and sets the desiring machine in motion. In Lacan, the entirety of desire is placed on the side of the *wish*, and the drive is regarded as something that needs to be fended off by the psychic apparatus, and that is rejected in the inaccessible Id.

To this primary narcissism, corollary of the birth of the primordial form of the ego and its opening of and to reality, Lyotard opposes something prior, which he finds in the notion of autoeroticism, which for Freud characterises infantile sexuality and consists in the free, objectless wandering of energies through erogenous zones of a fragmented body.

CINEMA AS A LIBIDINAL SET-UP

This is where the notion of libidinal set-up comes into play: this unbound, wandering energy, characteristic of primary processes, collides with the bound, stabilised organisation of energies characteristic of secondary processes. The role of the libidinal set-ups is to enable the encounter of these processes and to organise the channelling of the forces within the articulation of words, of colours, of sounds. These 'set-ups' capture unbound energies:

anything that is taken as an object (for example, thing, painting, text, body) is produced. That is, it results from the metamorphosis of energy in one form or another. Every object is composed of energy that is at rest, quiescent, provisionally conserved, inscribed. The set-up [*dispositif*] or figure is only a *metamorphic operator*. It is *itself* already composed of stabilised, conserved energy. (TP 15, translation slightly modified)

Through the notion of set-up conceived of as a 'transformer of energy' (TP 17), Lyotard attempts to account for the connection of the unbound force of the drive to the clusters of bound energy of language, of sounds, of colours.

According to this, the psychic apparatus is a libidinal set-up unto itself, as are social formations, the arts, discourse, and so on. In 'Painting and Desire', Lyotard states that there are profound libidinal configurations that generate artistic and social forms alike (MT1 53–75; see also Parret's Preface in the same volume). A libidinal economic aesthetics asserts that, much more than a simple analogy, there is a continuity between the various regions and the various ways in which energy is channelled; this continuity is conditioned by underlying organisations of desire. The existence of such matrixial set-ups (or 'matrix figures') (MT1 67) would then account for the correspondence of the psychic, economic, social and medial configurations.[1]

Thus, Lyotard's emphasis on the constancy characteristic of Eros, as opposed to the disruptive, non-recurring power of the death drive, is crucial for his understanding of the arts. Constancy is associated with the ideas of order, of repetition of the same and, therefore, of recognition, of return, of profit – traits that also define the workings of the capitalist system. It necessitates the exclusion of disorganised, non-recurring intensities. In the arts, the principle of constancy is linked to what Lyotard calls 'good form', be it the balance of colours in painting, the resolution of dissonances in a dominant chord in music, proportion in architecture. In cinema, this 'good form' consists in a plot with dénouement, in which each part of the framing, of the editing, of the script, is subordinated to the end of the totality (the film as a whole). In contrast, the avant-gardes in painting and music have dissolved good form. Such would also be the role of what Lyotard calls 'pyrotechnics' in cinema: to acknowledge a sterile consumption of energies that does not obey the regulative principles of the 'good form'.

Before analysing further Lyotard's elaboration of pyrotechnics in their link with the death drive, let us first examine how the 'good form', associated with Eros and the principle of constancy, can function for the viewer as an instance of identification. Unlike media such as music or painting, in which matter is added on a support of inscription, cinema, in each of its steps, consists primarily in operations of subtraction, which Lyotard also calls 'a foreclosure of all that is judged unrepresentable because nonrecurrent' (Ac 39). In commercial cinema, thanks to the operation of recognition by the eye for which the film has been constructed, the image is accepted by the spectator as the double of a 'real' situation. In Lyotard's presentation, the recognition of the object as a recorded object precedes the accepting of the object as a part of reality. This is the function of representation, the work of directing, 'mise-en-scène', which consists in instituting that limit or frame between, on the one hand, 'reality' and, on the other hand, what is caught in the lens of the camera, 'the real'. But the staging operates at two levels simultaneously:

> in order for the function of representation to be fulfilled, the activity of directing (a placing in and out of scene. . .) must also be an activity which unifies all the movements, those on *both sides* of the frame's limits, imposing here *and* there, in 'reality' just as in the real, the *same norms*, the same ordering of drives, excluding, obliterating, effacing them *no less off* the scene than on. The references imposed on the filmic object are imposed just as necessarily on all objects outside the film. (Ac 38)

Just as the fragmented body of the child is unified through the mediation of an image by a movement of identification that implies the foreclosure of all unbound libidinal fluxes, the film normalises the flow of energy by foreclosing the unbound drives. The child admires his specular image and identifies with it: the *imago* is an ideal-ego. The film has a similar normative function: its images are offered as *good* images, normal-images. The *imago* of the child, the normative-formative image of the film, shows the viewer how things should look 'in reality'. It seems that both operations of putting in the scene and out of the scene are conditioned by a priori scenographic operators – defined earlier as matrixial set-ups. In commercial cinema and in the Lacanian model of the mirror stage, this operator is narcissism: the identification to an exterior image as the good image and the assumption of this image as the symbolic matrix that opens the relation to reality:

> *good* form, *good* lighting, *good* editing, *good* sound mixing are not good because they conform to perceptual or social reality, but because they are a priori scenographic *operators* which on the contrary determine the objects to be recorded on the screen and in 'reality'. (Ac 38)

We do not perceive film as we perceive reality; we perceive reality as we perceive film, and we do so according to specific a priori operators. This could be true of all the arts. In *Discourse, Figure* already, in a section entitled 'Parenthetical Remark on the Lack of Reality', Lyotard made this claim about the work of art, reminiscent of Lacan: 'Reality is constituted from the imaginary. What is given at first is the phantasmatic object' (DF 281).

According to this statement, medial configurations can have a direct influence on our relationship to our perceptive and social reality and are therefore eminently political.[2] If we think of this unification of the polymorphous body into a total object as something that is not necessary, but actually contingent, and if it is true that the a priori scenographic operator determines the objects that have to be recorded on the screen as well as the way in which we register or perceive reality, then this means that, if we transform this operator, it is not only the filmic material that will be transformed – it will also have an effect on reality itself. If the filmic material is disposed not according to propagation, capital and unification, but rather according to the free and sterile expense of energy that Lyotard calls pyrotechnics, then our social and economic reality could be configured differently. To this end, one needs to call into question the univocity of narcissism as a necessary a priori scenographic operator:

> the real problem, missed by Lacan due to his Hegelianism, is to know why the drives spread about the polymorphous body *must have* an object where they can unite. That the imperative of unification is given as hypothesis in a philosophy of 'consciousness' is betrayed by the very term 'consciousness', but for a 'thought' of the unconscious (of which the form related most to pyrotechnics would be the economy sketched here and there in Freud's writings), the question of the production of unity, even an imaginary unity, can no longer fail to be posed in all its opacity. We will no longer have to pretend to understand how the subject's unity is constituted from his image in the mirror. We will have to ask ourselves how and why the *specular wall* in general, and thus the cinema screen in particular, can become a privileged place for the libidinal cathexis . . .
>
> A libidinal economy of the cinema should theoretically [*littéralement*] construct the operators which exclude aberrations from the social and organic bodies and channel the drives [*impulsions*] into this set-up [*dispositif*]. It is not clear that narcissism or masochism are the proper operators: they carry a tone of subjectivity (of the theory of the Ego) that is probably still much too strong. (Ac 39, translation slightly modified)

To Lyotard, Lacan can only account for the moment of the articulation of the primordial form of the subject because he presupposes it, 'pretend[s] to understand' it. But this model only accounts for the channelling of the life drives towards their propagation, thereby operating the foreclosure of all the death drives. In order to find a model that would account for the whole of the world of the drives, Lyotard turns once more towards Freud, through Pierre Klossowski, and attempts to see if perversion could be a suitable scenographic operator, one that would allow a bypassing of the normative operator of Lacanian narcissism.

In this context, perversion is defined as a sterile pleasure, which does not obey the circuit of reproduction.

Lyotard associates 'perversion' with formal operations of immobilisation and excessive movement – the two components unique to acinema as opposed to commercial cinema. My purpose here is not to analyse how he defines a certain reversibility of the libidinal relation between the film and the viewer in terms of the intensity of the movements. In 'The Idea of a Sovereign Film', looking back on his early hypothesis, Lyotard formulates the following reservation:

> I tried in ['Acinema'] to show the respective implications of these two polarisations on the libidinal relation between the work and the viewer. It was a little naive: I suggested that the immobilisation of the subject leads to the extreme passionate agitation of the viewer, while the latter was struck by sensory-motor paralysis in the face of incessant and disorderly tiny movements inscribed on the support. (ISF 64)

Rather than questioning this reversibility of movements, I want to shift the focus and investigate the modalities of cinematographic perversion in so far as it is linked to the question of the death drive's relation to a unifying totality that is mediated by the specular wall. What is at stake in the opposition of the tableau vivant and lyrical abstraction at the extreme poles of movement is still the opposition between a representative and a non-representative art, guided by the following question: is it possible to go beyond representation and its correlate of subjectivity?

Lyotard indeed associates the pole of immobilisation with the tableau vivant and illustrates it with the Swedish practice of *posering*. In posering, women take the pose that the client desires – the client is not allowed to touch the model. Perversion consists here in using a total person as a partial object. Posering would be the representation of the 'price, beyond price . . . that the organic body, the pretended unity of the pretended subject, must pay so that the pleasure [*jouissance*] will burst forth in its irreversible sterility' (Ac 40). It shows that corporeal unity is only achieved through an alienation, a renunciation of the pleasure of the polymorphous perversity and its erogenous wanderings. This practice therefore necessitates the reference to the total body that it undoes:

> The object . . . (is) offering his or her self as a detached region, *but at the same time giving way and humiliating this whole person*. The allusion to this latter is an indispensable factor in the intensification . . . Thus representation is essential to this fantasmatic; that is, it is essential that the spectator be offered instances of identification, recognisable forms, all in all, matter for the memory. (Ac 41)

The client experiences intensities as a total body, as a constituted subject, enjoying the sight of a person offered to his gaze not as a total person, but as a partial object, an erogenous zone. The pyrotechnics of the perverse fantasy may allow for extreme intensities in the spectator; it may summon the action of the death drive that comes to disrupt the ordered circulation of intensities. Yet it still belongs to the order of representation, in so far as it requires both the recognisable image and the constituted subjectivity of the viewer that it troubles (Durafour 2009: 56).

The second possibility for cinematographic perversion consists in perverting the medium itself, i.e. in contravening all the operations of exclusion that define 'good form' in order to thwart any possible 'synthesis of identification' or 'mnesic instances' (Ac 41). There is nothing 'represented' on the screen anymore, no form that could be recognised. The screen refuses any recognition as *Gestalt*: it elides itself in its function of specular identification. To Lyotard, this set-up of perversion of the medium comes down to decomposing the organism of the spectator now struck with immobility. His body is not an organism that operates syntheses of time and space any longer; it is reduced to regional, partial connections of energy. This perversion of the medium provokes an effect on the viewer that is analogous to the polymorphous perversity of infantile sexuality. The scenographic operator in this case is no longer the phantasmatic perversion, which, because it is still representative, is genetically posterior to Lacanian narcissism; here we have a pre-theatrical perversity, a perversity that addresses the body not as a unitary form, but as a polymorphous collection of zones.

According to the initial hypothesis, we should be able to see in this cinema of lyrical abstraction the model of cinema that would circumvent the orthopaedic action exerted by the film on the subject, on the organic and on the social body. Such a cinema would correspond to these pyrotechnics that Lyotard advocates, in so far as it would construct libidinal investments that are not guided by the finality of a return on investment, and in so far as these energies would not invest a unified instance, but detached regions. However, Lyotard refrains from victoriously proclaiming that this cinematic set-up is the alternative to representative cinema, for the kind of pleasure that it provokes is very far from reaching the level of intensity that Lyotard associates with the death drive (Durafour 2009: 69s). The whole question becomes, therefore, to know whether it is possible to experience *jouissance* through the medium or if this is solely possible through a set-up of identification via an object caught in a representative, phantasmatic structure. The series of questions that close 'Acinema' bear witness to Lyotard's discomfort at the time:

> The question, which must be recognised as being crucial to our time because it is that of the mise-en-scène and therefore of the staging of society [*la mise en société*] (outside scene), is the following: is it necessary for

the victim to be in the scene for the *jouissance* to be intense? If the victim is the client, if there is in the scene only the film, the screen, the canvas, the support, do we lose to this *dispositif* all the intensity of the sterile discharge? And if so, must we then renounce the hope of finishing with the illusion, not only the cinematographic illusion but also the social and political illusions? Are they not really illusions then? Or is believing so the illusion? Must the return of extreme intensities be founded on at least this empty permanence, on the phantom of the organic body or subject which is the proper noun, and at the same time that they cannot really accomplish this unity? (Ac 42)

Is it possible to have a cinema that would not be representative-figurative and that would still produce extreme intensities in the viewer? It does not seem possible to oppose so radically representation and its possible 'beyond'. Narcissism may not be a necessary operator, but subjectivity and its imaginary structure cannot simply be done away with. In *Libidinal Economy*, published the year following 'Acinema', Lyotard states that it is impossible to escape representation, that a beyond of representation can only ever be achieved from within representation. We cannot escape signs (LE 50). Acinema is only possible within the edges of figurative cinema. Yes, we must give up on getting over illusion. The images of cinema, the social, the political, partake of the illusion, the lure that constitutes reality and its imaginary structure according to Lacan. But, if the model of the death drive does not seem sufficient to overcome representation, does this mean that the idea of using cinema as a new kind of operator of libidinal investments, one that would have an efficiency in reality by having a formative power on the social body, should be abandoned altogether?

MISE-EN-SCÈNE AND SOMATOGRAPHY

In 'The Unconscious as Mise-en-scène', Lyotard shifts the approach to the question of representation and reality in their libidinal dimension and pushes the libidinal logic until it unties itself from within. It is no longer a matter of overcoming the illusion of representation, but rather of embracing the illusion that constitutes reality, of inverting the negativity that modernity associates with reality in order to assert the positivity of a statement of 'perspectives of reality' (UM 53) through works now envisioned in terms of 'diagraphy' and 'somatography', understood as an inscription of a message 'on bodies in order to give it to other bodies' (Trahair 2009: 228).[3]

The main point of contention of this essay is the Lacanian premise according to which the unconscious is structured like a language. Lyotard contends that if the unconscious operates a mise-en-scène, it is not according to linguistic operators (UM 46). This leads him to further radicalise his approach to desire as *force* and call into question the Freudian distinction between desire and the unconscious. For Freud, desire delivers 'primary messages', 'transparent libidinal messages', which the unconscious would then come to disguise in an act of staging. Lyotard states that Freud always interprets dreams, fantasies or hallucinations as symptoms of desire that have been staged by the unconscious – this even when Freud, in 1919, regards desire as a *force*, and no longer as a *wish*, as he did in the *Traumdeutung* of 1900. The analyst and the analysand have to dismantle the illusion that appears on the phantasmatic stage in order to recover the originary message of desire. Lyotard bases his analysis on the fantasy 'A Child is Being Beaten', which he describes, just like the practice of posering that constitutes the representative pole of acinema, in terms of tableau vivant. This may allow us to think of 'The Unconscious as Mise-en-scène' as an attempt to come out of the dead-end of the inefficiency of lyrical abstraction by a renewed, displaced investigation of representative-figurative art. Lyotard presents the fantasy as follows:

> The fantasy consists in a kind of scene or tableau vivant where the patient, placed in the position of spectator, sees an adult authority figure ... flogging some young boys. With the help of the patients' recollection, Freud 'discovers' that this scene hides another one, which he sums up with the sentence: 'The father is beating the child (that I hate).' This first phase constitutes the primary message, whereas the scene 'A child is being beaten' is similar to the final performance. In between there is the mise-en-scène.
>
> But it is not as simple as this. Between the first and the last phase, Freud says, it is necessary to postulate an intermediate phase which he calls: 'my father is beating me'. (UM 47)

The problem lies in the status of this second phase that is being reconstructed by the analyst and in the series of transformations that the desire has to undergo in order to form the 'tableau vivant' of the fantasy. Using once more Freud against Freud himself, Lyotard contends that a fantasy should not be regarded as the result of a chronological series of disguises of desire by the unconscious, but as the simultaneous presence of contradictory investments that cannot logically belong together, that are 'incompossible' (UM 50). The various phases of the fantasy are not linked by a relation of representationality, of causality, of mise-en-scène. Lyotard relies on Freud's depiction of the temporality of the drive developed in 'Drives and their Vicissitudes' through a comparison of the successive thrusts of the drive to successive eruptions of lava. Once the first eruption has burst out, the solidified lava flow persists unchanged and is not modified by the subsequent eruptions, which will simply come and superimpose themselves on the first one. Likewise, the first manifestation of the drive persists unchanged next to the subsequent thrusts that are often incompatible. Therefore, Lyotard states that

> A drive-siege never lets up; the opposite or inverse investment which accompanies it does not suppress the first, does not even conceal it, but sets itself up next to it. All investments are, in this way, contemporaneous with each other: one loves and hates the same object at the same time and in the same respect, which is contrary to the rules of intelligibility and chronology. (UM 50)

Each phase of the fantasy has to be looked at individually, not relative to the chronology of a mise-en-scène that would subordinate it to a general narrative according to the rule of return and whose programme would have been governed by the primary message of desire staged by the unconscious for the benefit of the totality. Here, even more radically that in 'Acinema', desire is not a wish; it has nothing to do with the intention to recover an object originarily lacking. It is a force that works. The unconscious tends to disappear as an instance of mise-en-scène and reintegrates the processual dimension of the 'primary processes': therefore, the unconscious and desire understood as force converge towards the limit where they become indistinguishable. The primary processes transform the drives. Of course, the drives can only appear through their effect, under the guise of their representatives: words, images, affects. But these representatives have not been staged by a director, by a *metteur-en-scène*, by an agency that would be more than mechanical. They have undergone metamorphism, or rather, what Lyotard calls 'diagraphy': they have been transcribed, their space of inscription has changed (UM 44). These drive-representatives appear side by side, without a relation of causality. The work of fantasy, just like the dream-work, does not think: Lyotard rids the unconscious and desire of any subjective residue, and shifts them entirely onto the positive model of the drive as dynamic process.

Lyotard shows that the mise-en-scène and its hermeneutic corollary is not necessary, but that its relevance appears contingent to a certain orientation of modernity, to a matrixial set-up. Psychoanalysis does not escape the influence of this matrix and is inflected by it. Lyotard directs his critique of representation towards the tool that has allowed him to express this very critique. If we undo the idea of mise-en-scène that, according to Lyotard, still inflects Freud's theory in spite of himself, then we obtain the coordinates of a new matrix set-up, which will define what Lyotard dubs, after Ihab Hassan, postmodernity. This incompossibility, whose model is found in the primary processes, will indeed become the defining feature of this trend, which Lyotard identifies, in 1977, as in the process of being articulated in literature, in the arts, in theory, and maybe in politics (UM 51). Postmodernity in this sense would be characterised by the dissolution of the idea of mise-en-scène understood as the activity that disguises an originary truth (UM 51). This dissolution implies a double and paradoxical movement: firstly, an expansion of the notion of mise-en-scène, since each drive can only appear as a drive-representative, and, secondly, the surpassing of mise-en-scène at the limit of its dissolution, since each representation is but one possibility amongst others that are simultaneously incompossible. And Lyotard concludes his essay by observing how Michael Snow's film, *La Région centrale*, functions in a way that is reminiscent of this Freudian metaphor describing the eruption of the drives. The film breaks with the central, unitary perspective and adopts multiplied perspectives; it refuses the constitution of a recognisable geometric space and radically breaks with traditional narrative expectations. Lyotard claims that while postmodern staging does not completely do away with mise-en-scène, it only aims at a diagraphy and a somatography (UM 53). Diagraphy: the film is the mechanistic realisation of a programme; somatography: there is an inscription of effects on the 'disconcerted body' of the spectator.

> Language is not made for telling the truth and film is not made to disguise truth on a fantasmatic stage. Both are inexhaustible means for experimenting with new effects, never seen, never heard before. They create their own reference, therefore their object is not identifiable; they create their own addressee, a disconcerted body, invited to stretch its sensory capacities beyond measure. (UM 52)

A film should not be considered as a phantasmatic scene where elements would be staged and, in turn, interpreted. It should primarily be envisioned as a set of devices conveying effects on bodies. The focus is no longer the orthopaedic foreclosure of aberrant perspectives that will in turn create reality and unify the body through specular identification, but the creative inclusion of multiple perspectives which 'disconcert' the body, address it as polymorphous, through the creation of its own reference and its own structure of address (UM 52). The film's attempt to 'state perspectives of reality' (UM 53) is no longer opposed to figuration, to representation.

The renewed engagement with the Lacanian model of desire in 'The Unconscious as Mise-en-scène' seems, therefore, to allow Lyotard to extend his approach to cinema in terms of a libidinal economic aesthetic up to the point where this approach starts losing its relevance. Once the unconscious and desire have been cleared of their residues of intentionality, representationality and causality that were linked to mise-en-scène, the economic libidinal model can merge with the Nietzschean model of a desire that would be entirely on the side of a creative force and give way to a pragmatics of effects, which will later allow, in turn, for a renewed investigation of the 'seductive' power of medial configurations in 'Two Metamorphoses of the Seductive in Cinema'.

NOTES

1. This idea seems to be rooted in Pierre Francastel's (1951) comparison of artistic forms and social formations, reframed through an energetic perspective. In 'Painting and Desire' (in MT1), in the wake of *Discourse, Figure*, Lyotard further elaborates the notion of 'matrix figure' as a machinery or set-up (*dispositif*) that would organise space and time, as a process that would determine where and how energies would be channelled and inscribed, across artistic and social formations alike.
2. In a different context, Jean-Michel Durafour also notes the militant dimension of acinema (2009: 61).
3. Lisa Trahair notes that this constitutes an '[expansion of Lyotard's] earlier thesis concerning the intensification of detached regions by the investments of libidinal economy' (2009: 228).

REFERENCES

Bennington, Geoffrey (1988), *Lyotard: Writing the Event*, New York: Columbia University Press.

Durafour, Jean-Michel (2009), *Jean-François Lyotard: questions au cinema. Ce que le cinéma se figure*, Paris: PUF.

Francastel, Pierre (1951), *Peinture et société: naissance et destruction d'un espace plastique de la Renaissance au cubisme*, Paris and Lyon: Audin.

Lacan, Jacques (2007), 'The Mirror Stage as Formative of the *I* Function as Revealed in the Psychoanalytic Experience. Delivered on July 17, 1949 in Zurich at the Sixteenth International Congress of Psychoanalysis', in *Écrits. The First Complete Edition in English*, trans. Bruce Fink, New York and London: Norton, pp. 75–81.

Nouvet, Claire (2009), *Enfances Narcisse*, Paris: Galilée.

Trahair, Lisa (2009), 'Jean-François Lyotard', in *Film, Theory and Philosophy: The Key Thinkers*, ed. Felicity Colman, Chesham: Acumen, pp. 222–32.

CHAPTER 9

Lyotard and the Art of Seduction

Keith Crome

Jean-François Lyotard's 'Two Metamorphoses of the Seductive in Cinema' comprises seventeen numbered paragraphs that range from observations on Gorgias and Plato's dialogue *Menexenus* (which also occur in a number of his other works) to remarks on two major twentieth-century filmmakers, Hans-Jürgen Syberberg and Francis Ford Coppola. Its subject is, ostensibly, two metamorphoses of the seductive in cinema, and Lyotard's aim is to describe seduction and its metamorphoses pragmatically. In what follows I offer a commentary on this treatment of seduction – or it might be more accurate to call them a succession of comments in that my aim is not so much to give an exposition of what Lyotard says, but to expose what he *does*, to make explicit the *force* of his argument. Eliciting the effect of Lyotard's argument through my 'reading', which is itself forceful, allows me to elucidate the complicity between what Lyotard calls 'seduction', the political and the philosophical.

SEDUCTION

In developing his linguistic pragmatics, Lyotard draws on the Wittgenstein of the *Philosophical Investigations*. As he remarks in *The Postmodern Condition*:

> Wittgenstein, taking up the study of language from scratch, focuses his attention on the effects of different modes of discourse; he calls the various types of utterance he identifies along the way . . . language games. What he means by this term is that each of the various categories of utterance can be defined in terms of rules specifying their properties and the uses to which they can be put. (PC 10)

Viewed from this perspective seduction is a game played by the seducer and the seduced, the addressor and the addressee of the seductive utterance.

However, it is not the thought of Wittgenstein that alone informs Lyotard's analysis of the specific pragmatic properties of seduction. His account of the seductive power of discourse is worked out via an appeal to Gorgias and Plato. Gorgias, Lyotard notes, in the *Encomium of Helen*, remarks the 'power of speech over the soul' and likens it to 'the effect of drugs on the bodily state' (TM 55). The spoken word – to which Gorgias attributes the power to seduce Helen – is, Gorgias says, 'a mighty lord': 'for all that it is insubstantial and imperceptible it has superhuman effects. It can put an end to fear, do away with distress, generate happiness and increase pity' (DK 82 B11).[1] And he continues, 'inspired incantations use the spoken word to induce pleasure and reduce distress. When the power of incantation meets the beliefs of a person's mind, it beguiles, persuades, alters it by sorcery' (DK 82 B11).

Of this power adduced by Gorgias, Lyotard says that it 'consists in the metastasis of the opinions of the listener: their displacement, the displacement of their foundation' (TM 55). And he goes on to say that in the *Menexenus*, Plato has Socrates describe the pragmatic effects, the enchantment, of funeral oration, the *logos epitaphios*, the end of which is political – the identification of the living citizens with the dead heroes. The orator, proposed by the Council, addresses the Assembly of citizens. He speaks of those citizens who died in combat: their death, for the good of the community, is a beautiful death – 'they were virtuous because they were Athenians and died for Athens' (TM 55). However, beneath this discourse, co-presented but latent, as it were, is another: 'You are Athenians; you are virtuous.' The oration works through the metastasis of the pragmatic instances of addressee, addressor and referent: in the overt discourse, the orator (the addressee) tells the Assembly (the addressor) that the dead (the referent) are fine; in the covert or latent discourse, the orator tells the Assembly that *they* are fine. Through the identification of the living with the dead, and the dead with the living, the *logos epitaphios* makes of the death of the heroes a mechanism through which the community assures itself of its virtue. Here, then, Lyotard finds the pragmatic apparatus of seduction: beneath a descriptive, narrative, utterance 'They (our dead) were good' (TM 56) is a latent prescriptive utterance – 'Be good!' Similarly, he says, the interrogative 'where will I find affection?' means 'Love me' (TM 56). Seduction, he says, seen from the point of view of the seduced, would have, by virtue of this latent prescription, the effect of 'making a discourse, even if non-prescriptive, into *an obligation*' (TM 56). The prescription obliges the addressee in that it 'suggests that he or she carry out what it orders, demands, beseeches, implores' (TM 56), and this execution effects what the structuralist narratologist Gerard Genette has called a *metalepsis* – 'a change in the level of one's take on the referent' (D 25). Take the statement 'Our dead were good' – accepted in its patent, descriptive, sense, it positions the addressee as a potential addressor of a new utterance confirming or denying it; however, at its latent, prescriptive level, it moves the addressor onto the scene of the referent, where he or she will act in the way prescribed.

Political discourse is eminently seductive. The *logos epitaphios* is a preeminent example, but all political discourse could be said to have such an end inasmuch as its aim is not only to situate its addressees vis-à-vis reality, but also to turn them into actors on the stage of reality. Indeed, is this not what 'ideology' is – not a power to conceal reality, to falsify the truth, but a power of effectuation, of actualisation?[2] Of course, this too, historically at least, has been the function of art, or of a certain kind of art, not least, of narrative art of the *mimetic* kind, where the pragmatic relation of narrator to addressee is almost completely, or is entirely, effaced – narratives that are a showing rather than a telling of their stories. In such instances, there is a staging of the narrative of an almost theatrical kind. As Lyotard says with a certain degree of caution, if not coyness, this hiding of the positions of the addressor and the addressee is a condition that is 'favourable to the transmission of a non-explicit prescriptive discourse. We see and we hear the history of Tristan, we register the demand: *Suffer and enjoy an impossible shared love*' (TM 57).

DUPLICITY

His title, he says, 'is doubly deceptive' (TM 55). On the one hand, 'Two Metamorphoses of the Seductive in Cinema' would be better if it were phrased in the interrogative and not the indicative mood. It would be better, that is, if it were shorn of its certainty since, in truth, it is an open question 'whether anything escapes seduction' (TM 55). On the other hand, despite indicating that he will consider two cases of the metamorphosis of seduction in cinema – the work of Syberberg, and the sequence of the attack on the Vietnamese village by the American dragoon helicopters in Coppola's *Apocalypse Now* – he admits he 'will say hardly anything about the work of Syberberg' (TM 55).

What is the meaning of this admission of deceit? Is it simply the transcription of an oral apology made when the paper was presented for Lyotard's belated realisation that the assurance implicit in his title, given to the conference organisers before the paper was written, was inappropriate? Which begs the question of why Lyotard did not take the opportunity to change his title before publishing his essay. Idle speculation! A rhetorical hypothesis is more fruitful. Is this not Lyotard's way of remarking the artifice of the essay? Which would make it a deceptive declaration of honesty, a dishonest dissimulation of honesty, a strategy frequently employed by the sophists and rhetoricians who, if tradition can be believed, frequently prepared their supposedly spontaneous speeches in advance. Or to put the point more properly, it would be the simulation of this sophistic strategy, and it would then amount to a paradoxical honesty about artifice. The effect is to precipitate the reader into an unending play of contrivances. In any case, the deception of the title, to which Lyotard deliberately draws attention, is a deception concerning deception, a deception about art – which by its very nature, or in truth, is deceit. More specifically, it is a deception concerning that deceitful art that cinema is, since cinema, inverting Zeno, conjures movement from out of static images. Moreover, the question that poses itself beneath the title, or which Lyotard introduces as a corrective for the deceptive assurance that the title offers – the question 'whether anything escapes from seduction' (TM 55) – is posed, or proposed, 'apropos of *political* cinema' (TM 55). Contemporary cynicism – which is perhaps merely a type of credulity – would have us say that, like cinema, like art, politics too is a *tekhne* of deceit. Lyotard's essay takes its place in this milieu of deception; it plays games with deceit – which is not the same thing as lying, which cannot occur without a reference to a pre-existing reality or true state of affairs.

Gorgias shows us, Lyotard says, the power the *logos* has to deceive. Sophistry is, he says elsewhere, 'the art of making … duplicitous speeches, *dissoi logoi*' (DT 82). In translating *dissos* or *dissoi* as duplicitous Lyotard is, if not being duplicitous, at least playing on the duplicity of the word, which has the principal meaning of 'twofold or double', and in the phrase '*dissoi logoi*' is usually taken to mean 'opposing arguments' – arguments for and against something. However, *dissos* can also mean ambiguous, and in the context of the arguments of the sophists, would, from the perspective of the partisans of truth, denote the illegitimate and paralogical procedures of argument practised by these 'artists of the word'. In citing Lyotard's remark, I take 'duplicitous' as equivalent to 'deceitful', since deceit here, at least in so far as it is allied to seduction, means saying one thing whilst meaning another – at least if we are to adopt a locution imposed by our everyday habit of speaking.

As if to convince us of Gorgias' complete mastery, his total grasp of this art, Lyotard goes on to tell us that there is not one fragment attributed to the great sophist that 'does not rest on the *peithô* (the persuasion), the *goètéia* (the sorcery) of language, on its deception (*apatè*), its power (*dunastès*)' (TM 55). He cites, as if in evidence, an obscure fragment from Plutarch which testifies that Gorgias had said that 'Tragedy is a deception' (TM 55), and that 'the deceiver is more honest than the non-deceiver, and the deceived is wiser than the non-deceived' (TM 55). That the 'deceiver is more honest than the non-deceiver' is a sentiment that Lyotard alludes to in an essay from 1973, 'A Short Libidinal Economy' (in LRG). There he contrasts the deceitful honesty of the historian with the honest deceit of the fabulist or storyteller. The historian, he says, sees her task to be that of undoing the various narratives that are the documentary sources that are her evidence, in order to recover the original story that provoked those narratives: 'the work proper to historical science [is] to undo what is done by narration in order to attain, by critical analysis (of the document, the text, the sources) the fact that is the raw material of this production' (LRG 200). By contrast, the storyteller, he says, 'knows' that he produces the story along with his narrative: 'the storyteller does not begin from the reference; he produces it by means of his narrative' (LRG 201). The storyteller proceeds 'by way of an artistic inversion': 'the object that the reader or auditor of the narrative receives as the story which has provoked the narration is, on the contrary, for the one who recounts it, the story that his narration engenders' (LRG 201). This artistic inversion of the narrative act – the referent, the story, is a product of, and not what produces, the discourse that is supposed to denote it – situates the activity of the historian within the field of the storyteller. The latter, the fabulist, the fantasist, the deceiver is more honest than the former, the historian, who 'does not want to know anything about this' productive activity (LRG 201).

NIHILISM

This artistic inversion is a specific form of the more general affirmation that the false does not distort the true, but that the true is a modality of the false. It is an affirmation that disabuses us of our philosophical credulity, and which is an expression of the decadence of the true, and not simply its paradoxical or contradictory reinstatement ('the declaration "all is false" is itself true'). It is an expression of the historical destruction of values, most notably the value of truth, which Lyotard, like Nietzsche, called *nihilism*.

Nothing escapes nihilism. It is the horizon of our age, and that age is, as Lyotard observes, long-lived. Instituted with the advent of philosophy, it has endured since Plato, and it endures as Platonism. There is no alternative to nihilism; there is only the necessity to act against it without the possibility of stepping outside of it. Consequently, Lyotard advocates the 'aggravation of the decadence of truth' (RP 119):

> Harden, worsen, and accelerate decadence. Assume the perspective of active nihilism. Do not stop at simply observing – either depressingly or admiringly – the destruction of values. Take a hand in their destruction; go deeper into incredulity; battle against the restoration of values. Go quickly and far in this direction; be proactive in decadence; accept, for instance, to destroy belief in truth in all its forms. (RP 122)

To expedite this decadence – the decadence of truth – it is necessary to turn the sting of knowledge against itself, to ask the question of the truth of truth.

Knowledge must be made to wonder, in the name of truth, if it is true. This would be 'active nihilism'. Passive nihilism, by contrast, retains or maintains an obstinate belief in 'the unity, the totality, and the finality of meaning' (RP 120).

Lyotard's 'linguistic pragmatics' – his concern with 'the pragmatic efficacy of discourse' (TM 56) – has, as he says, a modest place within the current of active nihilism. The appeal to Wittgenstein, the use of the idea of language as a game, is expedient. It is at one and the same time an expression of the decadence of truth and its expedition. As a method it supposes that the meaning of language cannot be located in an instance or order outside of itself, but rather is a product of what it does. By virtue of this supposition it is able to show how the referential instance that will to truth supposes, and that its discourse is supposed to represent, is but the effect, the product, of a series of rhetorical procedures carried out by that discourse.

It is this approach that he adopts in 'Two Metamorphoses of the Seductive in Cinema', and which motivates, or is motivated by, his appeal to Gorgias. The rhetorical analyses undertaken by the sophist, his concern with the persuasive powers of the *logos*, its sorcery, 'the power of speech over the constitution of the soul' which 'can be compared with the effects of drugs on the bodily state' (TM 55), are doubtless, for Lyotard, before Wittgenstein, identifications of the pragmatic efficacy of discourse. Since the sophist does not speak in order to discover or communicate a truth but simply for the pleasure of speaking, then sophistry could be said to initiate a pragmatics of the *logos*: the sophist's practice of speaking does not ground in an extra-linguistic truth but in language itself, and the meaning of what is said is not to be found anywhere than in language and what it does.

But sophistic rhetoric is much more than a simple foreshadowing of Wittgenstein's approach to language. When the sophist speaks he or she is guided not by what she speaks about, but by speaking itself, and the ends he or she pursues rather than the origin of what he or she says. In other words, the sophist practises the *tekhne* of speaking in terms of its effects on his or her interlocutor, and consequently the sophist begins to formulate rules for achieving these effects. Philosophy offers one way of speaking about things, but is nothing more than one way of doing so, and as the sophist recognises, there are many others. That is why sophistry is the art of the *dissoi logoi*; it is in the *dissoi logoi* that Lyotard finds an idea of language, of the *logos*, freed from its subordination to the theological principle of the unity of meaning. As he says, 'to speak is to fight, in the sense of playing, and speech acts fall within the domain of a general agonistics' (PC 10). If Lyotard can come to see in the analyses of the sophists a pragmatic approach to language, it is not simply thanks to Wittgenstein, it is because of the decadence of that idea of truth to which language, under the spell of Platonism, has been in thrall.

As is well known, Lyotard sided with the artist – an observation that is powerfully reaffirmed through the publication of the magnificent multi-volume series of *Writings on Contemporary Art and Artists*. He did so in order to reopen and renegotiate the *differend* between philosophy and art that was both instituted and settled in Plato's *Republic*. Similarly, siding with the sophists, the 'artists of the word' (TP 62), 'partisans of agonistics' (D 26), is a way of displacing or complicating Platonism, of unveiling the pragmatic principles by which it plays its game of truth. Thus Lyotard's abiding concern to expose the machinery and machinations by which that discourse that is philosophy produces itself as a true discourse, a discourse of truth, on truth, rests on an appeal to sophistry: for example, 'we could show', he writes,

> that the Platonic dialogue is forged from a series of decisions, some explicit, that is to say, announced in the dialogues, others implicit, or made on stage by the interlocutors, that these decisions taken by the director are all tricks infiltrated in the text that the Platonic heroes recite or as indications of the game that they have to respect, and that the effects which result are not different in nature from those that could be obtained by an orator, a sophist, a poet or a dramatist. (RP 235)

Philosophy is revealed as an art; but because, as Plato says, art, like sophistry, makes things appear as they are not, it is an art that, in its pursuit of truth, wants to forget that it is an art. As Gorgias observes, 'the deceiver is more honest than the non-deceiver' (TM 55), to which we might add – suspecting that this is what pleased Lyotard – that the 'truth-status' of Gorgias' statement is radically un-knowable.

THE SEDUCTION OF PHILOSOPHY

An example of Plato's use of the mechanism of seductive metalepsis can be seen in Socrates' telling of the Allegory of the Cave, in Book VII of *The Republic*. This example is perhaps more than an example because in some senses it is the archetype of this process, of this staging, inasmuch as the myth of the Cave – which as Philippe Lacoue-Labarthe says is a myth without any mythic source, a myth which is 'self-formed and self-grounded' – 'lays the foundations of Plato's political project' (Lacoue-Labarthe 1990: 81). And this project is, in a sense, the archetypical political-philosophical project, the project on which, and in response to which, the politics of the West is founded.[3]

The Allegory is held to provide a representation of the idea of a philosophical education. It pictures people as dwelling in a dark, underground cave, and as fettered by chains. According to its interpretation, these people represent human beings; they are depicted as being in a state lacking in enlightenment. Moreover, they do not recognise the state they are in; they are ignorant of their condition, and held captive by their own ignorance. Philosophy is represented as offering an escape from this condition, and as having the potential to free humans from their own state of captivity, turning them away from their immediate concerns that captivate them, and leading them to an understanding of the truth of their own situation and their own being.

Socrates has to recount the idea of a philosophical education as an allegory so that those to whom he tells the story in the dialogue can have some understanding of what he is talking about. But over the characters' shoulders, so to speak, and by way of Socrates, Plato is addressing the readers of the dialogue. The Allegory aims to show us, Plato's readers, what, in essence, a philosophical education is, namely a turning around of the soul, its movement away from the given world of appearance towards the world of the Forms or Ideas.

At first glance, and as it is ordinarily understood, it appears that all we, as Plato's readers, need to do is interpret the Allegory (as I have just done, albeit rather quickly and crudely), substituting for its pictures and images the meaning that they represent. But this cannot quite be all there is to it – not least because the Allegory does not simply make use of the accommodation of metaphor to convey an abstract meaning, but institutes the metaphysics that make sense of metaphor – this transport from the sensible or the material to the abstract and ideal.

In other words, if the Allegory is to work it needs to do something more than just picture to us, its addressees, the essence of philosophical education, it needs to lead us to that education, it needs to seduce us. It must effect an introduction to philosophy, it must produce that repositioning of the soul that it pictures in the reader, positioning the reader in the scene it describes.

Socrates begins the Allegory saying, 'Imagine – picture this! Men dwelling in a sort of underground cave . . .' (Plato 1969: 514a, translation modified). The imperative 'Imagine' is indeterminate in its addressee – it addresses both the characters that Socrates speaks to in the dialogue, and also us, the readers of the dialogue. Glaucon, one of those characters to whom Socrates speaks, responds to Socrates' picture by saying that it is an 'uncanny, out of place, image' that he gives of 'uncanny, out of place, people'. Glaucon's response is an anticipation of the reader's – who is initially positioned outside of philosophy – and the picture is uncanny because it does not immediately accord with the non-philosopher's experience of the world.

To Glaucon, Socrates responds by saying that the prisoners are like us. In this exchange is the mechanism that effects the metalepsis – the change in take – that I want to get at, that moves or seduces the reader of the dialogue from outside the scene of philosophy, into it or on to it. Like Glaucon, the reader, positioned as a non-philosopher, shocked and disbelieving, looks on the prisoners as uncanny, alien beings, and denies herself any kinship with them, only to then realise that in resisting the identification she acts as would the prisoners themselves. The more that she refuses to see herself in the image that Socrates presents of these strange people, the more closely she resembles them. However, as soon as she realises that her own attitude not only reflects Glaucon's astonishment, but also the hostility of the prisoners depicted in the Allegory towards the philosopher and towards philosophy, then she ceases to do so. The less that she thinks she is like the people pictured the more she is, and the moment she sees herself in them, she then distances herself from them.

It is no exaggeration to say that the Allegory institutes the space or theatre of our experience, that it sets up and stages the historico-politico-philosophical scene on which our experience is played out: it is the narrative – the space-time – of our truth. On the basis of the account I have just given, it is possible, I think, to speak of the Allegory as seducing the reader. Its effect is a neither voluntary nor involuntary leading of the reader to the scene or space of philosophy, which is the space or theatre of our experience. Certainly, as an operator or apparatus of seduction, the Allegory of the Cave shows us the truth of politics: it is not in terms of what it says about the city, or about justice, that the *Republic* is a political work, but in terms of how it pragmatically sets the reader on the scene of the political, how it induces or seduces them to take up a certain relation to a reality that it institutes or produces.

CINEMA

Set against this historico-politico-philosophical horizon, the question of 'whether anything escapes from seduction', which Lyotard substitutes for the deceptive assurance of his title, is a question that must necessarily remain open for as long as that horizon remains in place. This is not to suggest that this horizon is absolute or all-embracing, that it circumscribes all possibilities; it is not to imply – and this amounts to the same thing – that there is nothing in our experience that does not in some way exceed Platonism or remain irreducible to it. However, admitting this, as it is necessary to do, does not in turn mean that we have escaped from Platonism.

Given this, what, then, can be said in this respect of a cinema that putatively breaks with or suspends seduction? Before addressing this question, it is necessary to note that according to Lyotard there is something seductive about both Coppola's *Apocalypse Now* and Syberberg's *Hitler: A Film from Germany*. Considered pragmatically, *Apocalypse Now* is a realist film, and as Lyotard says, realist cinema is particularly favourable to seduction. Narrating 'the story of a dangerous search mission in the theatre of operations in Vietnam' (TM 58), it presents a complex saga or mixture of sagas – the 'positive saga of the hero', the 'negative saga of the sought-after officer', the 'impossible saga of the war' (TM 59) – and in conformity with the cathartic imperative of the tragic genre, it presents its audience with the prescription, 'live the intense epic of a pointless combat' (TM 58). *Hitler: A Film from Germany* is, Lyotard says, 'obviously a reflection on seduction by the Nazi narrative' (TM 60). However, at the same time as it provokes, or seeks to provoke, such a reflection, it 'encourages' its audience (or some of them at least) to 'enter into the Nazi epic by the eloquence (if not Wagnerian, at least post-Wagnerian. . .) of the soundtrack' (TM 61), and in that respect, it seduces.

Now, both also break with seduction – or if they do not break with seduction, they at least manifest its metamorphosis. In so far as they do, they differ significantly between themselves. One corresponds to Lyotard's postulation of the possibility of a 'non-seductive pragmatic relation', to a discourse which 'engenders some pragmatic effects without "sorcery"' (Gorgias' *goèteía*) (TM 56); the other corresponds to the possibility of a 'suspended pragmatic relation', to a discourse that has as its effect a suspension of 'the pragmatic relation between addressor, addressee and referent' (TM 56).

Lyotard finds a possible instance of the latter, a possible instance of a cinematic suspension of seduction, in Syberberg's *Hitler: A Film from Germany*. By its use of 'text, layouts with illustrations (nearly immobile tableaux vivants, flaunting their seductive power), dividing up into thematic chapters (in the interview with Winifred Wagner)' (TM 60), the film provokes the audience to a 'reflection on seduction by the Nazi narrative' (TM 60). This 'putting-into-reading' induces a distancing or 'detachment' from the 'prescriptive-narrative givens' of the images that is, in some respects, comparable to Brecht's *Verfremdungseffekte* – his use of techniques such as the making explicit of the narrator or narrative function, the inclusion of stage-machinery, films, music, the chorus in the drama, inauthentic acting styles, to prevent the audience from empathising with the action and actors of the drama, blocking the effect of catharsis, and breaking, or supposedly breaking, with the Aristotelian principles of theatre.[4] The question is whether this detachment is outside of seduction, whether it acts 'without "sorcery"' (TM 60). In answer to this question, Lyotard finds it necessary to observe the limitations of the parallel between Brecht's theatre and Syberberg's cinema. For whilst Brecht's epic theatre puts the effect of detachment into the service of the 'Marxist grand narrative', and Brecht remained seduced by it, Lyotard finds no such 'eloquence' in Syberberg. Yet, despite this, and as we have already seen, for Lyotard the film speaks with two voices, since by virtue of its soundtrack, 'the romanticism of a past monstrous epic never ceases to traverse musically the plastic meditation on it'

(TM 61), and its 'equivocity produces contrary effects on different addressees, and sometimes on the same one' (TM 61). The film is at one and the same time an example of seduction enacted and reflected, and Lyotard thus poses the question of whether, to the extent that it invites its audience into seduction at the same time as it distances them from it, it constitutes 'a case of suspended seduction' (TM 61).

Perhaps this equivocality makes apparent the predicament of what Lyotard calls here 'reflection', or what we might call, despite the difference that Lyotard detects between the Brechtian aesthetic and Syberberg's cinematic practice, the 'critical function' of art.[5] 'Reflection', which is made possible by detachment, is *critical* in that it makes possible an unmasking of the apparatus of power, in this instance the unmasking of the apparatus of seduction. Criticism in this sense – criticism in the sense of *critique* – is itself suspended from a political project, as Brechtian theatre demonstrates, and that is the case even if the political project remains in abeyance. Take the case of seduction: its critical unmasking consists in the disclosure of the pragmatic operations that serve to insinuate the seduced into an order of reality that is open to practical action, to an order of reality that is the object of *praxis*. Distanced and disclosed, these pragmatic operators cease to exercise their charm upon their addressees. Yet, the critical disclosure of this pragmatic apparatus is itself governed by a demand for transformation, and so it always supposes – even if it defers or suspends it – the operation of seduction. It is for this reason that Syberberg's *Hitler: A Film from Germany* is equivocal, its reflection on seduction being cut across by the seductive operation of its soundtrack, which fills, as it were, the vacuum left by the suspension of seduction at the plastic level. At a critical level, then, seduction is put into question in the name of a transformed order of reality that is yet to be brought into existence, or it suspends this projected order of reality but nevertheless leaves itself open to inhabitation by seduction.

According to Lyotard, a different break with seduction is at stake in *Apocalypse Now*. Whilst the film is for the most part realist, and if for the most part it operates seductively, one scene, Lyotard says, breaks with the technique of realism, and so breaks, or appears to break, with seduction – the scene of the attack on the village by the American helicopters. The technique used in this sequence is one that Lyotard, adopting a term applied by 'Europeans' to a 'current of American painting at the beginning of the 1970s' (TM 58), designates as 'hyperrealist'. Lyotard understands hyperrealism as a novel solution to the problem of the relation between photography and painting. Amounting to a series of experiments arising from the mechanical reproducibility of the image, hyperrealism 'plays whole-heartedly with reproduction' (TM 58). In doing so, it exacerbates the destruction of eloquence that Bataille said was first effected by Manet (TM 58). The work of art is 'eloquent' – is endowed with a sense or significance – to the extent that it inscribes, or permits the inscription of, the scene it presents in a virtual narrative of a 'mythological, religious, historical, intimist, or even simply intimate . . . character' (TM 59). By dint of being so inscribed, the image speaks; or better, something – the divine, Spirit, Liberty, Being, the Self – speaks through the image. If the narrative that situates the scene is itself mimetic, then the work operates seductively, transmitting one or more prescriptions to its spectator. By contrast, through its exploitation of the reproducibility of the image, hyperrealism drains the image of its significance, destroys its eloquence; based on the photograph, the 'snapshot' would be an appropriate term, it captures a moment frozen in itself, immobilised, without past or future, a moment in suspension. It relates to time only 'through entropy or repetition' – the multiple reproduction of images in Warhol, for example, present only an each time repeated – and gives no place to history (TM 59). Presented 'without past or future', the hyperrealist image ceases to solicit the intervention of the viewer, denying her the authority to transform the scene.

Hyperrealism's destruction of eloquence still allows a reality to present itself, but denuded of a past or future it is a reality presented with what Lyotard calls 'a sort of blinding stupidity' (TM 59). In the sequence of the helicopter attack on the village in *Apocalypse Now*, where the scene is not painted or photographed but filmed, and hence where everything is in movement, the quality of blinding stupidity with which reality is presented – or with which it presents itself – and the correlative 'stupefaction' of the spectator, are produced through the excessive visual and sonorous saturation of the sequence with elements all in ultra-rapid displacement. There is, Lyotard says, a 'chaos of data' (TM 59) since the auditory and visual intensity of the sequence overwhelms the capacity of ear and eye to synthesise the sensible elements by which they are assaulted. The spectator, suffering 'an excess of reality' (TM 59), is traumatised as it were, is put into a state of shock. A sense of panic pervades the scene since by virtue of its sensory excess, it eclipses all 'the little stories concerning the principal and secondary characters' (TM 59), and it loses all meaning as the implicit prescriptions associated with narrative eloquence 'founder in the excess of information' (TM 59). Placed in a 'state of loss of obligation' (TM 59) by the visual and sonorous excess of this sequence, the spectator is outside the 'game' of seduction (TM 60).

By virtue of its aesthetic intensity, this chaotic excess of the sensory wipes out the narrative function required by seduction and operates an-aesthetically, as it were. It amounts to something like a sensible paradox – an event without impression, an event that has the effect of having no sensible effect upon the senses, or that has the effect of leaving no effect. The chaotic excess of this sequence is, then, an an-aesthetic act by virtue of which reality – which philosophically speaking is that which is present – presents itself not merely with a lack of significance, with a meaninglessness or stupidity, but with a *blinding* stupidity. It is so overwhelmingly present that it blinds; it cannot present itself. In presenting itself, it effaces itself.

The intensity of the scene allows what I would like to call an 'insensible-sensible' to occur. There is something of the sublime in all of this.[6] For, according to Lyotard, the aesthetics of the sublime, as Kant analyses it in the *Critique of Judgement*, amounts to an anaesthetics. The sublime sentiment is occasioned by the incapacity of the faculty of imagination to form an image adequate to the manifold of sensation. With the sublime, he says, the mind suffers a shock, in that it is constitutively unprepared to accommodate the manifold of sensation by which it is touched, and of which it cannot therefore make representation (HJ 31). This failure of the imagination to make representation of the manifold of sensation that besets it gives rise to a pain; it suffers because of its incapacity. At the same time, however, it also provokes pleasure, since the impotence of the imagination reveals the potency of reason. As Lyotard puts it, 'in the sublime "situation", something like an Absolute, either of magnitude or of power, is made quasi-perceptible (the word is Kant's) due to the very failing of the faculty of presentation. This Absolute is, in Kant's terminology, the object of an Idea of Reason' (IN 136). Questioning whether this disaster of the imagination leaves any room for nature to address itself to us, since on the occasion of the sublime the mind 'feels only itself' (IN 136), Lyotard argues that the principal interest that Kant sees in the sublime sentiment is that proper to ethics. For Kant the sentiment of the sublime is the aesthetic sign of reason assuming the vocation (perhaps one might say the sublime vocation) proper to it, namely its realisation of its own interest in its freedom (IN 137). By contrast, for Lyotard there is nothing of this vocation realised in the paralysis occasioned by what I have called the insensible-sensible, and which Lyotard, in later works, calls an 'immaterial' matter (IN 140). Rather, the disaster of intelligence it betokens, the paralysis of all projects and activity it provokes, the radical passivity that it makes possible, allows that something give itself – *that there be* some something, Lyotard says (IN 140).

What is at stake in this insensible-sensible is a sensitivity to an affective event or intensity that is intrinsically recalcitrant to the mastery of the intellect, that insists and resists the mind's imposition of form on matter, an imposition instituted by philosophy, and which has shaped the history of the West. It realises its truth in and as nihilism, which is aptly named in so far as it is incapable of finding anything in the given except what the mind has ordered itself, and which submits all beings to the dictates of the understanding. It is for this reason that in his later work Lyotard invokes the necessity to bear witness to something like this insensible-sensible, and which he claims is all that 'remains as "politics"' (IN 7). Often seized upon, this claim has served to legitimate many criticisms directed towards Lyotard's supposed political defeatism, the inevitable, final, consequence of his drift away from Marx in the late 1960s, and his abandonment of the revolutionary project. This, however, is less the mark of a political failure or the sign of political defeatism, than the consequence of Lyotard's radical understanding of the current predicament that thought must face, the predicament of nihilism. Lyotard grasps nihilism from its roots in that decision of the West that is opened with the advent of philosophy, and that means that he sees nihilism as a complex historico-politico-philosophical phenomenon. And whilst there is something seemingly paradoxical in his appeal to what, from the perspective of the understanding, can only be thought of as nothingness in order to resist nihilism itself, this discloses the truth of nihilism, namely that it is nothing else than the insensitivity to the insensible-sensible that is matter, the annihilation of the nothingness that is the 'there is' of existence itself.

NOTES

1. The reference DK refers to Diels and Kranz 1952.
2. This observation about ideology is one that Lyotard himself makes in the introduction to *The Inhuman* (IN 6).
3. It is worth noting that the Allegory of the Cave also institutes a model on which cinema has been frequently understood, and, perhaps, in terms of which a certain form of cinema has been made – the form that in 'Two Metamorphoses of the Seductive in Cinema' Lyotard calls 'realist'. Thus, the profound co-implication of cinema and politics, a co-implication that predates the technological possibility of cinema, which both Lyotard's essay and this essay attempt to explore.
4. See Brecht 1974 and also Benjamin 1998.
5. The term 'critical function' is taken from Lyotard's essay 'The Tooth, the Palm'. The essay addresses the 'crisis of the theater' (Lyotard 1976: 106) induced by the experience of modern capitalism, and the 'crisis of modernism' (108). Lyotard considers this critical function of theatre to be the solution pursued by Brecht.
6. As Peter W. Milne noted at the *Acinemas* conference.

REFERENCES

Benjamin, Walter (1998), *Understanding Brecht*, trans. Anna Bostock, London: Verso.
Brecht, Bertolt (1974), *Brecht on Theatre*, ed. J. Willett, London: Methuen.
Diels, Hermann and Kranz, Walther (eds) (1952), *Die Fragmente der Vorsokratiker*, 6th edn, Berlin: Weidmann.

Lacoue-Labarthe, Philippe (1990), *Heidegger, Art and Politics*, trans. Chris Turner, Oxford: Basil Blackwell.

Lyotard, Jean-François (1976), 'The Tooth, the Palm', trans. Anne Knap and Michel Benamou, *SubStance* 5:15, pp. 105–10.

Plato (1969), *The Republic*, trans. P. Shorey, Cambridge, MA: Harvard University Press.

CHAPTER 10

Authorisation: Lyotard's Sovereign Image

Peter W. Milne

It may seem strange to begin a discussion of Lyotard and film with a reference to Lyotard and television. But if one were to attempt, as I would like to do here, to open up some of the 'political' stakes of Lyotard's interest in cinema, it may be worthwhile to do so. The text I have in mind is that curious little piece entitled 'Tribune sans tribun' in French and published in *Political Writings* under the title, 'A Podium without a Podium: Television according to J.-F. Lyotard'. Though I have the greatest respect for Bill Readings and Kevin Paul Geiman and their work in translating this important collection of Lyotard's writings, I should point out that the title is perhaps a little more complex than their rendering might make it seem. Surely 'tribune' can be translated as podium; the word comes from the title of the television programme on which Lyotard appeared on 27 March 1978, *Tribune Libre*, a kind of 'free platform' or 'open forum' where intellectuals could appear – for fifteen minutes – to discuss events of the day or, I suppose, whatever else might be on their minds. (*Tribune* can also be translated as 'opinion column'.) It's the second word, 'tribun', that's a little more tricky. It's clearly linked to the feminine noun 'tribune', but formulated as it is in the masculine it would appear to designate not a podium (or platform or forum, etc.) but a (male) 'tribune', that is, a kind of orator or even, in the archaic sense, a champion of the people. So while it doesn't retain the etymological link between the French words in the way that Readings and Geiman's translation does, another, perhaps more literal, rendering of the title of this little work might be something like 'A Podium without a Speaker'.[1]

And this would appear to be exactly what is in play here. The text is a transcription of the soundtrack of Lyotard's appearance on *Tribune Libre*, where he was invited to speak in the capacity of an 'intellectual'. Now, Lyotard's attitude towards intellectuals is well known: linked to the thinking of a universal subject, the intellectual is someone charged with describing situations or courses of action that would lead to the 'fullest possible embodiment' of this subject (PW 4). In this sense, the intellectual is an authority, someone with a specific kind of knowledge, taste, sensibility or means of expression that the general public is lacking. Given Lyotard's view that since the end of the eighteenth century no such subject (or even 'subject-victim') has been identifiable, it follows that there should be no more intellectuals either: thinking, along with painting, writing, and the other arts, no longer speaks for any specific community and does not 'seek to cultivate, educate, or train anyone at all' (PW 4–5). Such thinkers or artists experiment, and the experimenter is not an authority.

How, then, to appear on a television programme designed to provide a space for intellectuals? Lyotard's 'solution' to this problem is a humorous and novel one: for all but a few moments the soundtrack of his voice is out of sync with his image as it appears on the screen – 'a little mechanism of transmission', as he puts it, 'by which you don't see the one who is speaking and you don't hear the one you see' (PW 94). The 'tribune' is indeed absent from the podium: though there is an image of someone speaking, the link with the speaking voice is short-circuited, a ruse that has been employed in order precisely 'to destroy the image of authority that inevitably comes to frame itself in your screen, every time it makes you see anything other than fictions, films, or plays. . .' (PW 94). In refusing to comply with the image of authority produced by the screen, in tangling up image and voice-over and scrambling the message and its origins, the 'philosopher' (the third person is also employed throughout) thus 'refuses to appear before your eyes and ears as an authority, as he is asked to do' (PW 94).

Of course, Lyotard does not confine himself simply to this refusal to appear as an authority. One could say that he performs a certain philosophical questioning on the very nature of authority. For if a philosopher is someone 'who thinks about the common questions', we might note that in Lyotard's view (at least in this text), the questions that he or she 'reflects particularly and principally' on are questions of authority (PW 93). When the philosopher is then put in the position of having to assume this authority, is given the authority or is authorised to speak, he or she must then wonder at the very nature of this authorisation, this assumption of a certain kind of *competence*: for who can be said to be competent with regard to the questions that interest a philosopher, questions about love, work, society or health, but also questions on justice, beauty, happiness 'and perhaps even truth' (PW 93–4)? Who would be in a position to judge such competence? In a sense, then, the very idea of a philosopher appearing as an authority is self-defeating: 'If philosophers agree to help their fellow citizens to believe in authority in matters where there isn't any, to legitimate this authority, then they cease to ponder in the sense in which I spoke of thinking, and they thereby cease to be philosophers' (PW 95).

This problematic of authority is no doubt far-reaching, but let us recall that the context for this meditation on the competence and authority of the philosopher is occasioned by the invitation to appear on television, the 'slightest appearance' of which raises precisely these questions (PW 94). Despite what Lyotard seems to suggest here, the slightest perusal of the writings on film would indicate that the same questions beset cinema also. In its most basic terms, one could say that the issue for Lyotard would in part be linked to the representation of reality, or perhaps better – and more broadly – to the mediation of the real through narratives, images, discourses and even perception itself. It is a familiar theme in his work, and as we will see it can be tracked, in one form or another, through many of the turns and inflections that work has taken. If I choose here to track it through a few of his writings on film, using the figure of authority as a kind of guiding thread, this is not only in an attempt to examine these relatively few writings in terms of the broader figures that appear throughout Lyotard's many and diverse writings – though this in itself would probably make such an effort worthwhile. But, as I've already suggested, it might also turn out that certain political stakes appear in the question these writings raise, through various inflections, about the relationship between the viewer, the real and the image of the real of which film might only be one, but perhaps an exemplary, example.

Perhaps it is less a question of the image of authority, then, than it is one of the authority of the image – that of the cinematic image as much as the TV image. Indeed, it would appear that the first English publication of the text on television, in the journal *Framework* in the Fall of 1979, was included in a section called 'That Part of Cinema Called Television' (see Lyotard 1979). Perhaps I might take advantage of this fortuitous fact, then, to move these considerations on authority, and therefore on the political implications of the cinematic image, more firmly into the orbit of Lyotard's writings on film.

ACINEMA AND THE INTERRUPTION OF DESIRE

One might be willing to hazard the claim that the problem of the authority of the filmic image is to be found, in one form or another, in all of Lyotard's writings on cinema, not least in 'Acinema', one of the earliest and certainly one of the few sustained discussions on the topic. Still working in the register of what we might very generally refer to as the 'libidinal', Lyotard considers filmmaking here in terms of a series of inclusions and exclusions operating in the interest of producing a certain order, itself imposed to counter the intensities produced by incongruities of movement. Film direction thus acts 'as a factor of *libidinal normalisation*', 'the subordination of all partial drives, all sterile and divergent movements to the unity of an organic body' (Ac 39). It is no accident that the stakes of this 'libidinal normalisation' revolve around the 'so-called impression of reality', an impression that depends on a 'real oppression' of non-productive images (Ac 34). Direction (mise-en-scène), as 'a technique of exclusions and effacements' linked to the production of this impression of reality, thus opens problematics that far exceed the confines of film. Indeed, in this text Lyotard not only associates it with politics — it is, according to him, 'a political activity *par excellence*' (Ac 34).

The law that governs this order follows both the rules of representation for 'spatial localisation' and the rules of narration (*narration*) for what Lyotard here refers to as 'the instantiation of language' (Ac 34) but which we, following *The Postmodern Condition* or certain passages in *The Inhuman*, might also think of as a principle of temporal organisation.[2] What is here called 'acinema' is to be found at the two 'poles' Lyotard describes in terms of cinema's 'writing of movements': extreme mobilisation and extreme immobilisation (Ac 39), each of which contributes to the distortion of the forms of the image and to the blocking of any 'synthesis of identification' (Ac 41). In other words, they introduce 'arrhythmies' that disrupt the authority of the law of narrative-representation. In this text, these arrhythmies contribute to the interruption of desire: what is represented ceases to be a libidinal object, 'while the screen itself, in all its most formal aspects, takes its place' (Ac 41).

Although the language of acinema is not yet operative, this description seems to be largely in keeping with Lyotard's slightly earlier discussion of Resnais' *Je t'aime, je t'aime* in 'The Critical Function of the Work of Art'. In most cinema, Lyotard tells us in this text, the image 'functions as a scene in which my desire is caught and comes to fulfillment' (DW 71). In Resnais' film, however, in which a man who is chosen for experiments in time-travel undergoes non-sequential journeys into his own past, the spatio-temporal framework of the secondary processes are disrupted through the confusion of these 'flashbacks' (*retours en arrière*), which effect 'a real deconstruction of normal editing [*montage*]', 'a total deconstruction of sequence' (DW 75). Though in general the public goes to the cinema to 'forget' and to 'fulfill its own desires' by identifying with the phantasy projected on the screen, the non-sequential temporality of Resnais' film 'obliges the public to stop phantasizing', an interruption of the economy of desire that reveals the potential 'critical function' of the work itself: 'The spectator finds himself in the reversing, critical, function of the work and his desire collides with the screen, because the screen is treated as a screen and not as a window' (DW 75). The public is not permitted to 'find itself again' through the mediation of the image. Instead, the gaze runs up against the image itself. Another reality appears in this collision with the screen; objects, actions, or movements lose their familiarity. The gaze in thus reversed, from the image back on to the viewer. In the case of *Je t'aime, je t'aime*, this 'critical reversal' is brought about through 'cutting and editing' (*montage*), though this would only be one way in which the order and unity of the film might be disrupted, the spatio-temporal framework altered or skewed.

The critical work thus achieved is nonetheless particularly difficult as far as the cinema, 'mass media par excellence', goes, since the cinema 'belongs to "culture," and three-fourths of its function consists in stirring up and in recovering phantasy by having it find fulfillment through the screen' (DW 75–6). This suspicion regarding 'three-fourths' of cinema is echoed, perhaps interestingly, in the (roughly contemporary) 'Sketch of an Economy of Hyperrealism', a text to which we shall return. But there is that other '25%' (along, perhaps, with Lyotard's fifteen minutes on *Tribune Libre*). We can perhaps begin to see why Lyotard's interest is often considered to be almost entirely directed towards avant-garde or experimental cinema, a conception that has thus far meant that his work has had a greater impact on theories of experimental rather than mainstream film.[3] Though it may not hold in all cases, the same could easily be said for his interest in painting and other arts. The 'critical function' of any art, including cinematic art, would appear to lie precisely in its power to reverse and disrupt what might be thought of as its 'proper' or normal function – that is, in undoing the representational and narrative laws that give it its appeal and its authority. The critical function of such work is to release the viewer from the various economies (of capital, desire, meaning) in which he or she is situated, to undo the power of those economies, for however brief a time. Such a task would appear to fall largely to those works that refuse these economies, the very meaning, in many of Lyotard's texts, of the avant-garde. If the 'authority' of cinematic works is derived from the reinforcement of the norms of representation, the avant-garde's own power, perhaps even its own 'authority' (but we will see that this is not an authority if authority is to be associated with command or interdiction), lies in the willingness to forego these norms.

DEAUTHORISATION: HYPERREALISM

It is possible that at least some of this 'critical' power survives the transition from the work on the libidinal to the work on the 'postmodern' and later.[4] Let us recall Lyotard's claim in 'Answering the Question: What is Postmodernism?', for example, that the task that academicism assigns to realism is to 'preserve various consciousnesses from doubt', to create images with readily recognisable meanings and thus to allow the individual 'to arrive easily at the consciousness of his [or her] own identity' (PC 74). What Lyotard here calls 'industrial cinema' completes the task of narrative literature in 'rounding off diachronies as organic wholes', just as photography puts the final touches on 'the program of ordering the visible' elaborated for painting in the quattrocento (PC 74). The avant-garde artist, however, resists the demand to paint, write or film with this end in mind, refuses to allow his or her work to be put to 'therapeutic use'. And the stakes here are not so far from those described in many of the 'libidinal' texts: like the experimental filmmaker, the avant-garde artist more generally is described as being occupied with questioning the rules of representation or of narrative and with asking the question what is painting, writing, film, etc. But in so doing he or she also refuses to communicate, 'by means of the "correct rules," the endemic desire for reality with objects and situations capable of gratifying it' (PC 75).

Nonetheless, there is a change, and perhaps this is revealed most clearly in the text from 1980 on 'Two Metamorphoses of the Seductive in Cinema', a text that, despite its title, is closer to the orbit of the 'postmodern' and the work on language games and phrase universes than it is to the libidinal. For while the reference to seduction would seem to invoke the register of desire, Lyotard is very clear that in discussing seduction in terms of language games, 'we no longer scan the depths of desire and pleasure. We stick to the categories of linguistic pragmatics' (TM 56). Following Gorgias' description of tragedy as a deception able to produce a metastasis or displacement of the opinions of the listener, seduction here is a kind of 'game' played by both addressor and addressee. Rather than an appeal to desire or to libidinal drives, then, seduction 'would be a case of the pragmatic efficacy of discourse' (TM 56).

In what does this 'efficacy' consist? What is the nature of this metastasis or displacement? The effect of seduction, Lyotard tells us, would be to turn any discourse, 'even if non-prescriptive', into a 'non-formulated prescription' (TM 56). When a pragmatic situation obscures the place of the addressor and even of the addressee, the conditions are particularly 'favourable' to the transmission of such non-explicit prescriptives (TM 57). This is why he privileges narration, especially in so far as it has a high or even completely mimetic content: the perfect mimesis is the effacement of the writer, the presentation of an action or state of affairs as if there were no 'intermediary informant' (D 25). In representing a prescriptive relation on the 'referential stage', 'grand narrations' (*grandes narrations*) obscure the pragmatic relations between addressor (director, dramaturge, etc.) and addressee (audience) in favour of those between the heroes of the story (TM 57). Absorbed by the relations in the narrative itself, the pragmatic relation between the creator of the scene and the audience is elided. The framing of the image, the process of inclusion and exclusion giving order to a certain reality, is missed. And if the set-up in question here is initially that of the 'classical theatre', Lyotard will immediately stress that 'the same goes for Hollywood cinema' (along with Wagnerian opera) (TM 57). In each case, speech takes place between the characters; the director/dramaturge does not speak as such to the audience. The pragmatic relation is thus indirect and open to confusion or obfuscation.

Let us note that this obfuscation operates through narration's relation to realism. The realist image is here taken as a kind of distraction that hides the addressor/addressee relation in a way analogous to that of the obscuring of the economy of desire through the phantasy image. In this text, realism in cinema designates that 'perfect occultation of the places of the narrator and the narratee' that is the 'perfect mimesis' (TM 57). What prevents the audience from perceiving the intervention of the director is this realist 'spatial and temporal frame' in which the drama unfolds. In order to be successful in this ruse, the frame must appear natural and thus be invisible. It must therefore be 'as consistent as possible with the cultural norms of perception in space and time' obeyed by the spectators (TM 57). The latter are then 'seduced', and it is realism taken as a specific spatial and temporal frame that facilitates this metastasis.

If, given what we have seen, it is avant-garde film that might be thought most likely to undo this 'normalising' spatio-temporal framework, the example Lyotard gives here in fact suggests that 'industrial' or commercial cinema might also harbour moments that defy this framework. The majority of Francis Ford Coppola's *Apocalypse Now* is indeed realist in the sense described above; nonetheless, Lyotard will make an exception for one particular scene: the attack on the village by the American army helicopters. This scene is produced by quite another technique, one that he ventures to call 'hyperrealist' (TM 58) – and hyperrealism is not simply more or greater realism. It engenders other and different effects. Being filmed rather than painted or photographed, and therefore 'in movement', the hyperrealism of this scene comes from a kind of acinema, from its being saturated with 'sonorous and visual elements all in ultra-rapid displacement' (TM 59). Among the effects that this displacement engenders, the most important departure from realism is that it 'ceases to seduce' under the conditions just described; indeed, it might just stop seducing altogether – or at any rate, that is the 'hypothesis' (TM 58).

As the short text entitled 'Sketch of an Economy of Hyperrealism' makes clear, the hyperrealist image, in the very excess of its presentation, in fact remains cut off from any narrative of reality or 'discourse on the world' (MT1 103). Though the 'Two Metamorphoses' text is somewhat later, Lyotard seems to hold a very similar view there. Hyperrealism does not allow the viewer to lose him or herself in the familiar: the 'real' is made uncanny, as if in being too apparent or present it raises the question of its own possibility, even its own origin. If, according to Bataille, painting loses its eloquence with Manet and ceases either to 'dazzle the masses' or to express sentiments and relate anecdotes (Bataille 1955: 38, 52ff.), the hyperrealists' blind affirmation and repetition, says Lyotard, further destroys this eloquence (TM 58). Its images, relentlessly 'real', overdetermined and thus underdetermined or even undermined, isolate themselves by overloading and overdetermining in turn the cultural norms of perception. This is why they contribute to the undoing of the possibility of inscribing the image or scene in a narration, of giving it 'reality' by connecting what it depicts to other facts or events to form a world. One might say that this image or scene doesn't speak sensibly, and thus forges no links with what has already been said and what will come to be said, with what is, was, or will come to be. A 'reality' continues to present itself in this hyperrealist case, but one 'without past or future' and thus without any task for the addressee (TM 59). The hyperrealist image 'gives no place to history' or to historical development; it relates to time only 'through entropy or repetition' (TM 59). As for the addressee, he or she receives no prescription from it, but on the other hand is thus also devoid of the authority to transform it, an ambiguity that does not appear to be thematised in the texts from the early 1970s. How to understand this ambiguity and its implications for the cinematic viewer?

Let us first note that hyperrealism comes about as a 'novel solution' to the problem of painting's relation to photography (TM 58). It is thus the result of a series of experiments in painting and in the industrial production of images more generally, as well as for the addressor, the painter him or herself (TM 58). The hyperrealist artist is therefore not an authority in the sense invoked above; the hyperrealist image has no role to play in the fulfilment of any programme external to the production of images itself. In the context of the 'metamorphosis' of seduction, one implication would seem to be that the role of the addressor is no longer elided in the 'pragmatic' situation set up for the addressor of the hyperrealist image. The viewer is not manipulated by the hyperrealist image in the way that he or she is manipulated by the hidden prescription of the realist image, for example, or by the 'eloquence' of the soundtrack in Syberberg's *Hitler: A Film from Germany* (the other of the two 'metamorphoses of seduction' in this little essay) (TM 61). The viewer is thus freed from seduction and in this sense finds a kind of 'liberation' from the authority of the image in a way similar (and indeed linked, TM 58) to acinema's power to free the viewer from phantasy in the libidinal texts. Perhaps one could go so far as to suggest that the hyperrealist image makes it impossible to efface the fact that the image (and therefore any narrative of which it purports to be a part) is constructed, is not in the least 'natural'. If the construction of such an image is indeed a political act (and even the political act *'par excellence'*), its role here becomes impossible to forget. This means that one's role or place with regard to this construction also cannot be forgotten. This could be linked to what Lyotard elsewhere calls 'the Brechtian aesthetics of distanciation', that is, the hindering of the audience's ability to identify itself with the characters or action of the scene and the ensuing need to accept or reject what is portrayed at a conscious level (TP 111).[5] One might even be tempted to see a certain agency open itself to the viewer, along with certain critical possibilities.[6]

There are certainly elements of this reading in the 'Two Metamorphoses' essay, particularly with regard to the relatively few things said about Syberberg in the closing paragraphs. At the very least, Lyotard will suggest that the addressee can be called to reflect by or through the very nature of these images (TM 61). Nonetheless, the focus here is more on the force of the images and the very different pragmatic situation that is thus set up than it is on any 'message' of the addressor. The question is less one of coming to recognise or reveal a once-hidden obligation in the hyperrealist image than it is of an interruption of the pragmatic situation through which the viewer is not only 'freed' from seduction but also loses the authority to transform the scene. He or she is 'freed' from prescription but also from the responsibility or even the ability to act. With the loss of anything to do, to project, to remember or to sense, one is powerless, even thrown into a state of panic over the fact that 'no narrative can take charge of this chaos' (TM 59). By no longer playing by the rule that cinema should seduce, the sequence of the attack on the village 'brings back madness and injustice' (TM 59).

The effects of hyperrealism, then, are affective, even if this term might perhaps be somewhat anachronistic with regard to this text. Lyotard refers to a friend of his, 'a young American researcher and a Vietnam veteran' who became powerless to speak whenever the war came up. The scene from *Apocalypse Now*, says Lyotard, 'allowed me to understand this difficulty' (TM 60). There are many images, it turns out, that are 'placed outside obligation' (TM 60). This young man was also deauthorised, 'had lost all authority' to take what he had witnessed 'back up into a narrative, into a theory'. He was immobilised by another kind of 'hyperreality', struck with a silence that Lyotard does not hesitate to associate with the 'deportees on their return from the camps' (TM 60).[7]

AUTHORISATION AND THE SOVEREIGN IMAGE

If the 'Two Metamorphoses' piece appears closer to the Lyotard of the postmodern, language games and phrase universes than to the Lyotard of the libidinal, the presentation given at the Institut français in Munich in 1995 on 'The Idea of a Sovereign Film' would seem to count among those series of 'late' texts devoted to the affect and to a general 'supplementation' of *The Differend*.[8] Nonetheless, there may at first glance seem to be little reference to the affect here. What is sovereign in this text would appear to be the image itself, or what Lyotard calls 'the pictorial or filmic fact' (ISF 69). 'Reality' in this case is not associated with realism pure and simple, and thus does not simply appear as a construct of the representative-narrative form. Instead, it is described as enjoying a 'kind of autonomy' in relation to the narrated story; it can even escape or elude (*se dérobe*) the role given to it by narration (ISF 65). What the films that are the subject of this text do is to allow a 'real' to surface 'which seems to emerge from reality itself' (ISF 68). If there is an unconscious in play here, then, it is not the unconscious of the filmmaker or the viewer, 'but the unconscious of reality' (ISF 68), the opening of a world that is in the world, the passing of the 'ontological real' (ISF 69).

It is this reference to the 'ontological real', which appears also at various times in many of the texts on the sublime, that perhaps opens a way to the affect. Invoking Bataille, Lyotard refers to a sovereignty that would not be *the* sovereign (God, King or People) but 'an experience which is not authorised and which does not appeal to any authority', one having no relation to right or law (*droit*) but which simply happens or appears (ISF 62). On the one hand, this sovereignty is associated with the artist, who always works without authorisation, asking nothing of authority and without waiting for the right to proceed. But this 'sovereign indifference to authority' also sometimes gives rise to a kind of 'communication'. The word is taken from Bataille and we have seen that it is a strange one for Lyotard to use, since communication would appear to depend on conformity to the correct rules of construction and exchange, the setting-up of a (relatively) clear pragmatic situation. It is precisely the demand that artists (along with writers and philosophers) be communicable that he rejects in the opening passages of 'What is Postmodernism?', for example. But communication here is not linguistic, not an act of signification (Durafour 2009: 85–6). Indeed, it is a 'communion' that is incomparable to any exchange of signs (ISF 62). What it communicates, instead, is 'intense instants, temporal spasms' between reader or viewer and artwork – that is, it 'communicates' affects.

The artwork in question here of course is film, particularly that film known as 'neo-realist'. Whether or not the neo-realist image can exactly be said to be hyperrealist, it plays a role similar to the one played by hyperrealism in the 'Two Metamorphoses' paper. It is again a question of a kind of 'excessiveness' of reality, a hyperbole or exaggeration that in this very excess goes beyond the rules of representation and narration that it nonetheless employs. What makes neo-realism unique is that it is linked with a new 'relation to time', one which, in the Deleuzian terms invoked here, 'causes the filmic material of the movement-image to pass to the time-image' (ISF 63). In the 'classical' representative-narrative form, the image is subordinated to a very particular organisation of time, that of the movement of the narrative, in which 'it is framed and assembled in order to follow the story that the film tells' (ISF 63). In classical film, all movements 'are placed under the authority' of this general form 'and are authorised by it' (ISF 63). Around the time of the Second World War, however, a new mode of film began to appear – largely in Europe, although Lyotard, following Bazin, does not hesitate to add Welles and Ozu to the likes of Rossellini, De Sica and Fellini (ISF 63). Although in neo-realism the general form of movements continues 'to exercise its authority over the filmic narration', it also 'admits or tolerates . . . movements which do not flow to the same rhythm as the flux of the whole' (ISF 63–4). These movements produce 'blocks of temporality in suspense', 'arrhythmies' that are in no way necessarily linked with the acme of the narrative (as they are, for example, in *Joe* as Lyotard describes this film in 'Acinema') (ISF x; see Ac 64).

Acinema returns here, then, now in the attempt to understand neo-realism: Ozu tends towards an immobile acinema, for example, while 'certain scenes of Welles [move] in the direction of an excessive speed' (ISF 64). In the end, however, Lyotard now maintains that 'the two cases are little different sensorially': objects fixed at length can lose their bearings, while extremely rapid movements can come to seem immobile. What interests Lyotard in this case is rather the 'sovereignty' of these acinematic moments. Certain moments, necessary to the plot and thus 'functional' to the overall project, nonetheless also coincide with 'a space-time which is not finalised', but 'crude [*brut*]' (ISF 65). The capacity to identify people, objects, or situations is not usually lost in these cases. It is a question, rather, of the alteration of the space-time in which they are presented. Taking the word from Paul Schrader, Lyotard refers to these moments as 'stases', both an 'immobilisation of chronological time' and 'a kind of spasm' contracting the space-time of perception (ISF 66). What is presented is the 'transcendental condition of time', the form of time itself as a necessary condition for the perceiving of objects (ISF 66). Again following Deleuze, Lyotard distinguishes between time itself as a form, that is, as the 'capacity to grasp the flux', and that which changes and flows in this flux (ISF 66; see also Deleuze 1989: 17). It is only through the now that the flow of time is possible: what flows past and what arrives must be held and presented together in a present instant. It is the paradox of this instant of the already-over and the not-yet that 'allows us to see the indiscernibility of the movement and the repose as the two extreme instances of acinema' (ISF 66).

Jean-Michel Durafour is thus obviously quite right to identify 'strong Deleuzian accents' in this text (Durafour 2009: 79). Nonetheless, we can see that this invocation of the 'transcendental condition of time' also moves us into the orbit of Lyotard's reading of Kant as well as of Husserl. In certain texts on the sublime, and on timbre and nuance in music, Lyotard is interested in how the affect might escape or exceed this formative synthesis.[9] Acinema, on the other hand, would appear, at least in part, to make the conditions of this synthesis 'visible', even if only negatively, to present what is normally unpresentable: the conditions required for presentation. The stasis of the neo-realist image does not narrate, it takes all passed and possible events associated with the image and co-presents them 'in a virtual simultaneity' (ISF 67). In this contraction it reveals the operation of the camera, which works 'in the manner of the Kantian *Zusammennehmung*', acts as a 'blind and subtle eye which is immanent to visible reality and the human gaze' (ISF 69) – a condition of visibility that is not itself part of the visible. In relation to the narrative, Lyotard calls it an 'outcropping' (*affleurement*) of the visual on the surface of the visible (ISF 69).

Such outcroppings are not chosen by the author: the filmic fact 'happens' (*arriver*) to him or her. It doesn't take part in any programme. The filmmaker does not reveal these 'facts' so as to edify the viewer or to reinforce an individual or collective identity. As Bazin himself puts it, such facts, as 'fragments of raw reality', have no meaning in and of themselves; their meaning becomes apparent only afterwards, when they are linked to other facts and connected up by the mind (Bazin 2009: 239, 241).[10] These facts are not already given in an economy of meaning, readily exchangeable with other units in a process of circulating values. What they reveal is another world beneath or beyond the world given as 'reality'. Indeed, they produce a sense of the waning of the visible world (ISF 68), an image that would seem to reverberate with Lyotard's occasional references to the loss of faith in the reality of 'reality' – along with the accompanying need to invent other realities (see PC 77).

If we may follow Lyotard in following Deleuze a little here, we might note that the establishment of a new form of reality is precisely what the latter sees as the aesthetic stake of neo-realism for Bazin: 'Instead of representing an already deciphered real, neo-realism aimed at an always ambiguous, to be deciphered real' (Deleuze 1989: 1). If realism's normal effect is, paradoxically, to 'avoid the question of reality' (PC 75), neo-realism might be said to (re)open it. The pictorial or filmic fact does not serve reality. It is thus not 'servile' to the search for results, as Bataille himself puts it (1973: 163). But this means that, like the affect itself, its only right is death. The sovereignty of neo-realist 'moment-blocks' resides in this 'indifference to their fate' – recuperable to the movement of the narrative form, they cannot be contained within it (ISF 64). This is why sovereignty is 'allergic' to totality, and why it remains 'at the antipodes of authority', or rather, remains a stranger to it (ISF 69). It opens a world to us, but the world that it opens is 'neither permitted nor defended, neither good nor bad, neither high nor low, neither black nor white', or rather, 'is all this, indistinguishably' (ISF 69). The sovereign image thus does not attempt to replace one world for another, exchange an old reality for a new one. It does not assume authority. It opens what must remain beyond 'reality', outside of the narrative or of representation, available only on condition that the will be suspended, that there be no desire for results. We could perhaps say that what is here described as sovereign is very close to that 'absolute' of which the sublime is the negative presentation: that which remains stubbornly other to thought while nonetheless calling it forth.

Nancy may be right to see sovereignty in Bataille as more of an aesthetic or ontological than a political concept (Nancy 2003: 29). Nonetheless, I wonder if the stakes of this struggle over reality are not, in fact, quite close to it – slightly ahead, perhaps, or 'retreating' from the political, as Nancy himself puts it. In its indifference to authority, the sovereign image assumes its own authority, must authorise itself – as the philosopher, too, must do, in seeking a rule he or she does not already have. As Bataille suggests regarding Kafka, it is clear that this kind of sovereignty does not take its authority by criticising certain institutions with the aim of replacing them with 'other, less inhuman ones' (1973: 166). If it is in any way 'political' it would have to be in the sense invoked at the outset of *The Inhuman*: as resistance to the inhumanity of that certain kind of logic that Lyotard will come to call techno-science, a contesting of the authority of a certain 'reality' (see IN 1–7).[11] But perhaps it would be more precise to claim that it resists all such claims to authority.

A truly sovereign film remains an Idea in the Kantian sense, unachievable if by achievement we mean absolute sovereignty. But in brief moments, the sovereign image reveals the limits of the law. It therefore unveils that opening that is the 'space' of the *différend*. If this remains, at one level, a deauthorisation, it also remains a 'difficulty' for the authority of the law (see Bataille 1973: 167). What's more, this state of affairs would appear to be in some sense communicable, perhaps through the lending of an ear to the silence out of which it arrives. Out of the concrete, 'common' experience of what is taken for the real, a schism with that real can appear (Durafour 2009: 86–7). If this schism can be 'communicated', passed on, for instance through the cinematic image, this may not only serve to open the possibility for a kind of common sense, or perhaps dissensus, in the absence of a universal subject. It might also serve as a reminder that there is no final authority on the real.[12]

NOTES

1. Though perhaps the most faithful rendering, indeed, is simply 'Tribune without a Tribune', as Erin Obodiac translates it (2016: 173).
2. I am of course thinking in part of narration's role in organising historical time, but let us recall that myth also organises time, according to Lyotard, though it does so differently from narrative. For one of many texts relevant to this, see 'Time Today' in IN.
3. As Lisa Trahair, for example, points out (2009: 227). Trahair, probably rightly, as we will see, is cautious about this conception, referring to Lyotard's 'apparent' disinterest in the majority of cinema. Jean-Michel Durafour also refers to this common reception before going on to problematise it (2009: 3–4).
4. I try to make a case for this 'criticality' elsewhere. See Milne 2013.
5. See also Brecht 1964: 91. I'm grateful to Julie Gaillard for pointing out this link with Brecht.

6. This reading might even respond to a potential criticism of the libidinal texts, to the effect that if the political importance of works lies in the way they interrupt desire, then to have a 'political' experience of them would seem to require not enjoying them. The lack of any prescription, in this turn towards pragmatics, would not immediately preclude the possibility of aesthetic pleasure any more than would the sublime – the latter being, indeed, an *affirmation* of a kind of pleasure, even if it is one necessarily mixed with pain.
7. One wouldn't want to draw too close a connection between the viewer of the hyperrealist image and the sufferer of war or Holocaust, of course. What would seem to be analogous in these otherwise very different circumstances is the collapse of a particular pragmatic situation. For more on this, see D, particularly nos. 22–7, 131, 172–4.
8. For this reference to supplementation, see, for example, 'The Affect-phrase (from a Supplement to *The Differend*)' in LRG.
9. See, for example, LAS 105–6 and IN 158–60.
10. I have preferred to use this new translation of Bazin's classic text; nonetheless, given the importance of the word *événement*, 'event', in Lyotard's later works, I do not follow Barnard in translating the French 'fait' as 'event' here, but in the interests of avoiding terminological confusion retain the more common 'fact'.
11. We might note that Bazin himself sees neo-realist films as 'at the very least, pre-revolutionary' (2009: 221), implicitly or explicitly rejecting the reality they make use of.
12. This study was supported by a College of Humanities Research Grant, Seoul National University.

REFERENCES

Bataille, Georges (1955), *Manet*, trans. Austryn Wainhouse and James Emmons, Geneva: Skira.
Bataille, Georges (1973), *Literature and Evil*, trans. Alastair Hamilton, London and New York: Marion Boyars.
Bazin, André (2009), 'Cinematic Realism and the Italian School of the Liberation', in *What is Cinema?*, trans. Timothy Barnard, Montreal: Caboose, pp. 215–49.
Brecht, Bertolt (1964), *Brecht on Theatre: The Development of an Aesthetic*, ed. and trans. John Willett, New York: Hill and Wang.
Crome, Keith (2004), *Lyotard and Greek Thought: Sophistry*, Basingstoke: Palgrave Macmillan.
Deleuze, Gilles (1989), *Cinema 2: The Time Image*, trans. Hugh Tomlinson and Robert Galeta, Minneapolis: University of Minnesota Press.
Durafour, Jean-Michel (2009), *Jean-François Lyotard: questions au cinema. Ce que le cinéma se figure*, Paris: PUF.
Geller, Theresa L. (2007), '"The Film-Work Does Not Think": Refiguring Fantasy for Feminist Film Theory', *Gender After Lyotard*, ed. Margret Grebowicz, Albany, NY: SUNY, pp. 139–52.
Lyotard, Jean-François (1979), 'An Assessment of Television', *Framework* 11, pp. 37–9.

Milne, Peter W. (2013), 'Lyotard's "Critical" "Aesthetics"', *Rereading Jean-François Lyotard: Essays on His Later Works*, ed. Heidi Bickis and Rob Shields, Farnham: Ashgate, pp. 189–207.

Nancy, Jean-Luc (2003), 'The Confronted Community', trans. Amanda Macdonald, *Postcolonial Studies* 6:1, pp. 23–36.

Obodiac, Erin (2016), 'Autoaffection and Lyotard's Cinematic Sublime', *Traversals of Affect: On Jean-François Lyotard*, ed. Julie Gaillard, Claire Nouvet and Mark Stoholski, London and New York: Bloomsbury. 173–87.

Rodowick, D. N. (1994), *The Crisis of Political Modernism: Criticism and Ideology in Contemporary Film Theory*, Berkeley: University of California Press.

Sfez, Gérald (2007), *Lyotard: La partie civile*, Paris: Michalon.

Trahair, Lisa (2009), 'Jean-François Lyotard', in *Film, Theory and Philosophy: The Key Thinkers*, ed. Felicity Colman, Montreal and Kingston: McGill-Queen's University Press, pp. 222–32.

PART IV

Applications and Extensions

CHAPTER 11

Discourse, Figure, Suture: Lyotard and Cinematic Space

Jon Hackett

The focus of this chapter is on cinematic space – and how Lyotard's works on cinema and painting can illuminate this concept. First of all, I will discuss the way cinematic space was conceived at the turn of the 1970s in France (and thereafter in Anglophone journals such as *Screen*) in relation to film form and cinema as institution. This is the context in which Lyotard's early work explicitly on cinema, 'Acinema', was received in film studies. Subsequently, through a brief consideration of two films, I will consider the relevance of the *figural* to an analysis of cinematic space. These films are *Inception* (dir. Christopher Nolan, 2010) and *The Metamorphosis of Mr Samsa* (dir. Caroline Leaf, 1978).

My concern here is to show how some of Lyotard's writings served then as an intervention into various canonical debates about cinema and how others can serve now as a resource to figure cinematic space. The films analysed below depart from the types of cinema Lyotard himself wrote about: *Inception* is analogue cinema that utilises computer-generated imagery (CGI) to provide new experiences of space that we can frame in figural terms; *The Metamorphosis of Mr Samsa* is an independent animation whose perpetually shifting form spatialises the perpetual flux that Lyotard sees as one of the poles of what he calls 'acinema'. These choices may seem rather more pop cultural than the works analysed by Lyotard in his writings, explicitly interested in 'art' – but it is hoped that their relevance will be apparent in what follows.

One thing that most film and painting have in common is representation of a three-dimensional space on a two-dimensional support. This similarity is a commonplace, but one promising avenue of an engagement with Lyotard's work in relation to cinema is to extend his analyses of space and depth in visual arts to that of cinema. At first glance the relevance might seem limited – but only if we take cinema, as we often do, to mean live-action cinema based solely on photography. In fact, cinema also includes 'painted' forms – most obviously animation, but also a plethora of painted effects in live action, both analogue and digital, from the matte painting featured in many classic Hollywood films, to the construction of digital artefacts in today's mainstream cinema.

I am restricting myself to the figural and sometimes 'libidinal' works of the earlier Lyotard, which involves a certain licence in my selective use of his arguments. My interest here is foremost from the standpoint of film studies and how Lyotard's arguments can illuminate certain canonical and more recent debates there. However, it is my conviction that both the centrality of space and depth in the analyses of *Discourse, Figure*, as well as a concern for questions of desire and the libidinal, make this period of Lyotard's thinking most fruitful for engaging with cinema.

My contention is that the accounts given of the way space acts in cinema – whether on screen or more widely in terms of the apparatus of cinema production and exhibition – can be complicated through reference to Lyotard's writings. Furthermore, in the films I will be discussing, the unconventional spaces projected on screen require theorising from a perspective that eludes theories of suture and apparatus, which are based on spatial regimes deriving from single-point perspective as well as orthodox continuity editing.

SCREEN THEORY

Before drawing on the ideas articulated in *Discourse, Figure* in order to discuss the two films under consideration, it will be helpful to consider some canonical theories on cinematic space developed around this time. Many of the important theoretical essays on film published in this period in France were translated and also had considerable impact in film-theoretical debates in the US and the UK, often taking place in *Screen* and other journals. The important theoretical constituents were Marxism, psychoanalysis and structuralism – as with so much 'theory' in this era. I risk testing the reader's patience if this material is well known – but these ideas provide a useful counterpoint to the arguments made in this essay regarding Lyotard's own cinematic (and figural) writings.

In terms of film theory, the various articles and ideas that circulated at this time coalesced into what is often called in the Anglophone context 'apparatus theory' and 'theory of suture'. Such post-Lacanian theories emphasising subjectivity and ideology were the target of David Bordwell and Noel Carroll in their revisionist edited collection, *Post Theory* (1996), in which the ideas under discussion here were labelled 'subject-position theory' – one of the two 'Grand Theories' under fire, along with 'culturalism' (roughly, cultural studies).

Both suture and apparatus involve conceptions of cinematic space – both in terms of the space represented on screen and in terms of the spaces of production and exhibition of cinema. Ideas from structuralism, psychoanalysis and Marxism were used as frameworks in which to analyse the insertion of the spectator or subject into cinematic spaces – as well as the ideological and 'reality' effects produced there. What the concepts of apparatus and suture provided was a set of theories that, instead of being mere applied psychoanalysis, strove for cinematic specificity.

SUTURE

Jacques-Alain Miller's influential article on 'La suture' was first published in the inaugural issue of *Cahiers pour l'analyse* in February 1966, being taken from an exposé made in Jacques Lacan's seminar of a year earlier. It is an account of subject formation that has been particularly influential in film theory, as well as, for instance, Alain Badiou's theory of the subject. Drawing on number theory, it provides a framework for understanding Lacan's assertion that 'a signifier is that which represents the subject for another signifier' (Lacan 1977: 316).

Miller's main reference here is Frege, specifically *The Foundations of Arithmetic*, in which an account is provided of the generation of numbers on the basis of self-identity, with the constitutive exclusion of the object in the formation of the concept of the number zero, and thereafter, the series of natural numbers generated on this basis. Space precludes, supposing I were up to the task, a full account of this argument or of Miller's summary in the article. However, what is important is the concept of a series or chain of digits from which a non-identity is excluded, this gap or lack being 'counted as one'. Miller argues:

> If there are no things which are not identical with themselves, it is because non-identity with itself is contradictory to the very dimension of truth. To its concept, we assign the zero. It is this decisive proposition that the concept of not-identical-with-itself is assigned by the number zero which sutures logical discourse. (1977: 29)

Miller's point is that this also provides a model for Lacan's conception of the subject's insertion into the symbolic order. The subject enters this order through the exclusion, once and for all, of an object. This *objet a* is never to be recovered; the subject is a mere effect of the chain of signifiers that are constituted in this primary repression, to use Freud's earlier phrase for the emergence of the unconscious. So the zero of non-identity in Frege's theory is used as a metaphor for the lost object that is excluded from the psyche in the foundation of subjectivity according to Lacanian psychoanalysis. This is often seen as Lacan's updating of Freud's castration complex in terms of the language of structural linguistics, which Lacan considered a fitter metalanguage for psychoanalysis than the terminology used by Freud in his original conceptions. From this stems the familiar pathos of lack as decentring the subject and founding desire, as well as Lacan's assertion that the unconscious is structured like a language.

The term 'suture' is taken from medicine, specifically surgery, to signify the way in which identity is based on an effect of 'stitching' together the gaps in a chain of signifiers in order to provide an illusory sense of completeness. The subject, for Lacan, is founded on lack – and suture is one way of figuring the way in which precisely this lack is covered over or in which a seamless sense of identity, however illusory, may be produced through a linking together of signifiers in the subject's unconscious. When the individual is inserted into the symbolic order, suture is the operation that attempts to ensure the integrity of the individual by stitching over any appearance of lack.

Importantly for us here, suture was quickly adopted in film theory to provide an account of 'textual subjectivity' (as it has often been called) – the way in which the spectator is positioned by the cinematic text. This is an attempt to theorise the viewing experience along the lines proposed by psychoanalysis to account for the formation of the ego or self. The inaugural article here is also called 'La suture'; this time the author is Jean-Pierre Oudart. The piece was published in *Cahiers du cinema* in April 1969. It was translated along with Miller's psychoanalytic article in a 'Dossier Suture' in *Screen* journal in 1977.

Oudart's central argument is based on editing in cinema. The shot/reverse shot technique worked out in the second decade of cinema (emblematic of so-called 'continuity editing') is deemed to provide a mechanism for inserting the spectator 'into' the cinematic text in a way analogous to the process of subject formation identified in Miller's article.

Essentially, a single shot or point of view, such as that constructed in the early days of cinema in the static camera of the Lumière brothers or Georges Méliès, instantly raises the spectre of an 'Absent One' (the bearer of the camera's gaze, the notional person 'behind the camera'). What cinema developed thereafter in the silent era – and crucially, what audiences along with the producers came to recognise as a cultural code – was a mechanism for 'reversing' the gaze and replacing it apparently from the viewpoint of another character. The absent one 'behind' the camera is replaced by another shot identified with the viewpoint of the subject framed in the original shot, providing a notional position for the spectator 'in' the scene depicted. Oudart argues as follows:

prior to any semantic 'exchange' between two images . . . and within the framework of a cinematic *énoncé* constructed on a shot/reverse-shot principle, the appearance of a lack perceived as a Some One (the Absent One) is followed by its abolition by someone (or something) placed within the same field. (1977: 37)

So much so, in fact, that there results a 'hypnotic continuum' (1977: 38) in which the absent subject of the gaze is continually elided in the linking chain of shots – in a manner analogous to the elision of the subject in the chains of the signifier elucidated by Miller. This is the famous 'suture' of film theory of the 1970s, discussed by the likes of Stephen Heath, Laura Mulvey, Kara Silverman and others. As is well known, Slavoj Žižek and others have pointed out that these theories misconstrue the gaze as theorised by Lacan in his seminars – but this does not invalidate the broad points made about continuity editing and the spectator. My point here is that it involves a precise account of cinematic space – the discrete frames in continuity editing providing a pro-filmic space (before the camera) in which the actors, setting and props are mise-en-scène, an offscreen space and a notional point of view 'behind' the screen in which the viewer is positioned by implication.

What is crucial for the analysis in this chapter is that both suture and apparatus theory presuppose a cinematic space that is analogous to perspectival and representational space, conceived according to apparatus theory along the lines of the camera obscura. This might be adequate to provide an account of space familiar from live-action cinema that obeys the conventions of continuity editing. However, when film departs from these representative schemata, the pertinence of suture and apparatus are limited. Those advancing and developing the theory of suture often did valorise filmmakers who interrupted the allegedly seamless experience of being sutured into film narrative – but rarely in terms of unconventional uses of space itself. Here, as we shall see, Lyotard's figural conceptions can provide alternative conceptions that can account for non-standard uses of space in cinema.

It is also worth considering the implications of the function of suture in psychoanalytic terms to its extension for cinema spectatorship. According to Miller, suture provides an account of the exclusion of a constitutive gap in the subject from the chain of signifiers that make up that subject's symbolic order, the order of language and the unconscious. If this is the case, then suture guarantees, however provisionally, that the ego not unravel and come apart. Perhaps, then, suture in cinema is better suited to account for types of cinema that privilege the ego and consciousness – perhaps, say, classic Hollywood – than cinema that embraces the primary process. If this is the case, then the figural logic outlined by Lyotard – in which the dream-work does not think but rather acts – may be helpful in theorising the alternative spatial logics in more oneiric modes of cinema.

DISPOSITIF

One of the most influential anthologies of cinematic apparatus theory in English, entitled *Narrative, Apparatus, Ideology*, reproduces Lyotard's 'Acinema' as one of the six essays in the 'Apparatus' section of the book. There can be no clearer indication that Lyotard's essay was received at the time as an intervention on this question of the apparatus and *dispositif* of cinema.

Perhaps the two classic articles that set up the *dispositif* as an object of study for film studies are by Jean-Louis Baudry (1986a and 1986b). In these works Baudry considers the 'basic apparatus' of cinema in relation to its possible ideological function. The earlier essay, 'Ideological Effects of the Basic Cinematographic Apparatus' is one of several in France responding to a book by Jean-Patrick Lebel, *Cinéma et idéologie* (1971). This book, from a PCF writer, notoriously argued according to its detractors that the technology of cinema, qua *science*, was immune to ideological contagion – the content of the representations alone constituting ideology. Baudry's article argued instead that the positioning of the subject by the apparatus is inherently ideological: 'it is a question of preserving at any cost the synthetic unity of the locus where meaning originates [i.e. the subject] – the constituting transcendental function to which narrative continuity points back as its natural secretion' (1986a: 293). We can see here a clear continuity with Oudart's article on the suture, in terms of an analysis of 'textual subjectivity'. For Baudry, the apparatus 'on the model of the camera obscura' (1986a: 288) positions the spectator as if in front of a moving canvas, as a 'transcendental' subject.

The second article on the *dispositif* continues the analysis in terms of the impression of reality in cinema. Here we find Baudry reading Plato's Allegory of the Cave as a precursor to the cinematic set-up – provided we read the Allegory more in terms of Freud's analyses of dreaming. Baudry draws on conventional notions of Hollywood as the dream factory: 'The cinematic projection is reminiscent of a dream' (1986b: 308). This alludes to the immobility of the spectator's body in a darkened room, with the fantasy projected on screen analogous to the hallucination in dreaming. Again, this is a spatial account of cinema exhibition: the viewer is positioned concretely in a viewing space, in which a certain libidinal investment takes place.

Graham Jones has reminded us of the affinities of Plato's Allegory with both Lyotard's construal of the theatrical space of representation in *Libidinal Economy* and with models of the cinematic apparatus (Jones 2013: 77). The parallels between Baudry's apparatus theory and Lyotard's own *dispositifs pulsionnels* are evident, though we must bear in mind Lyotard's warning against the reduction of film representation and narratives to 'a simple superstructural function of an industry, the cinema, the products of which, films, would lull the public consciousness by means of doses of ideology' (Ac 35). Though Lyotard's spectator of 'Acinema' is much more intensely agitated by tableaux vivants than immobilised, Jean-Michel Durafour points out that Lyotard is in some ways 'quite close to Baudry': for both of them, figurative and narrative cinema involves a reworking of the western canonical pictorial scheme (Durafour 2009: 63).

'L'acinéma' was first published in the *Révue d'esthétique* in 1973 in a special issue of this journal entitled *Cinéma: Théorie, Lectures* (republished in 1978). It is worth quoting the dedication to 'Acinema' by Lyotard: 'These reflections would not have been possible without the practical and theoretical work accomplished for several years by and with Dominique Avron, Claudine Eizykman and Guy Fihman', colleagues of Lyotard at Vincennes (Ac 42 n). In fact, each of these colleagues has an article in the special issue, each of which acknowledge their debt to Lyotard's own conceptions of the figural. I shall consider two of these briefly below to highlight the common concerns with Lyotard's 'Acinema'.

Eizykman's article starts analogously to 'Acinema' by pointing out the liberatory potential of the then more recent experimental cinema: 'cinematic space, which has always invested the figure representation-narration, . . . is abandoning this figure and working other figures' (1978: 159).[1] Traditionally, cinematic space in Marxist theory is subservient to class struggle; in structuralist analyses to connotation and denotation (in Christian Metz for instance). Here Eizykman makes reference to Lyotard's critique of the closure of signification in *Discourse, Figure*. In each case, she argues, there is a channelling or parcelling of energy and force (we can see clear parallels with the 'libidinal' Lyotard): 'The two scenes cover two regulations: exclusion determines the regulated circulation, which implies the reabsorption of that which overflows regulated circulation' (1978: 170).

Fihman's article engages even more closely with the apparatus theory mentioned above, while claiming that it is Lyotard, in fact, who has opened up the *dispositif* as object of study (1978: 202 n.). As with Baudry, but with a libidinal economic lexis, Fihman argues that cinema is 'the extension by technical means of the representative desire of the Renaissance' (1978: 198). As with the Marxist critics of *Cahiers du cinéma* and *Cinéthique* at the time, Fihman scorns Lebel's attempt to parcel the cinematic apparatus off from ideological content; however, Fihman also rejects ideology critique in favour of an analysis of force and desire. The following assertion reveals how close the analysis is to Lyotard: 'Desire invests the *socius* from all sides, right through, without the distribution of these investments being able to order themselves according to the determination of any one instance, without this investment even being able to be localised on the surface of the social body' (1978: 205).

Therefore, when Lyotard's article comes at the end of *Cinéma: Théorie, Lectures*, we can read it as inserted into these problematics of the cinematic apparatus in its relation to politics and desire, the position of the spectator, mobilised or immobilised, and the cinema's institutional space. Of course, 'L'acinéma' was reproduced in the collection *Des Dispositifs pulsionnels*, whose name alone is indicative of this.

FIGURE

It is my contention that, among Lyotard's works, *Discourse, Figure* provides the most promising resources for a consideration of cinematic space on screen. Certainly this is the case as far as the analysis of films themselves are concerned. As such, the conception of the figure as that which disrupts discourse with depth, as well as space with desire, has much to recommend it as a framework with which to analyse films in which space behaves in unpredictable ways.

The opening of *Discourse, Figure*, in particular, involves a critique of structuralism – and of psychoanalytic uses of structuralism. Lyotard's characterisation of the function of the figure as 'a spatial manifestation that linguistic space cannot incorporate without being shaken, an exteriority it cannot interiorize as *signification*' (DF 17) would be as good a description as any of that which in film resists reading in terms of signifiers, codes and so on. This is so especially given Lyotard's reference to 'the desire that produces the thickness of reference' (DF 18) – which we might understand in a straightforward way in terms of the ineluctable effects of depth on the cinema screen and their resistance to linguistic codification.

In the chapter entitled 'Desire's Complicity with the Figural', Lyotard gives an exposition of three types of figure. The first, the figure-image, is described as follows: 'what it deconstructs is the silhouette's outline; it is the *transgression of the contour* [*trace révélateur*]' (DF 274). Lyotard has earlier discussed the figure as the priority of line over letter and in the figure-image we have the incompossibility of the line with single-point perspective and 'real' space. The figure-form is 'the figure that upholds the visible without being seen: the visible's nervure' (DF 275). It is revealed through the transgression of *good form* that escapes Euclidean geometry. Finally we have the figure-matrix, which is difference as such, visible in neither plastic nor textual space. As *matrice* (meaning 'womb' among other things) would imply, it is prior to and generative of these other figures.

FIGURE-FORM: *INCEPTION*

Inception (dir. Christopher Nolan, 2010) is often taken to exemplify a contemporary trend in filmmaking, the so-called 'puzzle film' (in Buckland's edited collection (2014) *Inception* has its own section as the 'archetypal' Hollywood puzzle film). These films, other examples of which might include Christopher Nolan's other films, *Memento* (2000) and *The Prestige* (2006), are characterised by their departure from conventional narrative pattern and order. As with Lyotard's readings of *Joe* and *Apocalypse Now*, rather than analyse the narrative in its totality, we can discuss the transgressive import of one particular sequence in the film considered. The main scene I will discuss from *Inception* reveals a sense of space itself warping under what we might identify as the irruption of desire, in ways that might work fruitfully against other, more unified readings of the film as a totality.

Inception is a film about dreaming. The main characters in the film are 'extractors', involved in stealing secrets from people's 'subconscious' through entering their dreams using technology developed by the military. Kristin Thompson (2010) has argued that the film's prime innovation is its 'continuous exposition' – we spend much time with the characters in training, taking part in shared dreams or in one another's dreams, exploring the temporal and spatial differences between the dream-world and real life. In a typical move for puzzle films, the boundaries between real life and dream life are unstable and porous. Further, the 'theory' behind dreams and levels of reality in the film is foregrounded in the dialogue and the diegesis – in the characters' discussion, training and development of their dream-stealing techniques.

In many ways the film invites a psychoanalytic reading in terms of the dream-work. Leonardo DiCaprio's character, Dom, spends much time explaining the temporality and spatiality of dreams to their rookie dream architect, Ariadne, played by Ellen Page, who is to design dream architecture of sufficient complexity to snare their prey, Fischer, played by Cillian Murphy. The features discussed by the characters include the importance of memory, the temporal dilation involved in descending into dreams within dreams, diurnal residues as dream resources, and so on.

At one point, Dom urges caution: 'The seed that we plant in this man's mind will grow into an idea. This idea will define him. It may come to change . . . well, may come to change everything about him.' Here we are reminded of the Freudian mechanism of primary repression, discussed by Laplanche and Leclaire (1972) – the kernel that brings the unconscious into being with a key signifier, here the single seed or idea that will form the nucleus of Fischer's rebooted unconscious, the 'inception' of the film's title.

There are other resources, however, that allow us to read the film in the terms of *Discourse, Figure*. Such an approach will allow us to pay closer attention to how space itself works at certain crucial points. Ultimately, this is of more interest to us here than the intriguingly structured pop-psychoanalytical plot. The sequence I wish to discuss occurs twenty-six minutes into the film, when Ariadne is receiving her training in dream architecture from Dom, who has come to headhunt her in Paris. These scenes involve Ariadne and Dom in the training lab with their colleague Arthur (played by Joseph Gordon-Levitt). With their technological apparatus Arthur sends the other two characters between the lab and the shared dream-world that they are exploring.

In one scene, Ariadne is invited to let her oneiric architectural creation run riot. Walking along the streets, Dom informs her that as he is the subject of the dream, it is peopled by constructions of his 'subconscious'. After an abrupt cut, perhaps highlighting the temporal lacunae of dreaming, Ariadne observes: 'I guess I thought that the dream space would be all about the visual but it's more about the feel of it. My question is what happens when you start messing with the physics of it all?'

At this point the two of them stop in their tracks. In the distance, we soon realise, at a certain point ahead of them the street with its buildings and road is starting to fold upwards perpendicularly. This is cut with overhead reaction shots revealing Ariadne's fascination and Dom's disquiet. The street nearer to them starts rearing up in another fold, apparently creating a cube whereby the roofs of some buildings now come to rest, with a crunch, on the roofs of the street on which they are standing. Paris has arched its back and folded back on itself. Reaching the end of the street, after a brief hesitation, the two of them step on to the street rising abruptly ahead of them, before walking upwards at 90 degrees from their previous position.

My interest in this scene is in the relation between cinematic space, dream-work and desire. It seems to me that the best way to make sense of this scene is precisely through Lyotard's notion of the figure-form – the flexing of the invisible ribs or *nervure* behind plastic space that disfigures good form and Euclidean space. For this is precisely what happens at this point in the narrative. That this occurs in a dream makes clear that the primary process is at work. Though this is not overdone, Ariadne's rapt gaze, raised eyebrows and transfixed posture also imply the irruption of desire into figural space. It is crucial to note that here the dream-work does not 'think' but rather works – description or metalanguage cannot capture the spectacular warping of space in this scene.

One might question at this point whether it is the cinematic representational space that is warped here, or whether it is instead the insertion of a 'warping effect' into an otherwise conventionally constructed cinematic space. The photorealistic sheen of the digital imagery in this sequence might make us wonder whether the spatial disruption is as radical as the foregoing account suggests.

But for this to be the case, we would nonetheless have to posit the insertion of one type of space into another, which would at any rate take us beyond the suture.

In addition, first of all, the folding back of geographical space into a cube is presumably not an experience that can be reconciled with any existing accounts of conscious experience. Second, the warp in the screen space does imply more than one notional viewpoint for the spectator: one on the level with Dom and Ariadne; another one rotating backwards along with the fold in the horizon. As we shall see in the next section, this places us in a viewing situation analogous, up to a point, with instances of pictorial space analysed by Lyotard, specifically in terms of the figural.

VEDUTA

The section of *Discourse, Figure* that illuminates this scene best is the 'Veduta' chapter. A veduta is, the Shorter Oxford tells us, 'a detailed, factually accurate landscape, usually a townscape showing buildings of interest'. Given the shared perspectival schema of renaissance painting and cinema according to the theories above, we might hypothesise that certain types of transgressive cinematic space will subvert the orthodox plastic scheme.

Lyotard selects Duccio's *Maestà* altarpiece in Siena as the last great painting that illustrates the mediaeval schema of the 'textual' plastic space; and Masaccio's frescoes in the Brancacci Chapel in Florence as the first great painting of the 'representational' picture space: 'It is there, in the spontaneous formation of the new plastic order, that we can properly see, and therefore fully signify, what we glimpsed in the theory, namely, the separation of the signifier from the signified and its anchoring in the designated – in

Still from *Inception*

short, the constitution of representation' (DF 184). For Lyotard there is a fundamental change in the relation of the support to the figural between these paintings and the traditions they represent.

Lyotard describes the shift from mediaeval 'textual' to renaissance 'representational' schemas in terms of a rotation, shifting the plastic signifier away from the 'flat', graphic signified, to the depth of designation. What we can see in Masaccio's paintings is the turn 'itself' rather than the fully realised new position:

> *I would like to suggest that it is thanks to this rotation that the repressed of medieval civilization – that is, difference as attribute of the figural – briefly emerges, and that it will immediately find itself rejected once more through the geometric organization of the field of vision.* (DF 187, emphasis in original)

It is beyond the scope of this article to discuss in depth Lyotard's construal of the differences between the largely Byzantine pictorial schemas of Duccio and the quattrocento ones of Masaccio. However, I do want to point out some similarities in Lyotard's analysis of the plastic organisation of Masaccio's works – how these occupy an in-between state between the mediaeval schemas and the *costruzione legittima* of the fully fledged renaissance – and how we might interpret cinematic space in the extract from *Inception* discussed above.

For Lyotard, the frescoes in the Brancacci Chapel are the most radical departure from the earlier plastic scheme. By contrast, the *Trinità* of Santa Maria Novella in Florence is a more modest disturbance of the representational scheme, 'on the sidelines where the shaken strata once again find their equilibrium and geometric order regains the upper hand' (DF 187). Nonetheless, it is the latter, with its nearly realised renaissance schema but where space is nonetheless inconsistent and askew, that best allows us to model the scene in *Inception*.

Lyotard highlights the relatively two-dimensional Gothic or Byzantine scheme of the donors near the front of the picture space, a remnant or legacy of the mediaeval schema, with donors in profile arranged more or less straight ahead for the spectator. By contrast, the trinity above them in the picture space is arranged according to single-point perspective, brought out by the famous coffered vault, whose orthogonals meet at the base of the plinth on which the Virgin and saint stand.

We appear to have two notional viewpoints, excluding the spectator as notional subject. These viewpoints place the viewer both horizontally level with the base of the plinth and well below the painting (due to the perspective of the vault). In fact, rather than posit this as an inconsistency in the painting, an incompletely realised attempt at single-point perspective, we might interpret this as an effect of a 'fold' in the picture space itself, at once positioning the viewer level with and far below the space represented. If this were the case we would be in a similar position to the viewer of the scene in *Inception*, where the characters are in one space, the horizon (Paris folding in on itself) in another. For Masaccio's picture to convey the same effect as the movie, the barrel vault itself would have to shift along a horizontal axis, then impossibly fold back again upon itself, while shifting the spectator's subject position 'inside' these folds.

It is worth pointing out that what facilitates this extraordinary scene in *Inception* is the development of visual effects that increasingly become indistinguishable from live-action footage in contemporary blockbuster cinema. Stephen Prince highlights Christopher Nolan's stress on location shooting, in-camera effects and real setting. He is also an advocate of film, rather than digital video. However, these are enhanced with post-production digital visual effects: 'Real locations with actors Leonardo DiCaprio and Ellen Page included Paris streets, which were then treated digitally for a spectacular scene in which the urban environment folds up into a cube containing the actors' (Prince 2012: 26).

This combination of live actors and settings with digital elements is increasingly the mainstream of filmmaking. The shot live action and created digital elements are just the start of a complicated process that involves digital painting of background elements, compositing digital with live elements of mise-en-scène. So much so in fact that, as Lev Manovich famously argues, 'digital cinema is a particular case of animation that uses live-action footage as one of its many elements' (2001: 302).

Reading the credits of contemporary blockbusters reveal the sheer personnel involved in compositing – combining live action and created digital artefacts. This implies that it is at least as difficult as designing the latter alone. In particular, ensuring that the lighting, colour and camera movement is consistent between live actors, sets and props – and the visual effects – takes teams of dedicated animators and crew. My point here is that though such effects are often denounced as empty spectacle or glossy commercialism, in this film they have the effect of creating new experiences of cinematic space that call for interpretation in specifically figural terms. In the same way that Masaccio's paintings are a return of what was repressed in the mediaeval plastic scheme, we might conjecture that the scene from *Inception* is a return of what was repressed in continuity editing – space itself as plastic and inconsistent.

FIGURE-IMAGE: *THE METAMORPHOSIS OF MR SAMSA*

There is of course another form of moving image that departs more fundamentally from live action, and which I will argue is amenable to analysis in terms of the figural, namely animation as such. Though this form of cinema has received comparatively little attention from film studies until fairly recently, it might seem promising in relation to Lyotard's thought in that its form is closer to painting than photography. Concurrent with the rise of CGI has been a form of animation that often aspires to photorealistic (if stylised) representation, associated with the productions of Pixar and DreamWorks, and so on. However, in this section I will consider a more 'painterly' (in the sense of privileging planes and textures over lines) animation by an independent animator, Caroline Leaf.

The Metamorphosis of Mr Samsa (1977) is a short film by Leaf from her time with the National Film Board of Canada, an organisation historically supportive of independent and experimental animation. It is notable for Leaf's technique of the stop-motion animation of sand on glass, underlit to produce a sepia-toned animation in perpetual flux of both figure and background. Leaf's animations provoke much interest when the painstaking process of manipulating sand (or ink) from frame to frame to produce the images is known. Her well-known animation from the year before, *The Street*, was an adaptation of a story by Mordecai Richler. As its title signals, the 1977 animation is based on 'Metamorphosis' by Franz Kafka.

One reason often advanced for the lack of critical attention to animation is its association with children's popular culture (for instance, Wells 1998: 187). *The Metamorphosis* in fact has a style that recalls children's drawings and books – figures are rounded, simplified and smudged, which provides a striking contrast with the terror of the narrative, with the original of which many will be familiar. The fact that an English translation of Kafka's story was unavailable to the animator for copyright reasons means that the characters speak an invented language, a *mitteleuropäisch* concoction which at times has a baby-like sound, enhancing the inherently uncanny nature of the narrative – including the radically other within the most domestic of spaces.

Aylish Wood, who has discussed animated and digital space extensively, has characterised this film as allowing 'reverberating space' to emerge, rather than using space as a repository for actors, props and setting, as mise-en-scène (2006: 137). That is, rather than suturing the viewer into a transcendent viewing position, space itself emerges as an intensive experience for the viewer, especially through the transitions between 'shots', which are effected through the swirling manipulation of sand into new configurations rather than through the cuts, dissolves and fades familiar from live-action cinema. The perpetual flux produced through the manipulation of sand on glass, we have said, embodies the pole of 'lyric abstraction' identified by Lyotard in 'Acinema' (Ac 40). We might also point to the often Cézanne-like compositions in the kitchen (and elsewhere), with tabletop, dishes and cutlery flouting the single-point perspective of live-action cinema or mainstream animation.

My contention is that Leaf's animations bear the trace of the figure-image: 'what it deconstructs is the silhouette's outline; it is the *transgression of the*

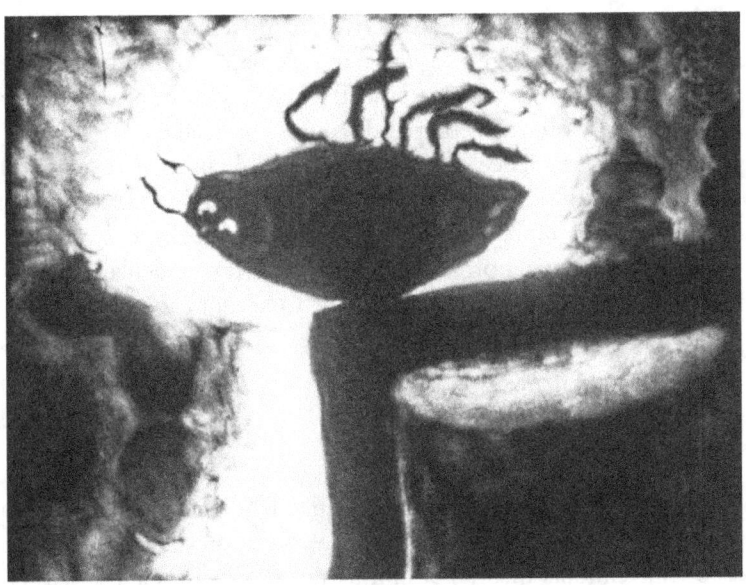

Still from *The Metamorphosis of Mr Samsa*

contour' (DF 274). As with the smudged faces of Masaccio's representations in the Brancacci Chapel, which Lyotard contrasts with the calligraphic international Gothic style of Duccio, Leaf's figures are not bounded by discrete lines but rather smudge into the background, or often leave blank traces behind them redolent of finger marks through powder. When Gregor as beetle struggles from his bed to the floor and to the doorway, his legs, carapace and antennae appear partially to erase the background, which nonetheless reshapes in the perpetual flow of sand that forms both figure and ground. The density and materiality of the space depicted, rather than being an empty container, calls to mind Maurice Merleau-Ponty's 'flesh of the world'; Gregor's body is intertwined with the rest of the plastic space of the animation: 'My body as a visible thing is contained within the full spectacle. But my seeing body subtends this visible body, and all the visibles with it. There is reciprocal insertion and intertwining of one in the other' (Merleau-Ponty 1968: 138).

For Lyotard, however, we have not said 'the last word on the subject of our spatiotemporal experience by characterizing it as an enwrapped depth, an immanent transcendence, a chiasm' (DF 130). The figure emerges as the chiasm or intertwining is disfigured – and Gregor in this animation embodies the unmasterable anxiety that this produces, a beetle on its back, as his own form and the pulverised background flail around him. We can discern here the effects of the figure-matrix, as the difference preceding the constitution of form and ground – but also of human and nonhuman, before sexual difference, the 'nonhuman sex' (DF 133) that precedes the symbolic order: 'The No of nonhuman, inhuman (*unmenschlich*) sex indicates difference, another position (stage) that unseats that of consciousness – that of discourse and reality' (DF 136).

Again, such an experience of space is unavailable in the live-action cinema theorised in classical film theory. In *The Metamorphosis* this break with perspectival representation is more radical than in the photorealistic *Inception*, where the transgression of spatial norms is temporary, albeit spectacular. In both cases, Lyotard's conception of the figural allows us to account for ruptures in filmic discourse and defigurations of cinematic space.

CONCLUSION

The new experiences of cinematic space afforded by digital technologies – as well as some much older ones afforded by analogue animation – are hard to theorise on the basis of conventional theories of film narrative and cinematic space. Theories such as the figural in Lyotard's work allow us to think some of the more transgressive ways in which space itself is subject to the primary process in cinema – and how the appearance of space that deviates from standard 'representational' schemes can be figured in terms of the irruption of the space of desire into filmic discourse.

NOTE

1. Translations from texts in French are my own.

REFERENCES

Baudry, Jean-Louis (1986a), 'Ideological Effects of the Basic Cinematographic Apparatus', in *Narrative, Apparatus, Ideology: A Film Theory Reader*, ed. P. Rosen, New York: Columbia University Press, pp. 286–8.
Baudry, Jean-Louis (1986b), 'The Apparatus: Metapsychological Approaches to the Impression of Reality in Cinema', in *Narrative, Apparatus, Ideology: A Film Theory Reader*, ed. P. Rosen, New York: Columbia University Press, pp. 289–318.
Bennington, Geoffrey (2013), 'Opening Up', *Cultural Politics* 9:2, pp. 203–11.
Bordwell, David and Carroll, Noel (1996), *Post Theory: Reconstructing Film Studies*, Madison: University of Wisconsin Press.
Buckland, Warren (ed.) (2014), *Hollywood Puzzle Films*, London and New York: Routledge.
Durafour, Jean-Michel (2009), *Jean-François Lyotard: questions au cinema. Ce que le cinéma se figure*, Paris: PUF.
Eizykman, Claudine (1978), 'Que sans discours apparaissent les films', in *Cinéma: Théorie, Lectures*, ed. D. Noguez, Paris: Klincksieck, pp. 159–71.

Fihman, Guy (1978), 'D'où viennent les images claires?', in *Cinéma: Théorie, Lectures*, ed. D. Noguez, Paris: Klincksieck, pp. 193–206.
Jones, Graham (2013), *Lyotard Reframed*, London: I. B. Tauris.
Lacan, Jacques (1977), 'The Subversion of the Subject and the Dialectic of Desire in the Freudian Unconscious', in *Écrits*, London: Routledge, pp. 292–325.
Laplanche, Jean and Leclaire, Serge (1972), 'The Unconscious: A Psychoanalytic Study', *Yale French Studies* 48, pp. 118–75.
Lebel, Jean-Patrick (1971), *Cinéma et idéologie*, Paris: Éditions Sociales.
Manovich, Lev (2001), *The Language of New Media*, Cambridge, MA and London: MIT Press.
Merleau-Ponty, Maurice (1968), *The Invisible and the Invisible: Followed by Working Notes*, Evanston: Northwest University Press.
Miller, Jacques-Alain (1977), 'Suture (Elements of the Logic of the Signifier)', *Screen* 18:4, pp. 24–34.
Oudart, Jean-Pierre (1977), 'Cinema and Suture', *Screen* 18:4, pp. 35–47.
Prince, Stephen (2012), *Digital Visual Effects in Cinema: The Seduction of Reality*, New Brunswick, NJ and London: Rutgers University Press.
Thompson, Kristin (2010) 'Revisiting *Inception*', www.davidbordwell.net/blog/2010/08/12/revisiting-inception (accessed 30 March 2017).
Wells, Paul (1998), *Understanding Animation*, London and New York: Routledge.
Wood, Aylish (2006), 'Re-Animating Space', in *animation: an interdisciplinary journal* 1:2, pp. 133–52.

CHAPTER 12

On Dialogue as Performative Art Criticism

Vlad Ionescu

> Am I seeing properly, or was I dreaming? Hallucination, or sharing? My madness, or our meaning?
>
> Jean-François Lyotard (WP)

TALKING ART

Besides the few articles that Jean-François Lyotard wrote on the seventh art, he sometimes employed the moving image as a means of experimenting with and talking about painting. I have in mind the few films where he engages in conversations with the painters Jacques Monory and René Guiffrey. In these cases, the filmed dialogue is introduced as a medium that combines the conversation about art with a careful gaze on the discussed paintings. With these two artists, Lyotard talks about their art and about art in general while moving around in their studio and literally touching and examining their paintings.

In Lyotard's work, film is more than a theme of critical reflection and even more than an experimental practice. At least one aspect of filmmaking, namely, the *dramaturgy* of the dialogue, became for Lyotard a type of art criticism. In the following, we examine these dialogues – cinematic and staged – as one of Lyotard's significant modes of addressing visual arts. Lyotard dedicated an entire body of writings (spread over seven volumes) to the visual arts, yet his films about the same subjects have gone unremarked. The hypothesis of this essay is, firstly, that the dialogue about visual arts functions as a form of *performative art criticism*. Instead of dictating the meaning of artworks, Lyotard allows this meaning to emerge by experimenting with language. Secondly, these dialogues also play an important role in the emergence of the viewer who encounters the paintings that Lyotard writes about. In a time when no pre-established poetics dictate the conditions of art, the beholder of an artwork is also not a given. Just as art has to invent its own rules, the beholder has to emerge alongside this artistic invention.[1]

This double hypothesis requires an analysis of these two instances: on the one hand, the films and the dialogues on artists, such as the filmed conversations with Monory and Guiffrey and, on the other, the written conversations where fictive voices account for other painters, like Valerio Adami, Daniel Buren or Shusaku Arakawa. Both cases respond to a fundamental issue in Lyotard's thought, namely the nature of art criticism. How do we talk about art? Is it a coincidence that Lyotard's first and last books on visual art both begin with an apologetic justification regarding the relation towards the artwork itself? *Discourse, Figure* defends and conceives the *aisthesis* as an uncontrollable plastic and libidinal force that disturbs the regular arrangement of discursive structures. While books are read, paintings are grazed because they make visible seeing itself a figural force. Lyotard argues that a good book deconstructs the time of reading (when signification is actualised), so that the reader can start it anywhere. And he apologises that *Discourse, Figure* is not such a book because it only signifies the deconstruction of the signifier: 'It is thus, still, a book of philosophy' (DF 12). *Karel Appel: A Gesture of Colour* also begins with an apology: 'The work of Karel Appel deserves a book other than this one. It seems here only to be serving as the occasion for the philosopher to reflect on his commentary of art' (KA 27). These are significant statements because they underline a central issue: can painting be approached as something more than as an illustration of metaphysical ideas? Many artists might even agree with this approach (KA 37), but the force of an artwork consists in confronting discourse with its precariousness, because how could discourse 'articulate coloured things that so clearly result from a gesture and are free of any finality?' (DF 27). In this sense, Appel's paintings confront understanding with the impact of an unformed matter that resists its schematisation.

Hence, we have to take stock of the way that Lyotard's dialogues are experiments, *within* the order of language, which have a double effect. Firstly, they offer an alternative to the canonical art commentary that traditionally delivers the iconological meaning of an artwork. They are also an alternative to the philosophy of art that addresses artworks as illustrations of metaphysical concepts. To the contrary, for Lyotard, the artwork is the outcome of experimentation with *figures* and it is linked to a form of criticism that is itself a type of experimentation with *discourse*. If the script belongs to the structure of the film, Lyotard's dialogues on painting read as dramatic experiments with language. When the philosopher stops thinking (that is, subordinating sensations to concepts) and starts writing (that is, experimenting with the written discourse), the commentary itself becomes a work made of words (DF 35). The dialogues on art *transpose* the sensations into discourse; they lack the rigorousness of the iconological analysis because they are meant as dramaturgical experiments that constitute a possible spectator for these paintings. Yet, because of their difference, any transposition from the register of sensations into the register of words generates figures of speech, phantasms, if not hallucinations. Lyotard's dialogues dramatise the activity of thought in the presence of sensations that overpower it. They are experiments that transform thinking in a theatre of voices.

Secondly, another question of art criticism – in film and words – is how to look at modern paintings, images whose rule of composition eludes us? What kind of original beholder do these artworks require? The original encounter with a modern artwork is never mediated by a set of rules that deciphers it. If the rule of making is absent, then the rule of seeing is also unavailable. Hence, art criticism debates this position of a beholder who is temporarily powerless in the original encounter with the work.

ARTISTS AT WORK

For Lyotard, writing about painting and making films about painters were complementary ways of thinking about the impact of visual arts in modernity. *À blanc* is a film that relates René Guiffrey's paintings to a classical Lyotardian theme from that period: that there is something unpresentable and invisible. The argument is well known: beyond the image as a material support and its identifiable forms, an immaterial sensation shivers on the surface of Guiffrey's paintings. This surplus is actualised in the aesthetic experience of the sublime. In the film, Lyotard refers to Guiffrey's white canvases as instantiations of this hypothesis. Just as the philosopher has to think the unthinkable, the painter has to paint the unpresentable.

Filmed in 1982, the documentary allows us to imagine that Lyotard's theory of the sublime emerged not only through a diligent close reading of Kant but also due to a consistent exposure to abstract painting. In the case of Guiffrey, the white does not present an object and the lines are not the trait of anything. Both the lines and the white, in combination with the light, reveal that there is something that transcends the perceptive field of objects. The line is an effect of the light that traverses the canvas. It is the field of light on a surface and it represents the possible (as opposed to the actual), just like in the *Autre blancs* of Pierre Soulages. The lines are comparable to the linear solos of Steve Lacy, the free jazz saxophonist.[2] Lyotard does not see in this a revelation of something beyond the sensible or a recuperation of a Romantic theme. To the contrary, these paintings present the viewer with paradoxes and tensions as opposed to figures and descriptions of phenomena. Guiffrey's whites demonstrate that the objects he identified in the field of vision do not exhaust the domain of *aisthesis*.

During the film, Lyotard avoids dictating these interpretations and his interventions are concise, allowing Guiffrey to talk about his paintings. A central visual aspect in these documentaries is that, as in the case of Monory, Lyotard takes a lot of pleasure in touching his paintings and moving them around the studio. Filming the artists at work means also exposing their works to different degrees of light, as if miming the *in vivo* experience of the paintings. The film does not reproduce the painting, as photography would do, according to the position of the body in space that determines the singularity of the beholder's experience. The interventions of the artist are even more present in the two short films on Jacques Monory. Lyotard appears rather reserved compared to a loquacious Monory who is eager to explain his *modus operandi*. He offers hypothetical interpretations, indicating his position regarding the relation of the philosopher to the painting. Lyotard's gestures and tone in these films prove that the philosopher is not a *cicerone* (to employ Burckhardt's title of his famous introduction to Italian art). The philosopher does not have a privileged access to the meaning of paintings that he is kind enough to transfer to an inexperienced viewer. To the contrary: artist, beholder and viewer are in a nascent state – there is no rule of composition and there is no rule of viewing the composition. There is no gallery guide that the viewer follows while passively listening to her illuminating explanations. When art is in a nascent state – another well-known Lyotardian theme – the philosopher cannot speak, like a ventriloquist, in the place of the painter, or make the painting speak.

In the documentary on Monory, Lyotard is filmed in what looks like a kitchen, smoking and introducing the painter as a 'spontaneous philosopher' who is interested in questions of meaning. A rather improvised scene, which contains a spontaneous yet generic remark: Monory's work is a *catalogue raisonné* of contemporary life, rendered as a Technicolor construct. Their dialogue concentrates around the choice between painting and film. Monory argues that he prefers painting in order to approach issues like women, deserts, death, murder and loneliness, indeed the signatures of his work. Film, on the other hand, is closer to the process of communication, and that is due to montage. As in the case of Gerhard Richter, Monory uses montage and photography as methods for his painting. In the presence of the camera, the painter becomes confessional towards Lyotard: he admits that while he loves life, he is afraid of death. The fact that for Monory painting functions as an iconology of existential angst corroborates Lyotard's hypothesis that the painter is also a 'spontaneous' and 'popular' philosopher.

Further, Monory describes his method as a way of 'returning' (*restituer*) the movement of life, which for him consists of boxes (TV sets and screens), stored on the canvas. The cinematic montage constitutes Monory's paintings for two reasons: first, each painting links various screens generating a visual montage. Referring to Orson Welles' *Citizen Cane* (1941), Monory argues that the montage inspired his work and his formation as a painter. Through his gesture of 'canning' or 'storing' (*la mîse en boite*), images originate in the cinematic montage that he interprets as a language and as the ability to narrate a story. Second, the montage returns in the multiplication of images, a serialisation that for Monory is a sign of life. Regardless of these speculative insights, Lyotard demonstrates that he has a solid knowledge of Monory's work and he chooses to focus on its formal analysis. For instance, the *Fausse Sortie* consists of twelve plans including images from Monory's life as painter and photographer. There are cosmological elements, like the sky and the earth, hence an interest in life (social and cosmological). A series presents the sky in images that are provided by radars, just as television mediates our social life.

David Carr-Brown's documentary (1982) presents the philosopher and the painter in a conversation about the visual aspect of painting. Can music and sound return (*restituer*) in painting? The transposition of media is a constant theme in both conversations with Monory. Lyotard is interested in the relationship between montage, painting and sound; the succession implicit in narrations as opposed to the simultaneity of painting. While Lyotard obviously has Lessing's *Laocoön* (1766) in mind, Monory's answers are intuitive and direct: music and sound belong to the film because a film without sound is horrible. However, for Lyotard, painting is also an art of time because one can cut out the painting in sequences and create a rhythm of its reading. The dialogue between the philosopher and the painter is improvisational and resists the programmatic search for a final meaning meant to explain Monory's work. Both Lyotard and Monory agree that the cinema employs time in a direct way, yet Monory adds that while in painting we perceive the totality of the canvas, in the case of film we need time to complete this movement.

For Monory, painting is a simultaneous synthesis of background and foreground, presented as a 'total sensation' that freezes time. Lyotard, on the other hand, wonders whether painting is not also subordinated to the rules of time. After all, it is the spectator that performs, in time, the unity of a Monory painting. His compositions are explosions made of shattered pieces where quotidian scenes are recognised. However, adds Monory, they have to attract and enthral the beholder's gaze. At this point, one cannot ignore the formal similarities between these conversations and Diderot's philosophy of painting. As we shall see, the relationship of painting to the beholder is central in both circumstances.

THE BEHOLDER

While the importance of Freud, Marx or Kant for Lyotard's philosophy has often been discussed, few commentators have addressed the influence of Diderot on Lyotard's aesthetics.[3] This research lacuna is relevant because literary genres play a central role in shaping Lyotard's philosophy. Before and after *The Differend*, a series of dialogues and causeries configure his philosophy of art. And the dialogue is central in the work of Diderot, who Lyotard described as his 'preferred author' and even a 'master'.[4] Through the fictional dialogue, the philosopher can experiment with thought because there are no pre-established positions and the course of the argument can always change. As we shall see, in his art criticism Lyotard employs this genre, which has a cinematic effect because these dialogues read like a script.

What is Diderot's role in Lyotard's philosophy of art? In his writings on art Diderot reflected on the status of the beholder. In his essay 'Philosophy and Painting in the Age of their Experimentation' (1981), Lyotard refers to the Salon of 1767 where Diderot discusses Vernet's landscapes which he admires in the company of an abbot, two young pupils and two servants. Diderot here performs a permutation because he interchanges reality and fiction, introducing facts and stories when he speaks to an abbot in the same way as to a virtual reader. Michael Fried also refers to these scenes where Diderot imagines that the viewer 'penetrates' the picture, a fictive stance that for Diderot is a criterion of artistic value for the genre painting (Fried 1980: 130–1). Diderot's interpretation takes the form of a dramatisation that includes a hypothetical viewer, the interpreter and other characters. It is a theatrical drama and, in *Entretiens sur le Fils Naturel* (1757) and *Discours sur la poésie dramatique* (1758), Diderot related painting to theatre. In these works, he asked that the model of dramaturgy should be painting (Fried 1980: 77). Instead of complicated plots, the spectator should be confronted with *tableaux*, these 'great mutes', as if he/she would look at a canvas. Permutations refer thus not just to what Lyotard detected as the switch between painting and nature but also to that between painting and dramaturgy. These permutations appear in Diderot's Salon of 1765 where Chardin's still lives are read as practices of staging tableaux vivants (Fried 1980: 82). The art commentary becomes a script where life dramatises painting and painting is a dramatisation of life. As Schmidt has shown, Hegel saw in Diderot's dialogue a fragmented world realised in the division of voices, oscillating between *He* and *I* (Schmidt 1996: 637). For Hegel, the dialogue is a staged dialectic where the nephew can take an opposed position in the conversation, a situation illustrative of the self-alienation of culture (Gearhart 1986: 1049). Lyotard, however, employs this staged dialectic – while referring to Diderot's *Salon* – as a strategy that generates unforeseen events precisely *because* of the friction between the individual works and a decoding system.

It is significant that the viewer is not a given but, like the art-critical discourse, is the outcome of experimenting with painting and its commentary. The beholder has to be discovered just as much as does the meaning of the painting. According to Diderot, the painting has to enchant the viewer and attract his/her attention because the painting itself establishes the beholder's gaze. However, as Fried explains, this engenders a paradox: paintings are to be viewed and they enthral the beholder, and yet, for Diderot, the best way to achieve this is to deny the presence of a concrete viewer, as something given (Fried 1980: 103). Precisely in order to enthral, the composition has to disregard the viewer. This indifference can enhance the fascination that the painting exercises (Fried 1980: 108).

Hence, there is no *continuity* between the painting and the beholder, just as there is no synchronicity between the individual and society. The unforeseen events that emerge from this discontinuity between the painting and the beholder, detecting in Diderot's *Salon* experimentations with voices that are 'post-Hegelian', resist the claim of a homogeneous and progressive dialectic. The *tableau* is a machine whose function is to develop, through an initial estrangement, a new beholder. In a sense, the same can be said of the experimental cinema or any artwork that rejects a pre-established rule of its composition: they all have to bring about a virtual viewer. That is why most viewers feel at ease when watching a Hollywood production but feel alienated when confronted with experimental films. The Hollywood productions are made with a prototype of a viewer in mind, namely a viewer who looks for distraction. The experimental film has no pre-given viewer in mind because it is itself the outcome of an experiment with time, acting, framing and montage.

This experimental position towards art criticism is significant for Lyotard, who recognises in it a *permutation* that disturbs the roles of communicability: the I (commentator) as addressor, the referent (the artwork) and the addressee (the beholder). As opposed to the *cicerone* (an addressor who transmits the information about the referent to the addressee), Diderot dramatises the relation between the viewer and the painting: the former emerges when the latter speaks *through* the art critic. I do not speak *about* the work but let the work speak *through* the voices that make up the art-critical discourse. This permutation is a dramatising strategy that produces fictive and cinematic effect that Lyotard cultivated in many of his writings on contemporary artists.

According to Lyotard, instead of showing how the artwork confirms a philosophical system, the art-critical discourse breaks this unity of artwork and system. It displaces the positions of philosophical concept, artwork and beholder while it experiments with them as incommensurables (MT2 157). Already in the 'Philosophy and Painting' essay from 1981, Lyotard argued that the theoretician has to stop using the artwork as a symptom that confirms the philosophical system, an erroneous strategy of which he himself had been guilty. Alternatively, art criticism should transfer the figural force that belongs to the artwork to the level of written discourse. In other words, Lyotard's categorical imperative is to *experiment* in language with the tensions that present themselves on the surface of the artwork. Philosophy becomes a work that connects to other works, like other commentaries that themselves are experiments with language.[5] The reflection *on* visual art is a theatre of voices. Instead of seeing the work as the stable 'illustration' of a pre-existing system (the artwork as realisation of the worldview), the philosopher becomes a writer who experiments with the figural forces of the canvas, which are transformed into art criticism. In art criticism, philosophy no longer re-establishes the unity of being by linking the artwork to its concept. Instead, because the artwork is an experiment, philosophy continues 'by means of reflexive experimentations' (MT2 163).

A THEATRE OF VOICES

The challenge for art criticism is to invent discourses that link to the impact that a painting can have on language. The experiment on canvas blends with the art-critical experiment so that both image and text reinforce each other. This strategy differs from the classical commentary where the text explains the image, thus subordinating the painting to the power of concepts. In his dialogues, Lyotard transfigures the visual into a performative type of criticism that appears as a theatre of voices.[6] The dialogues are scenarios that enact a critique of philosophical language. They 'mine' the activity of thinking, which appears as a performance consisting of questions and answers, affirmations and retorts, ponderings and gestures enacted by male and female voices. Instead of seeing an artwork as an illustration of a worldview, Lyotard cultivates the strategy of differentiating voices, male and female, affirmative and negative, descriptive and imperative. The goal is never to explain (in the sense of stabilising meaning) but to multiply the different positions towards the artwork, which is essentially that which resists totalising thought.

In this sense, the dialogue continues Lyotard's fundamental argument that there is an irreconcilable difference between the *structure* of language and the *power* of *aisthesis* (colours and timbres). Language signifies by subordinating the sensible to regular structures that the cognitive faculties code and decode. When reading, the figural power of the visual sign is insignificant. But as *Discourse, Figure* has demonstrated, the arrangement of lines in letters carries a visual force, in the 1970s often identified with the force of desire. In the case of dialogues, the timbre of the voice is already more significant, as the voice and its aesthetic modulations can radically change the meaning of the conversation. In the case of painting, if a sensation overwhelms the mind to such an extent that, for a short moment, it does not subordinate the sensation to a concept, then there is more in the sensible than what the mind can determine. The problem becomes one of logic: if the mind is so intensively overwhelmed in the case of Karel Appel's painterly matterism, then this minimal sensorial event is not recorded as a historical event that took place before or after another event. It seems that the *aisthesis* disturbs the temporal constitution of consciousness. Lyotard calls this strong and undetermined event the 'soul', indicating that the mind is temporarily deprived of its cognitive faculties.[7] How then can one address a sensorial event that actually deprives the mind of its cognitive efficiency? How can I remember this little shock of sensation that momentarily blocks my memory? This logical problem can be overcome if one accepts that the experience of a spontaneous sensation is felt – after the fact – as a mild hallucination. Depending on its intensity, an aesthetic experience is a momentary lapse of reason and a temporal loss of the self.

But how to speak of this event? Instead of subordinating its intensity to the communicative function of language, Lyotard allows it to affect the order of language. Instead of the search for a consensus, the fictive dialogues experiment with the intensity of confabulations. Instead of prescribing a meaning to the artwork, these dialogues dramatise the celerity of the affects that occur during that transient instant of the aesthetic experience.[8] Dialogues like 'Interesting?' and 'Paradox on the Graphic Artist' address neither the artist nor a specific artwork. These are scenarios that depict the process of experimenting with voices that debate the meaning of a notion (like 'the interesting'), but they suspend a consensus. The scenario signals the dynamics of thinking without a determinate criterion. Like the tradition of the essay (Diderot, Montaigne, Valéry), the tradition of the dialogue cultivates reflective thinking, without a rule or a prescribed finality. Thinking enacts a dramaturgy of faculties that interact on a stage. Thought unfolds like the intricate plaits of the acanthus ornament. We see the interactions of lines and the multiplicity of voices. Instead of presenting an idea, Lyotard's dialogues show how thinking itself is a theatrical arrangement that stages intricate and disquieting processes. *She* agrees and disagrees with *He*; retorts come and go in order to shape a sense of what 'the interesting' is.

These fictive dialogues can hardly be paraphrased; they present us with a series of scenes that address a sentiment that does not yet belong to historical time. The colour that we see in a painting is isolated from the chain of events in which it will be integrated: the story of art. Lyotard repeats Beckett's intuition regarding the paintings of Abraham van Velde: they are suspended things that present the extension (*l'étendue*) before it can be seen in isolated things (see Beckett 1991). The sentiment that these dialogues evoke is that of bracketing colours and timbres from the relations in which we usually organise them. In the language of 'Two Metamorphoses of the Seductive in Cinema', these dialogues do not inscribe the painted scene in the story of art, dating and explaining their meaning. The dialogues seduce because they suggest that, during the aesthetic experience, there is *no obligation* towards the artwork. The montage of voices that we read suspends the *aisthesis* and presents the dynamics – associative, imaginative and sometimes hallucinatory – that the *aisthesis* occasions.

STAGING PRESENCE

The dialogues entitled 'Presence' and 'Without Appe(a)l, Trance of Colour and Thoughts' both stage an essential moment that constitutes the aesthetic experience.[9] When faced with colourful sensations, like in the paintings of Appel, one can distinguish in them shapes that are integrated in objects of culture. The history of art is a story of actors (artists, curators, critics) that organise sensations into forms. Consequently, these forms are linked into a chronicle with beginnings and ends of styles: Romanticism, Realism, Impressionism, etc. Yet the presence of the artwork as a sensorial event escapes this historicising gesture. It refers to the moment when the mind surrenders its formative powers and receives a pure sensation. This presupposes a modulation of intentionality: the mind no longer intends an object and determines its adumbrations; it merely feels sensations without synthesising them. For an instant, before continuing to subordinate colour to recognisable forms, the mind feels itself as the reverberation of colourful matter. Lyotard's apology for presence marks a shift in his philosophy because it announces the abandonment of desire as a principle of art (which was central in the 1970s). While the artwork as instantiation of desire is now understood as a process where irregular forces transform the painted figures, linking them into stories and enhancing the plot, the artwork as presence is, according to Sfez, a terse *moment* of stupefaction that escapes the intrigues of desire (WP 460).

How to stage this event? Lyotard lets two voices speak about it: 'You' (*Vous*) and 'He'. The two characters do not always address each other because 'You' refers to 'He' as to a third person: 'as if he did not know that today commentary on the work is part of the work' (WP 113). On the other hand, 'He' addresses 'You' directly: 'I grant you all this, what you call reflection, in painting itself, keeps gaining ground' (WP 107). 'He' argues that today painting captures presence and 'You' retorts that this presence has always been deferred because thinking mediates between the gaze and the canvas. This deferral is due to the fact that the gaze is full of expectations and the painter is aware of the pictorial tradition. Yet sometimes, for 'He', instead of presenting an object belonging to space and time, the painting fractures space and time and presents an immediate sensation (WP 107). 'You' adds that painters have always reconfigured the way we look.

Buren's installations, for instance, disorient the gaze's relations to what it sees and reveal how the gaze is organised. Hence, Buren experiments in his work with what determines seeing in specific cultural contexts, such as the museum. The commentary becomes part of the work, or sometimes, as in the writings of Arakawa and Gins, the commentary *is* the work. These artists cultivate reflection more than visual presence (WP 115). Yet 'He' criticises 'You' because these writings do not imply that the artists gave up the issue of presence. 'You' seems to agree and adds that writings have always justified painting and that art history imposes a narrative structure on its objects, ascribing them a role in the story of art.

However, adds 'He', the figure perceived as presence escapes this diegetic structure. An Egyptian bas-relief can be explained as an object of culture. However, the same bas-relief is indifferent to the historical explanation if it is perceived as an apparition that 'interrupts all articulated thought' (WP 125). It is a powerful sensorial event that disrupts the chain of historical events. When it stupefies the mind, the work can only be presented through a parataxis: 'You do not know what to say; nothing, too much to say; not feeling like saying anything; only to stay. The coordinates of the destination are impossible, leaving an undisturbed space-time, a moment here, unexploitable by language' (WP 127). 'He' is aware that 'You' laugh at this kind of explanation because of the logical impossibility of testifying to an event that is not retained and reproduced by the mind. It is a philosophical embarrassment and 'He' even encourages the other to laugh (WP 129).

Consternation, mysticism, hallucination and stupefaction: these are possible notions to designate this moment when a form, a colour and a timbre happen *through* a sensation that suspends the cognitive activity of the mind. The sporadic scepticism of 'You' suggests that this event cannot be argued for because the mind ceases its determining power. 'He' and 'You' speak of an event that cannot be rendered like a historical event because presence refers precisely to the potential of the sensorial event to provisionally escape historical time. Confronted with the event, the mind is like an overexposed photograph: the form of the image is wiped out and it appears like a white field. That is why testifying to the event includes a tension between a strong sensation and an image that presents nothing, just whiteness. For both 'He' and 'You' presence implies a partial postponement of memory. That is why the confabulation is essential to the fragmentary reconstruction, and 'You' asserts: 'Mystical! Irrationalist delirium' (WP 134). There is no coherent memory of the event because its impact has the effect of a strong light and an incorrect exposure. The only visible memory is a blown-out image without an identifiable object. 'He' admits that testifying to presence means accepting that in art one is affected by no-thing, a non-place, an opening, a sensation without a support (WP 135). In this sense, presence is an acinematic event because it suspends a sensation, like a frozen frame that disturbs the course of the film.

EPILOGUE

Other dialogues, on Arakawa and Buren, continue this series of experimentations where the pragmatics of communication and the rigorous art-historical account give way to the intensity of confabulations. Paintings are staged and, like in Diderot, they become the model for dramaturgy. Yet, unlike Diderot,

Lyotard uses the painterly effects to generate two other artistic effects: first, the dialogic and fictive experimentations; second, to imagine the beholder of the discussed paintings. These dialogues subordinate communication to the dramatisation of the affect. That is their argumentative weakness and their dramaturgical power.

What does an affect sound like in language? To answer this question, Lyotard combines the tectonics of the philosophical tractatus with the convoluted performance of the affective phrase. These montages of voices form an alternative to the hermeneutics of art, i.e. the commentary that explains why and how to understand a painting. What is played in these fictive dialogues is not the iconological meaning of artworks but the emotional modulations that they are able to solicit.

The films on Monory and Guiffrey can be read as attempts to constitute this disempowered beholder of modern paintings, this viewer who – confused yet inquisitive – tries to make sense of what he or she sees. This is precisely one of the effects of Lyotard's dialogues: the beholder emerges by emulating the visual experiment that is at the core of painting with the commentary *on* painting. At this moment, their beholder can emerge not as an actual person but as the effect of the voices that 'speak in tongues' about their encounter with the discussed paintings. The dialogue links to the artwork and the beholder participates in the emergence of the artwork as such. This participation ensures the performative power of these dialogues: they are not just empty reflections but constitute a work through which the experimental character of art is maintained and cultivated. Finally, they can be read without a specific order, such as when looking at a modern painting, without a determinate direction. In this sense, Lyotard's dialogues on painting are montages that try to realise the deconstruction of the time of reading which he self-critically considered as the weakness of *Discourse, Figure*.

NOTES

1. On this point, I thank Jeroen Peeters for the fruitful conversations about Lyotard's art criticism, a topic he has addressed like no other in his essay 'Schrijven in het licht van de presentie. Het timbre van Lyotards kunstkritieken' (Peeters 2000).
2. The dialogues from the documentary *À blanc* run parallel to the long discussion with René Guiffrey of which fragments have been published in MT2 137ff.
3. Essential here is Suzanne Gearhart (1986) who reconstructs the broader context of the debate, namely Hegel's interpretation of Diderot's *Rameau's Nephew* (1761–2, revised in 1773–4) and Lyotard's use of the same dialogue as a mode of resisting the systematic Romantic philosophy. For a systematic insight into Hegel's interpretation of Diderot (which was mediated by Goethe's translation of *Rameau's Nephew*), see Schmidt 1996.

4. Lyotard stated this in an interview with Herman Parret that was taken in 1993 when he was invited to contribute with a publication for the 'Antwerp – Cultural Capital of Europe' event. Lyotard's contribution was the fictional dialogue 'Interesting' that was published in the same year in *Moralités Postmodernes* (see PF). It also appeared in a bilingual bibliophile edition, part of the 'Antwerp – Cultural Capital of Europe' series.
5. Lyotard writes: 'If the philosopher's phrases never stop beginning anew and folding back on themselves, leaving nothing, certainly not concepts, in his reader's mind, only the trail of a passing (*la traênée d'un passage*), it is because the philosopher's phrases must themselves make it perceptible in their form that they are a work. As a work these phrases seek out another work (that of the artist), and are displayed before other works (those of commentaries) that in turn seek them out' (MT1 163).
6. The fictive dialogue returns constantly in Lyotard's work throughout the 1980s and 1990s. The most experimental form it took is the commentary on Gianfranco Baruchello's notebooks (1980), where Lyotard writes on pages that face Baruchello's drawings (in MT2). 'Speech Snapshot' (1980) is a dialogue about photographs from the Salpêtrière (in IN). 'Paradox on the Graphic Artist' (1990) imagines two voices discussing the challenges of graphic arts (in PF). 'Interesting' (1993) is a dialogue between a man and a woman on this speculative notion (in PF). 'Karel Appel: A Gesture of Colour' (1998) (KA) also includes discussions between male and female voices, and the entire book *What to Paint?* (1987) (WP) is written as a series of dialogues. During the interview that Herman Parret made in 1993, Lyotard mentions that even though it might sound pretentious, he has different styles of writing and experiments with genres like the dialogue in order to avoid a dry discourse. The dialogue is a way of doing theory that is not theoretical. He adds that he invented many characters and this is a useful way to discuss contemporary arts because one is uncertain about their meaning. The dialogue makes possible a polytonality of possible meanings to such an extent that it is an essential procedure.
7. See for example 'Anima Minima' in PF.
8. Gérald Sfez argues that the dialogue in the philosophy of the late Lyotard is a strategy that allows language to become more than a means of communication and render experiences that are irreducible to language (WP 450). These dialogues then expand an intuition already formulated in *Discourse, Figure*, namely that the impact of the figural force on language disturbs its means of signification. Language has to then 'signify the other of signification' (DF 13). This other of signification is the sensorial event whose effect on the viewer these dialogues dramatise.
9. 'Presence' opens WP, and 'Without Appe(a)l' is chapter 17 of KA.

REFERENCES

Beckett, Samuel (1991), *Le monde et le pantalon suivi de Peintres de l'empêchement*, Paris: Éditions de Minuit.
Fried, Michael (1980), *Absorption and Theatricality: Painting and Beholder in the Age of Diderot*, Berkeley: University of California Press.

Gearhart, Suzanne (1986), 'The Dialectic and its Aesthetic Other: Hegel and Diderot', *MLN* 101:5, pp. 1042–66.
Peeters, Jeroen (2000), 'Schrijven in het licht van de presentie. Het timbre van Lyotards kunstkritieken', in *De passie van de aanraking. Over de esthetica van Jean-François Lyotard*, ed. Jeroen Peeters and Bart Vandenabeele, Budel: Damon, pp. 33–52.
Schmidt, James (1996), 'The Fool's Truth: Diderot, Goethe, and Hegel', *Journal of the History of Ideas* 57:4 (1996), pp. 625–44.

CHAPTER 13

Give Me a Sign: An Anxious Exploration of Performance on Film, Under Lyotard's Shadow

Kiff Bamford

The questions that arise when transcribing performance art onto film are fraught with anxiety and uncertainty, aspects of which also dogged this chapter's first iteration. It is important, therefore, to foreground these difficulties of translation in the present article and to apologise for the difficulties it may present to the reader. When giving a presentation it is bad practice to begin with an apology, but that is exactly how I began when I first presented this paper. It was at a conference,[1] the premise of which was exciting, and it seemed to fit with what I had been looking for: a way to take my research forward into a new terrain, away from that which has become perhaps a little too familiar to me over the last seven years or so.[2] And yet, when it came to the crunch – putting pen to paper, or rather fingers to keyboard – I found that, far from breaking away from that known territory, I barely left the shore, choosing to undertake a small intervention, a skirmish in the area of performance art, about which I feel most comfortable. And yet, in doing so I felt uneasy the whole time, which brings me back to my apology for apologising.

Why shouldn't you apologise at the outset of a presentation? Because it makes the audience feel uneasy? Because it undermines the position of (albeit temporary) authority given to the speaker? Because it betrays the trust of the host, shuffling uneasily in his chair, doubting the confidence exercised in extending the invitation? Is it then that in declaring my anxiety I might make you anxious and unsettle the expected proceedings? Particularly if I convey this anxiety not simply through a verbal apology but through other, physical manifestations: my mouth is dry, my body language is hesitant and perhaps you smell or sense the fear which takes over my body. Cinematically we cut to those indexical signs: beads of perspiration on the brow; close in on a slight tremor of the hand. Mark the silence in the room, which extends for just a moment – too – long before the music takes over as an attempt to express the feeling in the space; the space which has now opened up to engulf the audience, willing the narrative to give redemption to the troubled figure – be it schoolboy, priest, jilted lover. Or, perhaps invoking those sensuous qualities which have been the subject of Laura Marks' work, among others, and the 'sensory exploration' taken up in both experimental and commercial films to explore the sites, not simply of anxiety and hesitation but of trauma and cultural memory. What is important in this embodied approach to film is the acknowledgement that despite the mimetic basis of its function as a device for representation, it also has a materiality that affects its audience. As Laura Marks confirms, writing in the preface to *Skin of the Film*: 'Cinema is not merely a transmitter of signs; it bears witness to an object and transfers the presence of that object to viewers' (2000: xvii). In this remark we can hear the importance of Gilles Deleuze's thought to Marks' writing, as she acknowledges, but perhaps we can also hear the echo of Lyotard's own acknowledgement of Deleuze in the late essay 'The Idea of a Sovereign Film', in particular his contemplation of a specific object. Discussing the relationship between descriptive time and narrative time in neo-realist cinema, Lyotard describes how the intensity of a simple pot of water put on to boil allows the complexity of its multiple potential realities to rise up in a moment of simultaneous possibilities. But this aspect is not 'seen' by the director or the characters, says Lyotard; rather 'the pot is seen by a blind and subtle eye which is immanent to visible reality and the human gaze' (ISF 69). This newly translated essay is tremendously useful for opening up Lyotard on cinema – or Lyotard *to* cinema – and begins to account for the anxiety I have felt in writing this chapter. Marks speaks of the viewers' experience of cinema as being like a palimpsest – the layering of experiences being built up and passed on between audiences; so too is the experience of reading writings on art and cinema. All I offer to you here is a rather nervous top layer of my palimpsest which may, I hope, correspond in places to the 'outcrops of the visual or the vocal on the surface of the visible and the audible' which Lyotard identifies as the result of the 'free indirect narrative', with a nod to both Deleuze and Pier Paolo Pasolini (ISF 68).

The examples I am choosing to reference are not from a particular filmic genre but are aligned with my interest in those artists who work with performance and who, by the nature of their practice, also use film and video. There are three examples, of three different types: a film about a performance artist, a film featuring a performance, and a self-shot short video of my own.

MARINA ABRAMOVIĆ

I will start with the most mainstream example: that of Marina Abramović, who is the subject of the biographical film *The Artist is Present* (2012). It was given a limited cinematic release, shown on HBO in the United States and BBC4 in the UK and subsequently issued as a DVD. Directed by Matthew Akers, the film uses a conventional documentary style to follow the artist during preparations for the MoMa (Museum of Modern Art in New York) show of the same name: *The Artist is Present*. This 2010 retrospective of the artist's works included sound and video pieces, re-enactments of performances and the eponymous durational performance which received significant publicity in the mainstream press, particularly in New York. The performance *The Artist is Present* saw Abramović sitting in a chair in the atrium of MoMa for seven and a half hours a day, six days a week, for the duration of the show (three months, 14 March–31 May 2010). Opposite her was a chair which was occupied by different visitors in turn – visitors queued to sit opposite the artist and look into her eyes.

In an article responding to the exhibition and performance, but written before the film's release, the art historian Amelia Jones makes a swingeing critique of Abramović's exhibition, describing her as someone 'at the forefront of an industrial-strength institutionalisation of performance histories', driven by a desire to secure time, but failing: 'clinging to an outdated, modernist notion of presence that relies on a mystified notion of artistic intentionality and that ultimately relies on and reinforces the circuits of capital' (2011: 43). It is a brilliant article by someone who has written extensively on Abramović, signalling a significant change in their critical relationship, which is summed up in this reflection on her own experience of the performance:

> If anything, as a visitor to *The Artist is Present* I felt vaguely sorry that Marina was subjecting herself to something so exhausting. And depressed and a bit distressed at the spectacularization (albeit largely self-induced) of a 'body' and a 'body' of work I have long admired, as a historian of art and performance. If anything, I found myself wanting to revert to reading books about performance to escape the noisy emptiness of this 'real' live art experience. (2011: 18)

What the film gives us, that press coverage and still images do not, is a clearer sense of the set-up (*dispositif*) within which this spectacle of spectatorship took place – the lighting, the queuing, the recording and above all the pressure to be part of that set-up – exactly that set-up to which Amelia Jones reacts so strongly. Initially it seems that the film does not attempt to recreate the experience of the performance for the cinema viewer (this might have been more akin to one of Warhol's screen tests) but places the viewer in the conventional role of an observer of a ritual, mediated by cinematic conventions. However, the film also rehearses the layers of significant moments which are ignited for those viewers who do react positively to the performance, viewers who bring with them a knowledge not only of the myths surrounding Abramović but also of that wider modernist myth of the artist as shaman: a container of, or opening onto, an ontological originary presence. This is something to which Lyotard, some might argue, comes very close in his writings on art, except that here the focus is on the artist as interlocutor rather than on the matter or the gesture of the work which is Lyotard's concern.[3] Lyotard is quite clear in his discussions of presence that it is not the presence of being about which he talks. In writing on Daniel Buren in *What to Paint?*, Lyotard, or rather Lyotard's character 'You', explains that in Buren's work presence is merely used to 'show the falsity of presence' (WP 107). This is the same response Amelia Jones has to the MoMa performance where, unintentionally, the live event destroys presence.

The film, however, is more *about* the performance than showing the performance; it is careful to give the viewer the back story: a potted version of Abramović's history, including clips of past works emphasising the endurance that many involved. Then the expected talking heads of art-world figures who reinforce her art-historical significance and, in and amongst other things, a quasi-psychological interpretation of the work: her need for love as a consequence of her strict upbringing under Tito's regime in Yugoslavia.[4] We also see the worry, stress and illness in the lead-up to the opening of the show and this performance. The film gives us this information, these experiences, so that we, too, can be ready to be exposed to the culmination of the documentary: the performance *The Artist is Present*. But the film simultaneously exposes the inherent complicity of the artist with her own commodification and her insertion into the highly financialised world of contemporary art. And then there is our position as viewers of the film: watching, like the audience at the performance, but also as the product of the excess of visibility apparent in the set-up of the performance. Those seated opposite Marina look into her eyes while being watched by spectators and cameras, under huge lights in a space Abramović described as 'wanting to be like a film set', the entirety of which is being filmed.[5] The 'free indirect vision' referred to by Lyotard in 'The Idea of a Sovereign Film' plays on the ambiguity of positionality: when the speaker's or the observer's position is unfixed, ambiguous and in a state of productive flux. There is a perverse aspect of this at play in the film, aligned in part by the near-refusal to re-present the point of view of the viewer through the camera's eye, whilst doing everything to create the experience of that viewer through other means.

There are in fact only two moments when the camera adopts the viewpoint of the participant in the performance, the sitter in the chair staring directly at Abramović. One is in the opening sequence showing the artist's head and shoulders in a portrait pose, intercut with the head of a viewer, and the other – which is also used as the backdrop for the DVD menu – is a close-up of just the eyes. The eyes open, clearly slowed down, and stare; overlaid with evocative music – which crescendos slightly at the point of the eyes opening – together with her distinctive, heavily accented voice, stating:

> Performance is all about state of mind. The public is like a dog: they can feel insecurity, they can feel fear, they can feel if you're not there, so the idea is how can you bring the performer and the audience into the same state of consciousness here and now.

The film then cuts to several shots of visitor's reactions, building to a series of several in tears. There is a masochism at work in the relationship: 'The public is like a dog.' The artist is a dominatrix, the public is submissive (at least the public as shown in the film): submissive to the set-up, to the rules, to the role and power of the authority figure. But also written into the set-up is the possibility of the reversal of roles, something I will return to later.

What I want to compare this with is the figure of the onlooker as traced by Lyotard in his account of Freud's paper 'A Child is Being Beaten', in order to discuss the possibility of multiple and simultaneous positions operating within the frame of the film as recorder of performance. I am particularly interested in the figure of the observer who is ostensibly outside the game and yet becomes both implicated and imbricated in this and other filmic scenes.

'A CHILD IS BEING BEATEN'

The analysis of the phantasy 'A Child is being Beaten', written by Freud in 1919, is a frequent point of reference for Lyotard. His most detailed analysis appears in *Discourse, Figure* – over nearly thirty pages in the French edition – but it is also the central element of the presentation which was published in 1977 as 'The Unconscious as Mise-en-scène', one of the four texts which refer to film at length.

The focus of Lyotard's discussion is the staging of desire by the unconscious in order to describe the transformation of place, action and the temporal instances which constitute the complex operations which, in *Discourse, Figure*, he terms the 'figure-matrix'. In 'The Unconscious as Mise-en-scène' it is used similarly to explain the shift in the patient's relationship to the staging of the scene and the role of the active participant in the scene. What Lyotard highlights in Freud's analysis is the blocking together of different incompossible elements, incompossible according to the accepted logic of time, space and affective investment. He does this in order to emphasise the limitations of any attempt to 'read' desire as a translatable element. He also observes that Freud's use of a theatrical metaphor for the 'staging' of primary processes is based on the aesthetics particular to the conventions of late nineteenth-century opera and the proscenium arch. In both *Discourse, Figure* and 'The Unconscious as Mise-en-scène' Lyotard is making a clear critique of Freud's approach to art as a symptom to be translated, as the fulfilment of a phantasy which can be decoded. The proscenium arch, for example, effectively limits Freud's ability to recognise the importance of art as other than that which reveals a truth, as fulfilling desire, based as it is on the conventions of staging which hide the mechanisms of its production. Lyotard dispenses with the pretence of an inside and outside when writing about painting, the stage, theatre and, specifically in 'The Unconscious as Mise-en-scène', experimental cinema, through the example of Michael Snow's *La Région centrale* (1971). The concern is not revealing truths but setting up multiple perspectives and de-limiting the capacity to experience intensities, intensities that are transformed 'into movement and emotions on the spectators' bodies'. There is a conscious turn from Freud to Nietzsche, as made clear in these quotations from the end of 'The Unconscious as Mise-en-scène': 'When the force used to stage something has no goal other than to make manifest its potentiality . . . as attempts to state perspectives of reality . . . and draw it out beyond this old body' (UM 54). How is it to be drawn out? Not through a translation of the discourse of desire as a decodable message but by transcribing it on a virtual body: a transcription which effects the body of the spectator through what Lyotard names 'somatography'. Here it is important to emphasise the active process of transformation through transcription, not simply *on* the body but *of* the body, which is how Lyotard uses the term 'somatography'. As part of this process a new addressee is being created, one whose 'disconcerted body is invited to stretch its sensory capacities beyond measure' (UM 52).

One writer who takes forward this challenge, not only from Lyotard but also from Deleuze, and following D. N. Rodowick and Rosi Braidotti, among others, is Patricia MacCormack in her 2008 book *Cinesexualities*. We need to re-think our viewing bodies, says MacCormack, to undo and re-work them without dependence on 'genitals and gazing eyes as gendering and desiring organs' (2008: 133). Contrary to spectatorship theory, which honours the power of the gaze, that which MacCormack names cinesexuality requires the viewer to submit to the image, displaying rather an openness which is akin to that which Lyotard terms passibility: not a passive observer ostensibly outside the game, but one who is fully immersed and open to the transcription of the body through somatography. This takes us away from any fixation on the position of the camera as a viewer and away from those established codes of representation, often taken as the key indicator for works which document, record, or make an account of performance works. In Lyotard's comment on 'A Child is Being Beaten' it is the second stage of the analysis of the phantasy which takes us outside the traditional model of spectatorship. In the first and third the patient is the observer – of an adult beating a child – whereas in the second (constructed through analysis) it is the patient who is on the scene as the child, the subject who is being beaten, and therefore as 'an *unconscious* imaginal presentation: *the subject does not see himself seeing*' (DF 345). There are no witnesses, thereby no means by which to bring this stage of the phantasy to representation except through the intervention of the analyst, the implications of which Lyotard states as follows: 'Now as far as representation is concerned, if one doesn't see oneself seeing, one doesn't see' (DF 345–6). It is the consequence of this shift of the patient's position in Freud's analysis of the phantasy which preoccupies Lyotard. The viewer's eye is replaced by the body: 'when I am on stage I can't speak *about* what is happening on it', and this results in a somatographic displacement together with the attending discharge of libidinal force (DF 346; see also UM 48–9).

I am doubtful that Akers' film of *The Artist is Present* achieves this: it aims more at the fulfilment of anticipated suffering and witness to that suffering, rather than the masochism which comes from an opening up; not to the pleasure of known pain but to the indeterminate, which MacCormack terms 'cinemasochism'. It is the hesitation of the indeterminate which powers the writings of Sacher-Masoch – whose literary work and life inspired Richard von Krafft-Ebing to coin the phrase 'masochism' – and which makes it significantly different to the relentless, carnal sexuality in the writings of the Marquis de Sade. In *Coldness and Cruelty* Deleuze clearly separates the characteristics of sadism and masochism and rejects their elision into the single term 'sadomasochism'. For both Deleuze and Lyotard the characteristics of hesitation and indetermination fuel the *jouissance* of masochism, although Lyotard stays closer to Freud in emphasising a connection to the death drive. Lyotard ends the section on 'The Child is Being Beaten' in *Discourse, Figure* with an explicit articulation of the importance of the unknown in the hesitation of the death drive, whereby the intervals between the beat rely not on their regularity but their irregularity: the arrhythmic beat is fuelled by that which he terms the 'figural' and the tension of uncertainty. The same considerations return throughout Lyotard's writings on both art and film – the rapidity or slowness highlighted in 'Acinema' and the unexpected lingering on the object in 'The Idea of a Sovereign Film'. But perhaps more important is Lyotard's concern for that aspect of the figure in the phantasy which is neither an explicit stage direction nor a stable script to be decoded, but the unintelligible trace of the death drive which causes digression and rejection, not return. Meaning is not recalled by the figural but by that which closes meaning: discourse. The ghost as 're-venant' (returned) is called to meaning:

> The phantasy (the figure-image in this instance) is a ghost, a lost soul that discourse is called upon to redeem, because it is a meaning [*sens*] that is waiting to be signified [*signifié*], and that presents itself as a representation because it cannot find expression in words. (DF 347)

GHOST DANCE

The second example of a performance artist shown on film is Stuart Brisley's contribution to the 1983 film *Ghost Dance*. Directed by Ken McMullen as a co-production for the TV channels ZDF in Germany and Channel 4 in the UK, it is best known, perhaps, for the participation of Jacques Derrida and the subsequent discussions on 'hauntology' with Bernard Stiegler.[6] However, there has been little attention given to the collaboration between the director and the British performance artist, Stuart Brisley, and it is his performance at the end of the film which interests me here. It is highly unusual in that it functions neither as the record of a performance nor the subject of a film but rather as a constituent element within a wider filmic narrative. The performance is witnessed by the protagonist 'Pascale' who is represented by two actors, one of whom – the French actor Pascale Ogier – visualises her emotional response with tears. Whilst in Akers' film of Abramović, *The Artist is Present*, the tears of the participants are used as a key signifier of an authentic emotional response within the structure of the film as a documentary, the tears of Pascale are the tears of a character and therefore, on the face of it, 'acted', if not scripted – but here we are in interesting territory given that McMullen works with improvisations. As an insight into McMullen's way of working it is useful to refer to Derrida's comment about the preparation undertaken for a scene with Pascale Ogier. The filmmaker asked Derrida and Ogier 'to spend minutes, if not hours . . . looking into one another's eyes' (Stiegler and Derrida 2002: 119).

In the performance by Brisley, there is no attempt to show the literal point of view of the protagonist, who watches from the edge of the frame. Instead, what is exploited is the camera's own presence as an optical device manufactured to reproduce images in accordance with the dominant system of representation, based on that of Renaissance perspective. The orthogonal lines which order objects to appear as though in a three-dimensional field are here made manifest in the arrangement of the building, whilst simultaneously being questioned by their doubling, through reflection, and also through an ambiguity of the

Stuart Brisley in *Ghost Dance* (dir. Ken McMullen, 1983)

plane's orientation. When the figure of the performance artist Stuart Brisley is introduced into the scene, the pictorial result is to draw further attention to the illusion of the optical set-up. The more he touches the water, the more the reflection is broken. As he crawls into this space its consistency as a recognisable ordered space – that regresses on the horizontal plane – is momentarily questioned: the possibility of its axis is reconfigured as one that regresses vertically, the figure climbing not along, but downwards.

In itself this is a remarkable scene, but do we need the figure of the observer here, except as a link to the film's narrative? Pascale's role appears to be that of the Greek chorus: reacting to and narrating events, except that here we are also witnesses to the action, to which she is reacting, and the only communication she gives is to cry. She is, however, seen to be seeing. The crawling figure of the artist doesn't 'see' her, but the camera does and is distracted by her tears, prompting a cut to a close-up of her face, focusing on the tears. She doesn't speak except through those tears. Does she speak somatographically? Can we believe her tears more than those of the visitors to *The Artist is Present*? Can the film, if not the tears, provoke the '*désordre*' of which Lyotard writes in 'Acinema': the 'disorder [*désordre*] of the drives, as a composite of decompositions', which is picked up again in the essay on Paul Valéry – titled 'Désordre' – in *Lectures d'enfance*, whose very analysis is the consistency of inconsistency in the statement 'This is Art'.[7]

These tears are but a sign, now. Now, they are a sign.

'EMOTION'

To shift register, I would like now to describe a short video. You can search for it online, if you have the patience and technology available. If not, here are a few lines written in lieu of the sound and moving image. In this short video I am reciting the beautifully elliptical phrase written by art historian Donald Preziosi, paraphrasing Jacques Derrida's observation which challenges the romantic notion that the artist can somehow communicate emotions directly. In the background, elements from Mozart's *Requiem* play and the artist's eye dilates slightly as the phrase is repeated again and again: 'no artistic expression is an unmediated manifestation of emotion or thought'.[8] Following a silent section, during which a close-up on a single eye continues, the music returns with the Kyrie.

Central to Lyotard's discussion of film and theatre is the location of the viewer, their potential position psychically with(in) the scene, and their undoing by that which is insufficiently accounted for by signification. The role of somatography opens this up, as does the demand for intensity in 'Acinema' and the other libidinal writings. In an essay on theatre from the same collection as 'Acinema', titled 'The Tooth, the Palm', Lyotard ends his discussion of energetic theatre as follows: 'It's business is to produce the highest intensity (by excess or by lack of energy) of what there is, without intention. That is my question: is it possible, how?' (2004: 30).

Both 'Acinema' and 'The Tooth, the Palm' leave the same question – is it possible? – hanging. To some extent it is answered two decades later in 'The Idea of a Sovereign Film' with a 'no', at least not as a 'totally sovereign film', such sovereignty being 'absolutely allergic to totality' (ISF 64). The unauthorised occurrence which leaves the viewer waiting to be undone (*désordre*) 'happens' to the author as it does to the viewer. In his essay on Valéry, Lyotard describes the temporality of that which Valéry terms the poetic mind as 'a sort of spasm': 'It is a sort of spasm in which what has been done does not govern what is yet to be done' – hence the seeming expansion of Lyotard's concern for the cinematic from the niche of the avant-garde to more commercial genres (TP 170). Regardless of the genre, the director and the viewer wait: not for a completion of the form, but for its freedom from completion, its undoing, a disorder through the spasm of time, space and affective intensities: through 'a disseizure and a passibility in expectation of their end result' (TP 171). I feel I should end this with a return to tears: but tears by themselves *mean* nothing: so I will retreat under the shadow of Lyotard's words once more, from his last, unfinished text, *The Confession of Augustine*: 'The memory of a joy is not joyous, emotion is something actual, nothing is retained from it but the tasteless occurrence. That the affective quality is lost is at least not lost' (CA 30).

When this chapter had its first public iteration as a spoken paper I broke with the conventions of conference protocol by ending with an action. I cannot repeat this action in print, but will consider it no different to the task of commenting on a film through spoken or written work. We have to work through analogy to that which is not present; through the insertion of clips, still images or descriptions there is the hope that something of that on which the commentary is being made will remain. It is through such a reflection that I quelled the self-doubt – coexistent with the anxiety I expressed at the outset of the piece – which pervaded my desire to do something more physical than to read a paper and show a film. So I danced. Not a conventional dance, but one provoked by the rhythm of the words I spoke. Opening with a declaration:

'Art is Good!'

And an affirmative rejoinder:

'Art *is* Good.'

This was followed by a repetition, which begins to cast doubt on the confidence of the opening statement:

'Art is Good. Art is good enough for nothing.'

Then, trying out appropriate modulations of the voice to modify the statement:

'Art is Good, Art *is* Good; Art is Good enough for Nothing!'

After which the two statements can be repeated to rhythmic effect:

'Art is Good, Art is Good enough, for nothing; Art is good, Art is good enough, for nothing'.

I hope you try this at home – verbalisation is key.

'Art is Good, Art is Good enough . . . for nothing! Art is good, Art is good enough, for nothing.
Art is Good
Art is Good enough, for nothing
Art is Good
Art is good enough, for nothing!
Art is Good
Art is Good enough, for nothing
Art is Good
Art is good enough, for nothing!'

Once established – and here you have to pace, perhaps anticlockwise in a small circle or square; arms swinging in a quasi-militaristic fashion, if it helps, to move:

'Art is Good, Art is Good enough: for nothing, Art is Good, Art is good enough: for nothing, Art is Good, Art is Good enough: for nothing, Art is Good, Art is good enough: for nothing.'

Lose yourself momentarily, close your eyes; perhaps you are no longer being seen, perhaps someone will join you in your dance (no one at the conference did). Thrust your arms out as you recite, swing those hips with each iteration and continue until your words have lost sense or until you have a moment of somatographic displacement: when the anxiety disturbs your rhythm and you realise you don't know how to stop, how to bring this back, to return to discourse. You continue your repetition but allow it to slowly fade to a whisper – it has already become sounds detached from meaning, a series of sibilant hisses, and you seek to withdraw:

Withdraw, not so that I may desire you and wish to be as one with you to the death, but in order that in your absence, and thanks to your absence, there may come into being a memory of what made your presence and our scene possible.[9]

Hope for applause, that framing of representation which covers up the embarrassment, and sit down to face questions.

NOTES

1. 'Acinemas: Aesthetics and Film in the Philosophy of Jean-François Lyotard', University of Dundee, 7–8 May 2014.
2. See Bamford 2012.
3. See Costello 2000, a position which has been cited recently by Nigel Mapp (2013). I have questioned the simplicity of isolating Lyotard's approach as one which is 'impeccably modernist' (Mapp 2013: 100) because of the assumptions inherent in such terminology, particularly with regard to the use of Kant by figures such as Clement Greenberg in the history of art criticism (Bamford 2012: 93–7). There remains a need, however, to carefully contextualise the several voices of Lyotard's writings on art within those traditions that have been termed modernist within art history and criticism, particularly within the Anglophone academic community.
4. This interpretation echoes the biography outlined in the theatre work *The Life and Death of Marina Abramović*, staged with director Robert Wilson in 2011, in which Abramović took the role of her own, controlling, mother.
5. Quotes from Marina Abramović are taken from the film *The Artist is Present* (dir. Akers, 2012).

6. Stiegler and Derrida 2002. In this conversation Stiegler refers to Derrida's use of the term 'hauntology' as used in *Specters of Marx* (Derrida 1994).
7. Ac 35; 'du désordre des pulsions, comme le compose des décompositions' in the French. The essay 'Désordre' appears in the collection *Lectures d'enfance* (Lyotard 1991) and in English translation as 'On What is "Art"' in TP.
8. The full quotation, slightly modified in the video is: 'An "otherness" always inhabits a work, and no artistic expression can ever be an unmediated manifestation of emotion or thought' (Preziosi 2008: 271).
9. Lyotard, 'Anamnesis of the Visible, or Candour', in LR (228).

REFERENCES

Bamford, Kiff (2012), *Lyotard and the* figural *in Performance, Art and Writing*, London: Bloomsbury.
Costello, Diarmuid (2000), 'Lyotard's Modernism', *Parallax* 6:4, pp. 76–87.
Derrida, Jacques (1994), *Specters of Marx*, trans. Peggy Kamuf, London: Routledge.
Jones, Amelia (2011), '"The Artist is Present": Artistic Re-enactment and the Impossibility of Presence', *TDR: The Drama Review* 55:1, pp. 16–45.
Lyotard, Jean-François (1991), *Lectures d'enfance*, Paris: Galilée.
Lyotard, Jean-François (2004), 'The Tooth, the Palm', in *Critical Concepts in Performance*, Vol. 4, ed. Philip Auslander, London: Routledge.
MacCormack, Patricia (2008), *Cinesexualities*, Surrey: Ashgate.
Mapp, Nigel (2013), 'Lyotard, Art, Seeing', *Philosophy of Photography* 4:1, pp. 87–102.
Marks, Laura U. (2000), *The Skin of the Film: Intercultural Cinema, Embodiment, and the Senses*, Durham NC: Duke University Press.
Preziosi, Donald (2008), *The Art of Art History*, 2nd edn, Oxford: Oxford University Press.
Stiegler, Bernard and Derrida, Jacques (2002), *Echographies of Television*, trans. Jennifer Bajorek, London: Polity.

CHAPTER 14

How Desire Works: A Lyotardian Lynch

Graham Jones and Ashley Woodward

It is necessary to think of desire as an energy that works (Freud is explicit about this: I have in mind the brief note at the end of the chapter on the dream work, where Freud reproaches other analysts with only paying attention to the manifest content and the latent thoughts, whereas the only important thing is the work, how one passes from the one to the other, how desire works).

Jean-François Lyotard (LRG)

It's better not to know so much about what things mean or how they might be interpreted or you'll be too afraid to let things keep happening.

David Lynch

It has long been recognised that film may be approached through the model of the dream (the latter itself being, as Freud noted, the royal road to the unconscious), and this explains why psychoanalytic theory – among other things, a discourse on the function and meaning of dreams – has been so influential in film theory. It is hardly surprising then that the films of David Lynch, which are often praised for their overtly dream-like qualities, should have attracted the attention of so many critics armed with psychoanalytical tools of dissection. What we propose here is a challenge to the dominant interpretation of the film works of David Lynch – a challenge that turns around a dispute on how to interpret their dream-like aspects. The dispute is between Lacan and Lyotard: in effect, a dispute in interpretations of Freud, and of the unconscious and desire.

What is more widely at stake in this dispute is the nature of art, and in this particular case, the nature of *film* as an art.

When critics and aficionados liken Lynch's films to dreams they are usually referring to either one or both features associated with the oneiric: first, that dreams seem illogical in form and content (wherein things change shape or swap identities, strange juxtapositions occur, and the normal associations of time and space are transgressed or suspended), and secondly, that dreams appear highly resistant to sense (that they seem to involve many things without being *about* anything obvious – i.e. that there is no consistency, coherence or unity to their 'meaning'; they seemingly have significance but not signification).

The predominant approach to Lynch's work in cinema studies is to attempt to explain the *meaning* his films have, and what is more, to provide them with a unity and coherence that they purportedly 'lack', through extensive textual commentary and interpretative correlations.[1] Perversely, this is to miss what is most distinctive and powerful about these films. This mainstream interpretative tendency is overtly encapsulated in the Lacanian approach to Lynch's films, but is in fact generally evident in most critical interpretations of his work.

Against this thrust of interpretation, we wish to argue that the dream-like qualities, which are indeed often evident in Lynch's films, do not represent deficiencies, and thus need not demand some form of compensation or redress – that is to say, they mark neither a conceptual lack that needs to be filled (with an explanation) nor an obscuring veil that needs to be stripped away (to reveal a secret truth). On the contrary, our contention is that these aspects are neither lacunae nor infirmities in Lynch's artistic vision, and indeed that what is most distinctive about Lynch's films is their capacity to convey powerful effects through images *that defy meaning or signification.*

This chapter seeks to demonstrate that Lyotard presents a relevant understanding of desire – a plastic and affective one – which accounts for how images can convey or generate affects without encoding or imbuing them with any specific meaning. What is of particular interest to Lyotard is how desire expresses itself in *sensation*. This view of desire, we believe, constitutes a more faithful approach to the spirit of Lynch's films than the Lacanian one, and moreover, provides an encounter with them that does not ameliorate their enigmatic nature. Our argument, however, is not that Lynch's images escape all signification, or even that they are radically irrecuperable in terms of any narrative possibilities (Lyotard would insist that such a 'transgression' is itself a phantasy), but that this is not where their *force* resides. Rather, their force lies in their inherent resistance to signification and narrative recuperation, which is precisely what Lynch seems to do so well.

THE SEMIOTIC LYNCH

> It's a dangerous thing to say what a picture is. If things get too specific, the dream stops.
>
> David Lynch

Let us begin with Mark Allyn Stewart's *David Lynch Decoded* (2007). This text is more a populist commentary than a traditional 'academic' book, but is useful as a very clear example of the kind of reading – in this case, semiotic – of Lynch to which we wish to offer an alternative. Stewart's approach is announced in the blurb on the back of the book:

> What does it all mean? Surely all of those red curtains, strobe lights and dancing dwarves we keep seeing in David Lynch's films must mean something, right? Well actually, they do. In fact, not only do they mean something, they're all interconnected. Reading these symbols is the key to understanding not just David Lynch's films individually, but his body of work as a whole.

The core of Stewart's reading is that 'other-worldly' characters pervade Lynch's films, and they indicate an 'other world' which is divided from, but frequently invades, the 'real world'. He contends that 'over time Lynch has developed a visual language that we can interpret with regard to these characters and the strange world they come from' (2007: xiii). These characters are 'surrounded by distinct elements that have begun to define themselves. Like the visual language Alfred Hitchcock developed in his films . . . Lynch has been developing a world with its own language that can also be interpreted if we understand the language' (2007: 107). In the conclusion to his book, Stewart elaborates a series of repeated 'cues' in Lynch's films, which he treats as signs – signs supplying us with the meanings he believes are the key to their interpretation or decoding. These cues include Electricity, Dogs/Barking, Dreams and Visions, Blown Out/White Screen, Strobe Effect, Fire, Duality/Dual Characters, Painted Faces, The Colour Blue, and so on.

Stewart responds to the possible objection to his semiotic approach that Lynch in fact works in a more intuitive or meditative way as follows:

> when an artist does the same thing six or seven times, or as is often the case with Lynch, in virtually every film he's made, then intuitive or not, conscious or not, this is a pattern that obviously means something to him. When an artist does something again and again under the same circumstances and with the same results, this is something we can point at and say that it obviously has meaning. (2007: 121)

We see that for Stewart, *repetition* is taken as a basic marker of (semiotic) meaning.

For all his claims to uncover the secret system of signs and tell us what Lynch's films mean, Stewart's interpretations remain rather thin. The overall meaning of all Lynch's films (both individually and collectively) is given as little more than the existence of 'two worlds' (reality/other world), characters belonging properly to one world or the other, and visual-sonic cues for transitions between the worlds (such as Electricity or Dogs/Barking). (We will come back to the significance of this 'two-world' theory in relation to Lyotard's critique of semiotics below.)

The sort of interpretation offered by Stewart resembles that of many psychoanalytic critics in one important respect: in their common aspiration to establish one-to-one correspondences between 'symbols' and 'meanings'. This is the traditional popular conception of so-called 'vulgar Freudianism', with its obsessive search for interpretations and drawing of a long bow in the establishing of often improbable correlations.[2] Of course, psychoanalytic criticism has become more sophisticated in its interpretative strategies in recent decades. Nevertheless, its adherents frequently remain committed to Freud's self-contradictory striving to make comprehensible what is incomprehensible, to conceptualise what is a-conceptual, and to render the irrational rational, the illogical logical – even if this is now achieved through less direct means such as symbolic algebras and formulae, logical proofs, and structural models.

As we noted earlier, there have been many articles and books on particular films by Lynch, or even his work as a whole, which employ or cite such recent psychoanalytic concepts and approaches (involving discussions of the uncanny, fantasy, the Oedipus complex, castration, masochism, etc.). These include 'readings' by Creed (1988), Herzogenrath (1999), Bulkeley (2003), Coffeen (2003), O'Connor (2005), Schaffner (2009), Mctaggart (2010) and Akser (2012), to name but a handful. But perhaps the most sophisticated (and dubious) readings are those presented by Lacanian critics such as Slavoj Žižek and Todd McGowan. In the following section, we will present the broad interpretation on which Žižek and McGowan's efforts converge as indicative of the Lacanian reading of Lynch we wish to challenge.

THE LACANIAN LYNCH

What is interesting about the works of Žižek and McGowan is their resort to establishing correlations, not between filmic elements and particular meanings, but between filmic meanings and operative *structures*, and the related pedagogical function of establishing such correlations. Let us address the latter issue first. It is a distinctive feature of Lacanian engagements with both the works of popular culture and the more experimental arts that they do not treat such works as interesting or valuable in their own right but, instead, as opportunities for exemplifying fundamental theoretical concepts or insights. In short, artworks are merely instructive illustrations of Lacanian 'truths'. To his credit, McGowan is more nuanced in his rendering of such readings, but Žižek is both upfront and unabashed in his own (at best ambivalent, at worst contemptuous) view that what he calls 'imbecilic' popular culture serves little purpose in his work apart from illustrating psychoanalytical concepts (Žižek 1997) – that is to say, such products have no intrinsic value in and of themselves – such that Žižek could end each of his analyses with the letters QED.

Let us now turn to addressing the second notable feature of the Lacanian reading strategy. We see in Žižek's well-known essay *The Art of the Ridiculous Sublime* (2000) and also in McGowan's multiple commentaries on Lynch (but particularly 2000[3]) that, although both critics make numerous disparate claims on behalf of Lynch's oeuvre (for example, Žižek notes the emergence of a new type of femme fatale (2000: 9–12)), their respective positions ultimately converge on the significance of the Lacanian notions of desire, fantasy and the Real, and how the interrelated invocation of these in the text challenges the seduction or ideological solicitation predominant in Hollywood cinema. They interpret the 'dualism' – the 'two-worlds' hypothesis commonly attributed to Lynch's films – as exemplifying the operations of a psychical structure (an invariant and universal organising relation that persists despite its empirical – and often singularly contingent – content), and the bizarre, dream-like aspects of these same texts as signalling the intrusions of the Real into the fantasy that sustains the film protagonist's existence. Moreover, each accords *Lost Highway* an exemplary position within Lynch's *oeuvre*, and in outlining their interpretation of Lynch we will specifically focus on this film.

It is well known that while a 'first wave' of Lacanian film theory focused on the register of the Imaginary, the 'second wave', of which Žižek and McGowan are representatives, focuses on the Real.[4] In his later work Lacan grants the concept of the Real ever more importance, and revises his account of the Imaginary and the Symbolic to accord with this. Essentially the Real, no longer simply that which subsists beyond the Symbolic as un-symbolisable (and therefore unknowable), now constitutes the traumatic kernel that insists *within* the Symbolic yet constantly threatens it. The Symbolic itself lacks full consistency or coherency (after all the individual is only ever consciously attached to parts rather than the entirety of it) and the Imaginary provides the potential means of 'plugging' or hiding the holes within it. In essence, fantasy is the crucial means of papering over the gaps in the Symbolic, and by extension the fundamental void that resides at the heart of the split subject, but it also serves as a shield to ward off the potential intrusions of the Real, which would otherwise be experienced as terrifying and destabilising. This void, the awareness of which is repressed, *is* the Real – it is the potential threat of the failure or lack of meaning and coherence. This is why, according to Lacan, everyday social reality is necessarily infused with, even propped up by, *fantasy* (in short, there is little that is real about reality) and when we become aware of this then the Real is felt as a disturbance or distortion in the fabric of that same reality (i.e. as the uncanny or inexplicable sublime, closely linked to *jouissance* or surplus enjoyment). Or, even worse, when the fantasy falters then the chaos of the Real overwhelms the individual and this leads initially to an overwhelming sense of persecution and often thereafter the disintegration or dissolution of the subject's very social identity.

It is this notion of the Real and its disturbing intrusions into fantasy and social reality that largely determine the readings of Lynch's work (and particularly of *Lost Highway*) by Žižek and McGowan. There is some irony to this in as much as each of them strives to comprehend something incomprehensible, domesticating it by theoretical means (to ward off the Real by shoring up the Symbolic). In Žižek's case this has a further dimension in that, as we have noted, he rather reductively treats all cultural phenomena as grist to the Lacanian theoretical mill.

For both Žižek and McGowan, *Lost Highway* overtly depicts the tense juxtaposition between the fantasy that sustains a sense of everyday reality and the realm of the Real where the uncanny or incoherence insists, and the potential disintegration of the protagonist's identity that results from the collision between them. This is somewhat unusual in Hollywood cinema, McGowan suggests, as the so-called 'dream factory' usually functions to obscure or resist acknowledgment of the Real, despite the latter's spectral presence in the form of narrative or scenic distortions or lapses in coherency (McGowan 2007: 19–20; 2008: 17, 20, 32, 204–5). In *Lost Highway*, however, the underscoring of the Real through the contrast between these two domains is, he claims, primarily established through the use of *an uncanny doubling of the protagonist*: that is, roughly a third of the way through the film the protagonist suddenly and without explanation transforms into a different person with a different name (a transition reinforced through the use of different actors, and further reflected through contrasting scenarios of everyday life and a very different use of mise-en-scène). This is followed by a series of increasingly more bizarre events culminating in the film ending by repeating elements of its beginning, a circularity that Lynch, and his co-screenwriter Barry Gifford, have likened to a Moebius strip – which appears to present two distinct sides but ultimately is revealed to have only one – an emblematic image of repetition and doubling that is often cited in interpretations of *Lost Highway* (see Herzogenrath 1999 for example).[5] In both Žižek and McGowan's respective Lacanian readings of these events, the musician Fred Madison is viewed as the desiring subject who cannot divine the desires of his partner and kills her as a result. Unable to confront this deed directly, he constructs in its place a fantasy scenario in which culpability is erased and the question that prompted his desire (What does the 'other' want of me?) is addressed through his own replacement by the virile ego-ideal of Pete. However, the fabric of this fantasy is subsequently disturbed by irruptive traces of what has gone before (i.e. the repetition of the repressed traumatic event). By degrees this fantasy appears to corrode in the face of these disturbances and inconsistencies and thus, no longer shielded from the encroachment of the Real, Fred appears finally to lose not just his identity but also his sanity.

Perhaps surprisingly, both Žižek and McGowan ultimately see the events of the film in potentially useful terms, arguing that they prove, if not therapeutic, at least instructive for the audience – in as much as they lay bare the logic and structural relations between desire, fantasy, the Real and the gaze:

> Lynch's films demand that the spectator revaluate her/his relationship to the cinema. The cinema is no longer an escape without any connection to the outside world, nor is it a reality unto itself. Instead it is the reverse side of that outside world – the fantasmatic underside that holds the truth of the latter. If we escape at all in Lynch's cinema, we escape into the trauma that remains hidden but nonetheless structures the outside world. (McGowan 2007: 24)

As such, Lynch's films – and *Lost Highway* in particular – provide insight into *the traversal of the fantasy* through vicarious means (that is, through the filmic medium), whilst positioning the viewer in a certain (albeit painful) proximity to these elements without putting his or her own sanity at risk. Or, put slightly differently, Lynch's films provide a *relatively* safe means of approaching the traumatic Real and perceiving the fictive (yet necessary) role of fantasy without collapsing the distinction between them or eliding the viewer's implication in their effects. And more significantly, in doing so we – the audience – *are thus compelled to confront a fundamental Lacanian truth*. Indeed, a truth that Lacan's acolytes will didactically demonstrate to us if we fail to recognise or grasp it for ourselves.

A LYOTARDIAN LYNCH

If we now turn to Lyotard we find challenges to the accounts that we have discussed so far: irrespective of whether we begin with, on one hand, Lyotard's critique in *Discourse, Figure* of textuality and the types of reading practice which privileged the discursive and conceptual understanding, or his critique of semiotics and structuralism in his later 'libidinal' works, on the other, we nonetheless find a distinct resistance to the kind of reading offered above. Let us take the critique of semiotics in *Libidinal Economy* (LE 43–9) first, as a counterargument against the general tendency to see Lynch's films in terms of signs that need to be interpreted so that their supposed hidden meaning may be rendered apparent.

Lyotard critiques semiotics as a form of nihilism, rooted in a Platonic 'two-world' theory, in which one world is elevated at the expense of the other. Nietzsche argued that the assumption of a (Platonic, Christian) supersensuous 'true world' devalues the sensuous world we experience, and Lyotard argues that the semiotic theory of meaning repeats the same structure: when sensuous, material things are taken as signs of an ideal meaning, the value of the sensuous thing is negated. Against this nihilism, *Libidinal Economy* develops a 'libidinal materialism', in which the sensuous is accorded value by being seen as charged with *affect*. In various places in the writings of his libidinal period, Lyotard supplies an example from Hans Bellmer's writings which illustrates the difference between semiotic nihilism and 'libidinal intensity': A person with a toothache digs their fingernails into their palm. The palm can be taken as a sign for the toothache, or both the aching tooth and the palm can be taken as pains, as sites of intensity on the body; the clenched hand acting as an energetic transformer delocalising the pain, drawing it away from the tooth through a material bodily flow (Bellmer 2006; Lyotard 1976: 105; LRG 308–9).

Not only does Stewart present Lynch's films as a series of ciphers to be decoded, as replete with signs to be interpreted, but the very meaning he uncovers in Lynch's work is a kind of Platonic 'two-world theory'; that is, the very metaphysical view which Lyotard sees as paralleling the semiotic theory of meaning. What is laid out in Stewart is a path to what Lyotard calls 'disintensification'. Stewart introduces the basic procedures that Lyotard identifies as characteristic in the usual setting up of a rationally meaningful structure: for a start, find repetitions, and suppose them to be the meaningful elements. Treat them as signs – they refer to something. Then, advanced semiotics – what they refer to are themselves signs, so all the signs are interconnected in a meaningful web. In this way, Stewart treats not just individual films as narratives, but the entirety of Lynch's work as a kind of metanarrative. Moreover, what everything supposedly means is anchored in the other world, the 'great Zero', as Lyotard calls it, which can never be made fully present.

We see in Stewart's interpretation of Lynch a clear illustration of all semiotic approaches, in which the basic structure of the nihilism of semiotics as Lyotard understands it is evident: every time an intense effect (acinematic scenography) occurs in the film, Stewart treats it *not* as significant in itself because of its sensorial qualities and effects on our bodies, but instead as signifying some hidden meaning, typically the existence of another realm lurking behind this world. The nihilism could not be more clear: the sounds and images themselves are disintensified by being treated as signifiers referring to supposed signifieds, and ultimately to some supposedly transcendent meaning. From a Lyotardian perspective, this is a way of 'numbing' ourselves to the aesthetic experiences Lynch's highly creative invention of cinematic elements might otherwise allow: it directs us away from the sensuous, to the intelligible *meaning*.

Next, let us consider the attempts, such as those of Žižek and McGowan, to give Lynch's films a specifically Lacanian meaning. While Lyotard's own early works draw heavily on psychoanalytic theory, he opposes the mainstream, reductive psychoanalytic account which treats artworks as simply the disguised expression of phantasies (and thus as symptoms, or signs, of the psychopathology of the artist). Moreover, he explicitly develops arguments against Lacanian psychoanalysis, for reasons he perhaps most clearly articulates many years later, in his autobiographical *Peregrinations*:

> The anger I felt against Lacan's reading of Freud was related to the third term, the Symbolic, to which the entire field of language and knowledge belongs. . . . in such a schema, to apprehend . . . forms and appreciate them, as we once used to say, by feeling pleasure or pain, which is merely taste, would offer nothing but an occasion to be deceived by 'our' unconscious. I considered this to be an emergency situation and that something had to be done to save a place for beauty and sentiment, given the imperial preference granted by the Lacanian system to the concept. (P 10–11)

Lyotard's objection to Lacan is thus to a kind of psychoanalytic theory which conforms to the traditional philosophical devalorisation of sensuous forms, of the aesthetic, in relation to conceptual knowledge. While his explicit resistance is aimed at the 'structuralist' Lacan, and the readings of Lynch we surveyed above draw on the later Lacan, the thinker of the Real, we nevertheless see much of what concerned Lyotard as persisting in these readings.[6] That is, they do not treat film itself as an art, in which the aesthetic effects of the sounds and moving images are accorded value for their own sake. Rather, they are interpreted in terms of a meaning, where that meaning turns out to be Lacan's theoretical discourse. Although the theme of the Real is frequently invoked, it is made to play the role of a theoretical concept which completes the desire for a closure of meaning through theoretical interpretation, rather than be allowed to persist in the work itself (or in the theory) as that gap or lacunae in meaning which Lacan's idea indicates. Moreover, the nature of the overall meaning imputed to Lynch's films – the *traversal of the fantasy* – confirms Lyotard's objection that it is only the clarity of rational knowledge (Lacanian discourse) which is presented as allowing us to escape the lures of desire, lures constructed from filmic images.

The resistance to such readings that Lyotard's work suggests does not deny that Lynch's films, or film in general, can be interpreted along Lacanian lines, nor presume to offer a better interpretation of what any film 'means'. Indeed, one could suggest that *Discourse, Figure* is in fact not so much Lyotard's attempt to refute Lacan's ideas (such as the gaze and the Real) but rather to transform them in such a way as to free them from their negative and determinative aspects and thus render them more open-ended. In particular, the figural as a transgressive element that undoes wish-fulfilment provides an alternative possibility to the notions of desire as lack, the gaze and the Real, and a more productive way of approaching Lynch's works – but not in order to 'read' these works differently (in fact, *not to 'read' them at all*) or to derive from them a general theory of cinema or spectatorship. Rather, what is at stake in a 'Lyotardian Lynch' is a change of emphasis, from interpreted meaning to aesthetic experience on the level of sensation. The aim is not so much to offer an alternative theory, then, as to facilitate an encounter or 'event'.

The most striking thing about Lynch's films is *the way that they affect us at the same time as frustrating our attempts to make coherent sense of them*. The semiotic and psychoanalytic approaches attempt to explain this mysterious power by asserting that there *is* a coherent meaning, but one that lies beneath the surface and acts on us unconsciously. The Lyotardian approach, by contrast, argues that the unconscious and desiring elements work on the 'good' forms of narrative-representative cinema and *deform* them, in a manner akin to the operations of the dream-work in Freud. The power of Lynch's films is thus located in their irrationality, and on the level of the sensuous, of their formal and material qualities. Let us proceed now to a positive account of a 'Lyotardian Lynch'. We will briefly sketch two points from Lyotard's works to indicate how we think a Lyotardian encounter with Lynch might be developed.[7]

1. *The Dream-work*

Discourse, Figure mounts a powerful polemic against 'reading' artworks, against treating them as intelligible structures whose signs simply need to be decoded. The motivation of this polemic is a desire to uphold the sensuous specificity of artworks, to return us to an appreciation of art in terms of its aesthetic qualities. As we have seen, Lyotard points to *desire* as the 'figural' force which forms and deforms plastic elements, and works creatively to construct art. In *Discourse, Figure*, Lyotard mounts an argument against the Lacanian understanding of the unconscious as structured like a language, because such an interpretation seems to leave no room for desire in the transgressive sense in which Lyotard thinks it needs to be understood in order to account for art. This argument proceeds by way of an interpretation of Freud on the dream-work. He cites an important note by Freud to support his approach:

> Many analysts have become guilty of falling into another confusion which they cling to with equal obstinacy. They seek to find the essence of dreams in their latent content and in so doing they overlook the distinction between the latent dream-thoughts and the dream-work. At bottom, dreams are nothing more than a particular *form* of thinking, made possible by the condition of the state of sleep. It is the *dream-work* which creates that form, and it alone is the essence of dreaming (*das Wesentliche am Traum*) – the explanation of its peculiar nature. (Freud 1953–74, vol. V: 506)

Lyotard's central contention is that desire should not be understood as legibly constituted latent content, but as the plastic force which deforms such thoughts in order to produce the manifest content. Desire does not signify, but *works*. For Lyotard, in this period of his thought, this power of desire to produce forms, and to 'deform' the recognisable forms of both our habitual perception and unconscious wishes, is the secret power of art.

Against Lacan's assertion that the processes of the dream-work can be explained according to linguistic operators (he draws on Jacobson's analysis of metaphor and metonymy in order to explain condensation and displacement), Lyotard argues that we must understand them as *plastic* operators, working on forms (or 'things') instead of words. Freud names four such processes – condensation, displacement, considerations of representability, and secondary revision. Lyotard focuses on the first two as indicating the radical processes of desire, while the second two merely ready them for presentation in a form more acceptable to the 'secondary processes'. He explains them as follows.

Condensation names the way that multiple dream-thoughts may be 'condensed' into fewer dream-thoughts or images. Lyotard explains: '*Condensation* must be understood as a physical process by means of which one or more objects occupying a given space are reduced to a smaller volume, as is the case when a gas becomes a liquid' (DF 238). Against Lacan, Lyotard notes that Freud insists that condensation – far from applying operators that are properly linguistic – treats words as though they are things. In condensation, the transparency characteristic of signifiers is transformed into the opacity characteristic of vision: one side is shown, the other is hidden (yet in a sense they are still one). Lyotard explains this process with the image of a piece of paper, on which the 'primary text' of the dream-thoughts is written, being crumpled: what remains legible are only partial distortions of this primary text, like the manifest content of the dream. In this way, condensation appears as a *transgression* of rational discourse (and not one of its operations).

Displacement refers to the way that a libidinal investment (cathexis) can be 'displaced' from one thought or image to another (to take a classic example, feelings you have about your father might be displaced onto another authority figure, such as your boss at work). For Lyotard, displacement works in conjunction with, and as a preparatory step towards, condensation. It concerns changes in emphasis with regard to the initial text of the dream-thoughts. Taking the image of the crumpled paper, it is as if displacement acts to reinforce parts of the paper, to insure they remain legible while others are crushed into disappearance. Desire, for Lyotard, is thus both the force which crumples the text, and which reinforces parts of it, keeping them readable: in both ways, it is a force of plasticity, which works on forms.

The approach to Lynch that we propose here would see the 'strange' or illogical elements of his films as precisely the work of such plastic operators. In films such as *Lost Highway* and *Mulholland Dr.*, the narrative is subject to logical, spatial, and temporal distortions that defy its reconstruction in a rationally coherent and consistent whole. Condensation and displacement are evident in elements such as the identity-swaps evident in both films, in which two people are one (condensation), or when affects associated with one become attached to another (displacement). In these and other Lynch films, slurred speech and distorted images likewise 'crumple' the cinematic 'text', leaving some traces legible while others disappear (think for example of the distorted speech of the dwarf in *Twin Peaks*, or the disconnection between speech and action in *Rabbits*).[8]

2. Libidinal economic aesthetics

After *Discourse, Figure*, Lyotard develops his reflections on desire and art into what he calls a 'libidinal economic aesthetics' (Lyotard 2015). This aesthetics depends on a distinction between two sorts of desire discussed by Freud: desire as lack, as wish, associated with representation (of the absent object of desire), and desire as positive energy or force, libido, which Lyotard will exploit to discuss nonrepresentational art. In this second sense, which Lyotard emphasises, 'desire is posed as transformable energy' (LRG 303). He explains further:

> There are two poles. One pole is that of *Wunsch-desire*, wish-desire. It entails negativity; it entails a dynamic; it entails teleology, a dynamic with an end; it entails an object, absence, a lost-object, and it also entails accomplishment, something like wish-fulfilment. *All of this produces a set-up [dispositif] which requires us to consider meaning in desire* [emphasis ours]. The other pole of the category of desire in Freud is libido-desire, process-desire, primary process . . . it is a matter of a process of energetic fluxes and the liquidation of the fluxes in what Freud calls a psychic apparatus, which is also the body, or even zones of the body, elements, organs, or partial organs, of the body. (LRG 202–3)

With respect to cinema, we may note right away that the Lacanian theories of Žižek, McGowan and others maintain themselves on the basis of desire understood in the first sense, as wish and lack. The dialectics of desire and fantasy which structures their readings of Lynch is based on desire as wish (where fantasy is an imaginative fulfilment of that wish). According to Lyotard, however, energetic libido is the more fundamental nature of desire, and one that allows us access to a radically different aesthetic.

Libidinal economic aesthetics proposes several 'elements': the reservoir of libido; *dispositifs* or 'set-ups' which channel the libido and invest it in an organised way, which transform it, while themselves being composed of libidinal energy; and various general ways to describe the economy of the libido and the values attached to it. These latter include principally the distinction between what Lyotard insists are two 'regimes' of the drives, two ways of repeating affects or libidinal intensities: Eros repeats in a manner which maintains the structure in question in a well-regulated way, while the death drive is a repetition which deregulates the structure, producing irregularities and instabilities. In the terms of 'Acinema', commercial, or narrative-representative cinema involves a repetition of images and sounds under the regime of Eros, while experimental cinema is a repetition under the regime of the death drive, in which the two poles of acinema – extremely fast movement and immobilisation – are deregulating instabilities. Under the regime of the death drive, 'the flows of energy entering into the apparatus are discharged without regard for the principle of constancy that rules the apparatus' (LRG 303).

According to Lyotard, it is Eros that is primarily operative in narrative-representative cinema, where repetitions of identifiable images work to construct a narrative, allowing the viewer to stage their desire on screen through identification with a principal character or characters. It is just such a thematic of desire as *wish* which accounts for the possibility of the kinds of psychoanalytic interpretations we reviewed above. While not disqualifying such a thematic, the second kind of desire, that of force or libido, allows us to see film operating according to a different kind of economy, where what is of interest is the intensity of the sensorial qualities of the sounds and images and the impact they have on the body. According to Lyotard, this intensity is negatively proportional to the capacity of the film to recuperate the sound or image in a higher 'meaning'. Such intensities, the matter of *acinema*, are useless and sterile with respect to meaning, like a match struck for the fun of seeing it burn (Ac 34). (And, in fact, we see precisely just such an image of an incendiary match – irreducible to (though consistent with) a higher, narrative meaning – repeatedly throughout Lynch's *Wild at Heart*.)

In Lynch's films, where others look for signs and codes to interpret them, we see and feel libidinal energy and its transformations, desire inscribed in deformed and explosive images and sounds, and the affects they transmit to bodies. Lynch's acinematic moments – pyrotechnic images exploding with energy, cascades of dreamy smoke, incongruous sounds echoing from the depths of the unconscious – are the more powerful *the less they mean* with respect to the narrative. This accounts for the effect they have on us – which tends towards an unsettling rather than a development of meaning in the film – far better than treating such effects as 'signs'. There are a plethora of such 'acinematic' images and sequences in Lynch's films. Let us make a very brief and partial inventory, if only to reclaim them from the too eager ministrations of cinema's hierophants:

- Acinematic moments of excessive movement and immobilisation, and combinations 'between' them (as Lyotard notes (ISF 64), they are effectively the same), such as the 'staccato' effect of strobing lights, or the speeding up and then slowing down to create slowly moving 'streaked' images (such as in *Lady Blue Shanghai*).
- Over-lit sequences, or 'blowing out' into a blank screen, often associated with intense feeling – ecstatically smiling faces, or sex. *Jouissance*, pleasure so intense it appears as pain, and as excess with respect to narrative meaning.
- Light effects created with blurring of focus and other techniques, frequently with no apparent value for the narrative.
- Unusual camera angles, and close-up shots of 'things' associated with the narrative, but treated in excessive detail – such as the close-ups of the phone in *More Things That Happened*.
- Industrial sounds. A displacement of the ambient sounds of the factory environment to scenes of everyday life.
- Etc.

We may adapt Lyotard's conclusions on painting, which are equally applicable for our purposes here regarding Lynch, and for (a)cinema in general:

> Our hypothesis (and our conviction) here, based on the movement of polymorphism in contemporary [cinema] and economy, is that the force of what is [filmed] does not reside in its referential power, in its seduction, its 'difference', in its status as signifier (or signified), and that is to say, in its lack, but in its plenitude of switchable libido. (LRG 329)

THE MOEBIUS STRIP

In his reading of *Lost Highway* Žižek makes much of the structure of the film as a temporal loop – which ends by returning the narrative to roughly the same point where it started – thus evoking Lacan's characterisation of the psyche as compulsively repetitive in nature. And as we have already noted, Lynch himself likens this circular movement to a Moebius strip – an idea that has exerted much fascination over critics in respect to the numerous doublings that feature in Lynch's oeuvre. But what if instead we could turn and twist this image against even itself so that it no longer lent its power in support of such determinate 'meanings', or to interpretations concerning dual worlds, 'hidden' messages, or the reiterative structure of the unconscious? Indeed, such a possibility already resides within Lyotard's work, since the Moebius strip is a topological figure employed in *Libidinal Economy* to describe the workings of desire itself. There this figure, renowned for its seeming appearance as two surfaces that are in fact one, is invoked to account for how energy travels across and discharges itself on a single conducting surface (LE 2–3). Understood in this way, the figure of the Moebius strip (the figural at work) frees us from accepting the ontological dualism attributed to Lynch's films: for what appeared to be two distinct worlds are then but the two faces of a single continuum without depth, marked not by the traversal of a fantasy but by the *dispersal of intensities*. The constant filmic references to electrical sounds, sparking wires, flames and flickering lights mark the movements, the passage and the travails of these energetic displacements. As such they denote nothing, they mean nothing, and yet they are *not* nothing: valuable in and for themselves, they are the intensities – the acinematic potential – of the libidinal economy of cinema, and of the socius in general.

NOTES

1. Allister Mctaggart (2010) suggests that throughout the various commentaries on Lynch there are five main approaches: 1) a focus on Lynch as an 'auteur' – which tends to approach his works chronologically and debate whether the aesthetic form or content are either progressive or not; 2) readings that are firmly wedded to the view that Lynch's films are politically conservative or reactionary in both form and context (e.g. misogynistic, puritanical, nostalgic, etc.); 3) a reading of the films as attesting to some kind of 'New Age' or Jungian striving for 'wholeness'; 4) interpretations that allow for reading the films 'differently' or against the grain of normative readings, without automatically committing to the position that the films are inherently conservative (e.g. feminist interpretations); 5) and finally, psychoanalytic, although predominantly Lacanian, readings. To this list we might add possibly one more: a recent growing interest in the role of affect and sensation in Lynch's works. For assorted examples of these different approaches see the respective collections edited by Sheen and Davidson 2004, Devlin and Biderman 2011 and Gleyzon 2013.
2. For an excellent discussion of the history of, and difficulties associated with, psychoanalytic attempts at interpreting culture, particularly literary texts, see Wright 1998. It is worth noting that Lyotard himself wrote a critical summary of such approaches – see his essay 'The Psychoanalytic Approach to Artistic and Literary Expression' in TP.

3. This paper forms much of chapter 7 of McGowan 2007.
4. For historical overviews of Lacanianism in film theory see the introductions in McGowan and Kunkle 2004 and McGowan 2008.
5. Apparently, this claim was originally attributed to Lynch and Gifford in the official press-kit prepared for the film's release. However they have each confirmed it in a number of interviews over the intervening years – for recent examples see Barney 2009, Odell and Le Blanc 2007, and Nochimson 2013.
6. A great deal of work could be done around the relations in play here, of which Anne Tomiche's (1994) insightful article, which compares Lyotard's and Lacan's later positions, would form an essential beginning point.
7. In the space available to us here we can do no more than give a general indication of some of the many points that could be taken up. In particular, we regret not being able to develop Lyotard's concept of 'double reversal', which provides an alternative account of the role of phantasy – and its *unfulfillment* – in artistic creation and appreciation (see DF).
8. See also Delage de Luget 2010 for a brief but notable discussion of the figural in an essay on Lynch's films.

REFERENCES

Akser, Murat (2012), 'Memory, Identity and Desire: A Psychoanalytic Reading of David Lynch's *Mulholland Drive*', *CINEJ Cinema Journal* 2:1, pp. 59–76.

Barney, Richard (2009), *David Lynch: Interviews*, Mississippi: University Press of Mississippi.

Bellmer, Hans (2006), *Little Anatomy of the Physical Unconscious, or the Anatomy of the Image*, trans. Jon Graham, New York: Dominion.

Bulkeley, Kelly (2003), 'Dreaming and the Cinema of David Lynch', *Dreaming* 13:1, pp. 49–60.

Coffeen, Daniel (2003), 'This is Cinema: The Pleated Plenitude of the Cinematic Sign in David Lynch's *Mulholland Dr.*', *Film-Philosophy* 7:7, www.film-philosophy.com/index.php/f-p/article/view/728/640 (accessed 30 March 2017).

Creed, Barbara (1988), 'A Journey Through *Blue Velvet*: Film, Fantasy, and the Female Spectator', *New Formations* 6, pp. 97–117.

Delage de Luget, Marion (2010), 'La Fragmentation, ce monstrueux: Étude sur le décloisonnement disciplinaire dans l'œuvre de Lynch', *Appareil* 6, https://appareil.revues.org/420 (accessed 30 March 2017).

Devlin, William and Biderman, Shai (eds) (2011), *The Philosophy of David Lynch*, Lexington: University Press of Kentucky.

Freud, Sigmund (1953–74), *The Standard Edition of the Complete Psychological Works of Sigmund Freud*, ed. James Strachey, London: Hogarth Press.

Gleyzon, Franois-Xavier (ed.) (2013), *David Lynch: In Theory*, Prague: Litteraria Pragensia.

Herzogenrath, Bernd (1999), 'On the *Lost Highway*: Lynch and Lacan, Cinema and Cultural Pathology', *Other Voices* 1:3, www.othervoices.org/1.3/bh/highway.php (accessed 30 March 2017)

Lyotard, Jean-François (1976), 'The Tooth, The Palm', trans. Anne Knapp and Michel Benamou, *SubStance* 5:15, pp. 105–110.
Lyotard, Jean-François (2015), 'Freud According to Cézanne', trans. Ashley Woodward and Jon Roffe, *Parrhesia* 23, pp. 26–42.
McGowan, Todd (2000), 'Finding Ourselves on a *Lost Highway*: David Lynch's Lesson in Fantasy', *Cinema Journal* 39:2, pp. 51–73.
McGowan, Todd (2007), *The Impossible David Lynch*, New York: Columbia University Press.
McGowan, Todd (2008), *The Real Gaze: Film Theory After Lacan*, New York: SUNY.
McGowan, Todd and Kunkle, Sheila (eds) (2004), *Lacan and Contemporary Film*, New York: Other Press.
Mctaggart, Allister (2010), *The Film Paintings of David Lynch: Challenging Film Theory*, Bristol: Intellect.
Nochimson, Martha (2013) *David Lynch Swerves: Uncertainty from* Lost Highway *to* Inland Empire, Austin: University of Texas Press.
O'Connor, Tom (2005), 'The Pitfalls of Media "Representations": David Lynch's *Lost Highway*', *Journal of Film and Television* 57:3, pp. 14–30.
Odell, Colin and Le Blanc, Michelle (2007), *David Lynch*, Hampenden: Kamera Books.
Schaffner, Anna Katharina (2009), 'Fantasmatic Splittings and Destructive Desires: Lynch's *Lost Highway, Mulholland Drive* and *Inland Empire*', *Forum for Modern Language Studies* 45:3, pp. 270–91.
Sheen, Erica and Davison, Annette (eds) (2004), *The Cinema of David Lynch: American Dreams, American Nightmares*, London: Wallflower Press.
Stewart, Mark Allyn (2007), *David Lynch Decoded*, Bloomington: AuthorHouse.
Tomiche, Anne (1994), 'Rephrasing the Freudian Unconscious: Lyotard's Affect-phrase', *Diacritics* 24:1, pp. 43–62.
Wright, Elizabeth (1998), *Psychoanalytic Criticism: A Reappraisal*, 2nd edn, London and New York: Routledge.
Žižek, Slavoj (1997), 'Connections of the Freudian Field to Philosophy and Popular Culture', www.lacan.com/zizlacan3.htm (accessed 30 March 2017).
Žižek, Slavoj (2000), *The Art of The Ridiculous Sublime: On David Lynch's* Lost Highway, Seattle: University of Washington Press.

CHAPTER 15

Aberrant Movement and Somatography in the Hysterical Comedies of Roméo Bosetti

Lisa Trahair

> The time has come to consider the would-be symptoms as artistic creations.
>
> Jean-François Lyotard (UM)

In his books *Discourse, Figure* and *Libidinal Economy*, and in two very short essays on cinema, 'Acinema' and 'The Unconscious as Mise-en-scène', Jean-François Lyotard considers the stakes of intermeshing psychical operations, as they have been understood by the discourse of psychoanalysis, with aesthetic practices. A handful of ideas that Lyotard formulates over the course of these works – aberrant movement, the relation between desire and mise-en-scène, and the emergent concept of somatography – are particularly relevant to the aesthetics of early film comedies. In the films of cinema's first decades, the operation of the comic is put to the task of devising for film a kind of primitive poetics. Just as the hysteric performs a kind of somatography in order to 'speak' without the use of words, the comic poetics of so-called 'primitive' cinema eschews the use of verbal discourse and circumvents the regime of perceptual reference and cognition conventionally associated with the photographic image to make mise-en-scène coincide with desire. By creating a circuit that draws on the resources of automatism to impute and insinuate, the gag gives expression to the drive independently of discursive means. Its aberrant movement sets in play a kind of 'somatographic operation', transferring psychical energy from the mechanical and corporeal world to the audience to make us laugh.

And yet, we find ourselves in a position of both agreeing and disagreeing with Lyotard over whether 'symptom' or 'artistic creation' best captures the sense of the part played by the comic in this embryonic cinematic 'language'.

L'HOMME AIMANT (1907)

In 'Acinema', Lyotard contrasts the pleasure of cinematographic movement that derives from the subordination of movement to narrative purpose with the *jouissance* experienced in the observation of movement in-itself. Is there room in Lyotard's analysis of 'acinematic' movement to understand the peculiarity of comic movement? In his discussion of the 'paradox of immobilisation' in the writings of Sade and Klossowski, Lyotard acknowledges that the 'intensification' that humiliates the whole person must take place on the representational axis:

> representation is essential to this fantasmatic; that is, it is essential that the spectator be offered instances of identification, recognisable forms, all in all, matter for memory: for it is at the price, we repeat, of going beyond this and disfiguring the order of propagation that the intense emotion is felt. It follows that the simulacrum's support . . . itself must not submit to any noticeable perversion in order that the perversion attack only what is supported, the representation of the victim; the support is held in insensibility or unconsciousness. (Ac 41)

Significantly, Lyotard's argument is built on his identification of the cinema's support being the screen and the celluloid – that on which movement is inscribed – rather than movement itself. While the question of what actually constitutes cinema's support is the topic for another paper, here we can perhaps conceive another extremity of movement in the fascination with vectoral motion that subtends the comedies of cinema's second decade.

Roméo Bosetti's 1907 film *L'homme aimanté* (*The Magnetic Man*) provides a brilliant example of both compulsive linearity (or radical contiguity) and what we will come to understand as the hypercathexis of mise-en-scène to express desire. Moreover, this hypercathexis happens at the levels of both form and content, which is to say support and fantasy, both in order to tell the story and within the story. Physical movement is the basis for the audience's absorption into the story's anecdotal form. Anecdotes, it is worth remembering, traditionally differ from narratives in their digressive nature and in their intention to reveal a secret (Cuddon 1982: 42–3).

Bosetti's film delineates the strange predicament of a man whose newly acquired attire results in all manner of objects suddenly becoming attracted to his person. It begins with two young reprobates of the Parisian streets hiding in wait behind a stationary carriage for someone to ambush. When our man enters the frame as a likely victim, they trip him, try to mug him and chase after him when he escapes. Catching his breath after eluding his assailants, the man is then squeezed from the opposite direction by two other much more menacing thugs. Escaping again and finding safe haven in his house, the man observes an ornamental suit of armour standing guard at his door and takes himself off to purchase a chain-mail vest. In the sequence that follows, the boy charged with delivering the item undertakes some charging of his own. Making a detour to a factory where his friend works, the boy unwraps the vest and lays it on the platform of a magnetising machine so that when our man takes to the streets under the protection of his new armature, the reaction he elicits is nothing short of an indiscriminate enthusiasm of the world of objects for his person. Covered in the flotsam of the world – shop signs, pieces of furniture, pots and pans – the man eventually visits the *commissariat* to report the strange nature of this latest assault. The *préfet*, seeing his gendarmes' swords twittering nervously in the man's presence, isolates the active quality of the object, and resolves the man's problem by breaking its circuitry. Upon disrobing the complainant and sending him on his way, the *préfet* delights in demonstrating the operation of 'the law' to his subordinates by bouncing the vest in front of their swords so that they rise and fall in time with his bidding. Seizing on the resemblance of the swords' movement to the erectile function, the insinuating condensation delights in the causal relation between actions and objects in the physical world by opening this world to two others: one of contagion and laughter, the other of a peculiarly cinematic metaphysics.

This oddly self-exposing little film of less than ten minutes duration exemplifies a distinctively cinematic slapstick of aberrant movement. In the first place objects are diverted from their intended purpose because their autonomous existence allows them to be channelled into the covert discourse of desire. In addition, the camera itself is drawn to the performative bodies of the mise-en-scène just as much as any of the objects in the diegesis are drawn to the man in the chain-mail vest. Its resolve to follow this movement of energy prescribes the implacably linear course of the film's editing so that onscreen movement forms a single continuous trajectory. It is thus not the case of movement being subordinated to the story but of movement and story being one and the same.

What we have here is the almost perfect illustration of the joke as it is understood by Freud: an innocent line of thought concerning the quirky behaviour of an object, and of happenstance, unfurls before us, producing in the process an atmosphere of levity and mirth. A condensation of elements occurs, and before we know it a second thought has stolen the stage, so that the anecdote speaks not simply of some misadventure in the physical world, but more tendentiously of libidinal desire, on one level rather frivolously in a form that we all recognise as the law of attraction, and on a second level in the literalisation of the obverse side of objects intended to repel. More concerned with relaying anecdotes than telling stories, cinematic comedy from the outset sought to demonstrate the force of attraction in all its novelty rather than dramatise conventional social relations; it was more interested in spectacular effects than reasonable causes and in the action of aberrant movement than the representation of life-changing events.

ABERRANT MOVEMENT AND AUTOMATISM IN HYSTERIA

The cinematic gag is of course visual and performative rather than verbal and in this respect departs from the joke as it is discussed by Freud. As a form constituted by ideas that have no immediate access to words, silent cinematic comedy quite literally derives from gagged speech. Yet, early film comedy shares its obmutescence with cultural practices and psychical pathologies in existence long before the invention of cinema, not all of which were inclined towards the methods of insinuation and aspersion that define wit. Theatrical melodrama developed as a performative art that seized upon physical gestures and elements of mise-en-scène to express affect, emotion and thought precisely because the French monarchy prohibited the use of speech on stage except in its own repertory companies, where dramatic work was subjected to official review and approval (Belton 2005: 131). Far from suppressing the expression of political dissent, this prohibition of speech facilitated the emergence of an art form that bequeathed to cinema its means to tell stories long before it discovered its voice.[1]

In 1895, the very year that the first film comedy was projected to a public audience in France, Freud and Breuer published their collection of papers, *Studies in Hysteria*. As a disease that performs a kind of corporeal cathexis in order to 'speak', hysteria as it was theorised by psychoanalysis helps us comprehend how, why and with what consequences early cinematic comedy redefined the physicality of the profilmic world. Like the spectacle of the illness of hysteria that gives us 'mute access, but access nonetheless, to the question of forms and signifiers' (Didi-Huberman 2003: 3),[2] in early cinema the comic reterritorialises the indifference of the profilmic world to make it a medium for the imagination. Just as in hysteria, where the operation of the drive seizes the habitual functioning of the body, in these early film comedies the comic represents nothing other than desire, which, like a will to power, expropriates 'reality' to produce images.

As Lyotard has duly noted, we find in Freud's work a propensity to draw connections between psychoanalysis and aesthetics. Between 1893 and 1895, Freud and Breuer studied the methodology of the hysteric as though it were aesthetic in nature. As a disease precipitated by a lost connection between cause and effect, between the 'idea' and the symptoms that nevertheless express it, hysteria has been described as a 'malady of representation' (Laplanche and Pontalis 1988: 195). The 'aesthetic' is precisely this lost connection between idea and symptom that makes representation impossible. Broadly speaking, the 'aesthetic' entails the physical cathexis of regions of the body which comes into play because an 'idea', or precipitating cause, that is inaccessible to consciousness nevertheless retains its full quota of original affective charge, while the subject is unable to abreact it by normal actions, whether by tears, violent reaction, acts of revenge or talking about it. The aesthetic of hysteria particularises itself by producing spasms, contortions and paroxysms. What is especially pertinent to our inquiry here is that Breuer goes to some lengths to insist that while some hysterical symptoms are ideogenic, meaning that they bear some resemblance to the lost idea, others are strictly idiopathic in that they derive from strictly physical excitations. With respect to idiopathic symptoms, what is essential to note is that the 'aesthetic' has a mechanical or automatic component to it.

Breuer describes the automatism or mechanism of hysteria in his account of Anna O. Breuer's patient herself became ill while nursing her sick father and suffered from the onset of a *condition seconde* or *absences*, characterised by the emergence of a recalcitrant and abject personality completely split off from her normal consciousness and prone to wild hallucinations, sleepwalking, communicating only in English (although her mother tongue was German), and suffering from hydrophobia, a convergent squint and significant paralysis and contractures in parts of her body. Breuer identifies two psychical conditions that predisposed her to illness – an underemployed brain resulting from the monotony of family life and, related to this, a habit of daydreaming, constructing, as it were, her own 'private theatre' (Breuer and Freud 2000: 41). Breuer's method of treatment was a meticulous reconnection of causes to effects, symptoms to their traumatic incident. In Anna O.'s case the traumatic incident turned out to be an unusual occurrence when Anna drifted off to sleep while sitting up with her sick father waiting for the arrival of the doctor. In a 'waking dream', Anna sees a snake approaching her father, and finds herself unable to fend it off because of the normal paralysis associated with sleep. In terms of physical innervation, Anna's body in this instance was simultaneously beset by the contradictory conditions of paralysis and arousal – the waking Anna awaiting the doctor was physically passive, yet cognitively active – which carried into her dream as affect. From this time, Anna experienced with ever greater frequency both absences and accompanying hysterical phenomena. Breuer explains: 'the opportunity multiplied for the formation of new symptoms of the same kind, and those that had already been formed became more strongly entrenched by frequent repetition' (2000: 42–3). Eventually any distressing affect with a sudden onset resulted in absences: 'chance coincidences set up pathological associations and sensory or motor disturbances, which thenceforward appeared along with the affect' (2000: 43).

In his essay 'The Unconscious as Mise-en-scène', Lyotard explicitly compares the methods of the film director and the hysteric on the basis that both work within the general 'art' of mise-en-scène, and of 'somatography', as the inscription of messages on human bodies so that they can be transmitted to other bodies (UM 44).[3] Lyotard first of all marshals classical Hollywood cinema as the kind of filmmaking practice in which the director manipulates mise-en-scène as the unconscious would use the primary processes to *disguise* desire in order to secretly fulfil some wish, only to discard Hollywood in favour of the experimental or avant-garde cinema that exemplifies the indiscernibility between mise-en-scène and desire. Michael Snow's *La Région centrale* (1971) is called upon to demonstrate that the outmoded aesthetic that lies at the heart of Freud's conception of the work of the unconscious takes its model from the Viennese theatre and opera of the late nineteenth century (though it is arguable that his analysis of the film does this only indirectly by imputing that the modernist aesthetic practices that supersede classical ones retain them via negation) and how useless the discourse of psychoanalysis is for understanding the 'most audacious inquiries in the most recent arts' and 'the stakes of "postmodernism" as a whole' (UM 51). Lyotard's analysis of *La Région centrale* endeavours, in other words, to both show the dependence of Freud's work on aesthetics and 'diminish the import' of 'his discourse' such that the imperative to seek the truth 'within the closure of representation' will be displaced by the establishment of '*perspectives* within the return of the *will*' (UM 51).

The duration of *La Région centrale* is roughly three hours. As Lyotard describes, 'the spectator's gaze is carried along supple and irregular trajectories ... carried away on a both infinite and bounded voyage that opens up every perspective on sky and ground' with 'light and colour' and 'angles and distances' subject to continuous change (UM 51). To put it more prosaically, the film shows a series of continuous sequences of a natural landscape thanks to a pre-programmed mobile camera endlessly pivoting on both its vertical and horizontal axes to create a continuous series of image loops. The mise-en-scène's elements comprise blue skies, forest landscapes, lakes and rocky terrain. No sound issues from these natural environs; the only sonic elements are the mechanical noises of the camera adjusting its course in response to the program's instructions.

The aesthetic that announces the supersession of the oppositions between fantasy/reality and truth/deception by the 'will to perspectivism' derives from the fact that the camera's movements are pre-programmed, and hence automatic, with respect to both itself and to what it sees, while the velocity of the camera's movement on each axis is independent of the other. The camera's single concession to the contingency of the environs it photographs is an adjustment of focal depth in response to the ever-changing proximity and distance of the material being photographed. But this adjustment is automatic. The program that determines the movement of the camera independently of any living sensory-motor capacity is completely indifferent to the natural world it mediates.

What needs to be kept in mind in all this is that in using Snow's film to cast aspersions on the limitations of Freud's theatrical conception of aesthetics, Lyotard is entirely dependent on the developing sophistication of Freud's thinking about the relation between mise-en-scène and desire to draw out what he finds to be the most admirable and indeed exemplary aspects of Snow's cinematic aesthetics. For one thing, the imbrication of the 'atemporality of the film' and the 'multitemporality of these stories' imitate the 'dischronisms of Freud's primary processes' (UM 53). And in as much as 'the centre of the region is a labyrinth' (UM 52), the infinite variety of the camera's scannings are visual emblems of drive-eruptions, which collect together as a series of thrusts, much as Freud's drive-thrusts are understood as successive deposits of eruptions of lava, where the first thrust remains unchanged yet impacts the elements and the composition of the thrusts that succeed it. Thrusts are thus 'distinct from one another in the time of their occurrence but . . . [each is] homogeneous within its own period' (Freud 2001: 130; UM 50).

Lyotard thus calls upon Freud's conception of the drive to dismantle the commonly held conception that psychoanalytic theory holds to the opposition between truth and deceit and reality and fantasy and that it endeavours to fix interpretation in the manner of medical science. In so doing, he withdraws interpretation from intentional consciousness and hands it over to the automatism of the camera. He proposes that gone in Snow's film is the identity between the unconscious and the director as the one who stages mise-en-scène in order to disguise a primary text by transcribing the signifiers of one kind of text into another. Instead, mise-en-scène survives as somatography because the camera interprets the program Snow fed into it. Considered as 'analogous to the mise-en-scène of desire by the unconscious', the machine transforms 'the written signifiers' of the program 'into movements and into emotions on the spectators' bodies' (UM 53). One has to acknowledge here, he says, 'the strange character of the operations perform[ed]' on the drive-material (the camera's loops or thrusts) and visual material (the body of the world as it is filmed, profilmic reality) respectively, which is that 'the condition of understanding desire' is 'not as a set of instructions promoted by some love- or hate-wish but as the will to create realities' (UM 53).

In making his case, Lyotard insists that he wants to do away with or at least displace the 'problematic of the unconscious and mise-en-scène', but what he actually does is replace an unconscious that he thinks has a capacity to interpret the primary meaning of desire with a machinic unconscious that operates automatically – nothing less, that is, than the director as automaton, the director embracing automatism!

It is no less important to grasp that in Breuer's account of hysteria, in the hysteric's 'representation' of her illness on her body, her somatography as it were, what is designated aesthetic is in fact automatic.

Breuer invokes something like the condition of *film viewing* when he observes that patients suffering from hysteria have a predisposition to hyperaesthesia – a condition brought on by pastimes like needlework and other mindless activities that induce trance-like states – that impacts the onset of illness. With the occurrence of the traumatic event, the affect associated with it is displaced onto peripheral objects in the subject's environs and the sensations that emanate from it. The subject who transforms her affect by an unconscious cathexis of the world around her is *also* a *metteur-en-scène*, but significantly – and this is a point that Lyotard all but misses – one who operates at the level of automaticity, that is, without the reflective or intentional consciousness of a director. Because of her inclination to reverie or distraction, whether habitual or symptomatic, the subject distributes the psychical energy associated with the idea to the content of the scene. The trauma induces a hypnoid state in the patient that switches on a camera inside her and records her presence in a scene that will later either elude her entirely or that she will regard with indifference.

Evidence that Breuer believes that there is an 'automatism' at work in hysterical phenomena and that the body is the site of this automatism can be found in his insistence that not all hysterical phenomena are ideogenic. Hysterical causes may be ideogenic, but hysterical symptoms are idiopathic.[4] Indeed, a disconnection between 'idea' and affect such that the 'idea' is isolated and entirely lost to consciousness ensures that the idea is *not* directly transcribed into symptoms. It is rather the idea's affect, disconnected from its cause, that attaches itself automatically to *images* associated with the original context in which the troubling 'idea' presented itself.

In arguing that not all hysterical phenomena are ideogenic, Breuer cites the lack of connection between the paralysis of Anna O.'s arm and the precipitating idea of snake-like objects that led to the onset of her illness. He thereby concludes that in the case of hysteria, one and the same physiological process may be set in motion 'equally by ideas and by peripheral and other non-psychological stimuli' (Breuer and Freud 2000: 187). Non-psychological stimuli are purely physical, such as erythema produced as a result of being irritated or touched; peripheral stimuli are preconscious impressions of the subject's environs. In the case of Anna O., we could go so far as to say that the idea might appear to be a cause, but it is really an effect of a complex confluence of contingencies.

In trying to understand the psycho-physiology of the hysteric's hallucination of pain, Breuer insists that ideas alone are insufficient explanations, observing that 'mnemic images pure and simple' cannot 'even at their greatest vividness and intensity, attain the character of objective existence which is the mark of hallucinations' (Breuer and Freud 2000: 188). To Breuer this both suggests that the perceptual apparatus operates independently of the 'organ which stores up and reproduces sense impressions in the form of mnemic images' and leads him to posit the existence of 'some abnormal condition of the apparatuses concerned with the conduction and sensation of pain' (2000: 188). The hallucinations of pain from which hysterics suffer he concludes are caused by an 'abnormal excitability of the apparatus concerned with sensations of pain' (2000: 189). Such excitability comes about *both* by the 'spur of ideas' and the abnormal stimulation or excitation of peripheral stimuli (2000: 189). This abnormal stimulation or excitation of peripheral stimuli is what Freud will later call displacement. At this time, Breuer explains the hysterical conversion by comparing it with the movement of electricity through compromised circuitry. When an electrical system is overloaded, the weaker points of its insulation are susceptible to breaking, with the result that electricity will be conducted at 'abnormal points' and result in the occurrence of 'abnormal facilitations'. Moreover, because 'permanent change has been produced at these points', it is more than likely that the disturbance will recur whenever 'the tension is sufficiently increased' (2000: 203).

The treatment of hysteria is not therefore simply a matter of undertaking symbolic interpretations, as Lyotard at times implies. Certainly relations between symptoms and causes must be recovered, but an indirect chain of causal links obscures the original precipitating cause from view. What is important is that because the causes of the precipitating idea are received automatically, which is to say without conscious cathexis, the affect that rightly attaches to the idea cannot be expended. On entering into a veritable labyrinth of complex associations, the idea is transformed into unrelated ideas, and comes up against other experiences that can even contradict it. The affect of the original idea can thus be subject to rectification by other completely unrelated ideas. A complete hysterical conversion is said to have occurred when an abnormal affective reflex has 'become completely facilitated by frequent repetition', thereby obliterating 'the operative force of the [original] releasing ideas so totally that [in relation to those ideas] the affect itself emerges to a minimal extent only, or not at all' (Breuer and Freud 2000: 206). The precipitating idea, once lost to consciousness, is denied access to the dimension of temporality that would erode it in an orderly way.

Breuer's hypothesis of idiopathic facilitations or aberrant movements of psychical energy is confirmed in the pathology of Anna O., who experienced an entirely new set of symptoms once she began to manifest the *condition seconde*. The origin of such symptoms, which comprised a number of 'paralytic contractures in her left extremities and paresis of the muscles raising her head' (Breuer and Freud 2000: 44) could not be located in the original traumatic hallucination. The fact that they disappeared completely when Anna was cured, whereas others, only ever in abeyance, returned from time to time (undoubtedly, 'whenever the tension in the system was sufficiently increased'), is further confirmation that they had no ideogenic sources: 'their appearance was not due to the same psychical process as that of the other symptoms, but is attributed to a secondary extension of that unknown condition which constitutes the somatic foundation of hysterical phenomena' (2000: 45). The body, in other words, undertakes abnormal facilitations independently of thought.

And this means that the aesthetics of the symptom formation that Breuer and Freud attributed to the hysteric in 1895 was not as theatrical as Lyotard suggests.

ABNORMAL FACILITATIONS IN TWO MORE BOSETTI FILMS

The automatism that Breuer goes to such pains to insist upon in his account of the 'aesthetics of hysteria' is part of the metaphysics of cinema, whether it is actively taken up by filmmakers (as we see in reflexive modernist works and in cinematic comedy) or merely put to work in the utilisation of elements of the mise-en-scène as tropes for the development of narrative. Another two Bosetti films held in the Collection Parisienne at the Forum des Images in Paris show us further elaborations of the comic cathexis of the physical world that characterised early cinematic slapstick. The peripatetic formula of *L'homme aimanté* is retained in a second Bosetti film (this one co-directed with Louis Feuillade) entitled *Une dame vraiment bien* of 1908, only in this film the woman herself rather than any prosthesis is the cause of the mayhem that ensues, and, unlike the man of the previous film, the woman remains strangely indifferent to her undoing of the habitual operations of the world around her. Even though the camera follows her promenading through the streets of Paris, its interest lies in what happens to the men who are the unintended recipients of the image she projects and who pay the price of 'agitation and libidinal expense'. When she waltzes past a man cleaning the street outside his shopfront, his distraction causes him to sally a nearby woman with bucket of water, and when her path crosses the trajectory of a second man he walks into a post. As the anecdote plays out, the symbolic erection takes greater shape without ever (of course) becoming visible. A third man rides his bike into a table, a fourth falls over, another sets his hose on a passer-by, yet another sideswipes a man with the two-by-four that he carries. When the woman's presence results in a parade of soldiers falling into disarray, two policemen, again literal representatives of the law, dutifully chase after her, cover her with a veil, and accompany her to her destination.

The aberrant movement of a third Bosetti film, *Le tic*, also made in 1908, of a little over nine minutes duration, embraces subject matter closer to the concerns of psychoanalysis. Again the tale is anecdotal and its normal movement is peripatetic: a pair of newlyweds, the Lèridons, have decided to take in the sites of Paris for their honeymoon. What is again immediately noticeable is that the camera altogether forsakes the city's monuments to focus on the effects of Julie Lèridon's uncontrollably twitching eye. As the precipitating cause of the disarray, the tic itself is never made directly visible to the audience. In a hotel room, the couple unpack and prepare themselves to go out, when Monsieur Lèridon (in an intertitle) instructs his wife to mind her tic. The camera cuts to a medium shot of the couple, who kiss in agreement with each other as Julie bobs her head from side to side to show that she has her eyes under control. Out on the street, the Lèridons soon have a trail of men following them, each one believing that Julie has sent them a secret sign of some future promise. First an old man, then a 'calicot', then an omnibus driver, a beggar, a bookseller, a policeman, and finally an old war veteran and a whole lot of dogs. The dogs, like the automatism of the body that Breuer observes, comprise a surplus whose presence is not an effect of the originating trauma, yet serve to drive home the message that it is as if Julie were on heat.

Between 1906 and 1916 Bosetti made more than 300 films, most of them, one imagines, are short little tales of the kind described here. Of what are they symptoms? Why, nothing other than the drive itself. Formed within the ambivalence of the drive, in Bosetti's anecdotal films the cinematic gag unfurls itself to create irregular trajectories. It does not disguise desire but manifests it by seizing what is unconscious in the image. While each film evidences its 'thrust' distinctly from the others, taken together, 'homogeneous within its period', these films take the first steps towards finding cinema's non-discursive means of 'communication'.

CONCLUSION

In this chapter I have used Lyotard's writings on psychoanalysis and cinematic aesthetics to examine early cinematic comedy's penchant for aberrant movement. What these films demonstrate is a conception of the medium where 'the support' is neither the apparently neutral substance of the celluloid nor the blackness of the screen on which film is projected but the autopoietic movement of the physical world and its indomitable capacity to undo the bodies that inhabit it. In both his 'Acinema' and 'The Unconscious as Mise-en-scène' essays, Lyotard understands cinematography as a kind of writing of movement where the director attempts to disguise desire by restraining autopoietic movement through processes of ordering and exclusion. It is my argument that in both essays Lyotard too lightly heeds cinema's curiosity about the automaticity of aberrant movement. In the second essay he would have done better to more rigorously examine the mise-en-scène of the hysteric than suggest that Freud's conception of desire and its relation to the unconscious is limited by the dramaturgy of Viennese opera as an ordering of the various component arts to stage a story that was once a script. In his study of hysteria, Breuer makes it clear that the hysteric's unconscious is comprised not of thoughts so much as fragments of scenes and impulses that have no words, and that the conversion of the traumatic event is not a symbolic act but an automatic one, borne of both abnormal stimulation and aberrant movement as the means of facilitating idiopathic expression. These movements are not equivalent to the figurative linkages between signifiers and signifieds that make meaning possible but are expressive of a desire that has nowhere to go. If by replacing the cinematography of his 'Acinema' essay with the somatography of the hysteric in 'The Unconscious as Mise-en-scène', Lyotard succeeds in acknowledging more radical possibilities for the aesthetics of cinema, this is because Snow, like the hysteric, depends on the automaticity of the unconscious, whereby the idea of interpretation as a volitional activity, on which the notion of disguise depends, is put into question. But there is no particular reason why access to this aspect of movement should be the prerogative of the avant-garde alone. In the anecdotal form of the film comedies of cinema's first decades there is no question of the transcription of a literary medium that precedes the cinematic one. What drives these films is aberrant movement itself, in every instance an uncontainable eruption of desire and a determination not to let go of it.

Has the time come to treat symptoms as artistic creations? The catalyst of such a plea is surely admirable in its condemnation of the stranglehold that normative interpretations have on individuals and its determination to create scope for acknowledging the infinite differences that comprise civil society, but it is not clear that ignoring the trauma that lies at the basis of the symptom's production is a prudent course of action. Moreover, today such a plea smacks of all that was wrong with a certain postmodernism – though perhaps not the one that Lyotard makes reference to in his essay on mise-en-scène. Even so, the idea offers little comfort to a world racked by the violence that ensues from the exclusion of whole sections of civil society from effective and legitimate political participation and from a media that is wont to confuse symptoms with artistic creations and to capitalise on this very confusion as a means of sustaining itself. On the other hand, the scope of aesthetic *analysis* pursued in the name of psychoanalysis, including Lyotard's contribution, could be usefully extended to the disordered movements, or symptoms, of those political and social realities that ensue from such exclusions. Treating artistic creations as symptoms also seems like a viable proposition in the alternative it offers to the polarity between mainstream cinema as an ideological manifestation of capitalism's superstructure and avant-garde works as practices determined entirely by the 'good' intentions of the artist.

NOTES

1. In addition to developing a system of gestures, which were subsequently recorded by François Delsarte, theatrical melodrama used quintessentially pictorial means to make definitive statements by arresting action and composing actors in tableaux vivants, tableaux that were not unlike the 'attitudes passionelles' that Charcot observed in the behaviour of 'madwomen' at the Salpêtrière.
2. In *Invention of Hysteria: Charcot and the Photographic Iconography of the Salpêtrière*, Georges Didi-Huberman sums up hysteria as a 'pain that was compelled to be invented as *spectacle and image*' (2003: 3).
3. The director's work also involves 'diagraphy' as a change in the space of inscription.
4. Significantly, Breuer distinguishes his and Freud's position from Moebius', who argued that hysteria comprises a disease where all pathological phenomena are caused by ideas, only to subsequently qualify this assertion by admitting that some hysterical phenomena correspond to these ideas by resemblance whereas others do not (Moebius 1888: 39). The phenomena that correspond to ideas are those caused by auto-suggestion, as when the idea of not being able to move a limb causes paralysis, while other phenomena, although still caused by ideas, 'do not correspond to them in their content' (Breuer and Freud 2000: 186).

REFERENCES

Belton, John (2005), *American Cinema, American Culture*, 2nd edn, New York: McGraw-Hill.
Breuer, Josef and Freud, Sigmund (2000), *Studies on Hysteria* [1893–95], trans. James Strachey, New York: Basic Books.
Cuddon, J. A. (1982), *A Dictionary of Literary Terms*, Harmondsworth: Penguin.
Didi-Huberman, Georges (2003), *Invention of Hysteria: Charcot and the Photographic Iconography of the Salpêtrière*, trans. Alisa Hartz, Cambridge, MA: MIT Press.
Freud, Sigmund (1976), *Jokes and Their Relation to the Unconscious* [1905], ed. and trans. James Strachey, Pelican Freud Library, Vol. 6, Harmondsworth: Penguin.
Freud, Sigmund (2001), 'Instincts and their Vicissitudes' [1915], in *The Standard Edition of the Complete Psychological Works of Sigmund Freud*, Vol. XIV, ed. James Strachey, London: Random House, pp. 109–40.

Gunning, Tom (1986) 'The Cinema of Attraction: Early Film, Its Spectator and the Avant-Garde', *Wide Angle* 8:3–4, pp. 63–70.
Gunning, Tom (1989) 'An Aesthetic of Astonishment: Early Film and the (In)credulous Spectator', *Art and Text* 34, pp. 31–45.
Laplanche, Jean and Pontalis, Jean-Bertrand (1988), *The Language of Psychoanalysis*, trans. Donald Nicholson-Smith, London: Karnac Books.
Moebius, P. J. (1888), 'Uber den Begriff der Hysterie', *Zbl. Nervenheilk*, 11:66.

Appendices

APPENDIX 1

Lyotard's Film Work

Claudine Eizykman and Guy Fihman[1]

In his *Peregrinations*, which constitutes an intellectual anamnesis, Jean-François Lyotard insisted on the eclectic aspect of his philosophical approach. He had been reproached for this eclecticism, but here he claimed it as his own, specifying that this eclecticism is based on the demand to accord an equal importance to the aesthetic, the political and the ethical. Lyotard's successive works return to this fundamental triple equipollence, which he traced back to his three earlier 'vocations': 'I wanted to become a monk . . . a painter, or historian' (P 1). These represent 'three poles to which I have always been attracted' (P 6), and Lyotard specified that 'all three entities are active, unavoidable, in the three fields with the same force, even if not present in the same way' (P 5). 'Acinema' is thus given as an example of an approach relevant to a 'comparison of politics with art'.

The exigency of this unprecedented philosophical triad is significant for all Lyotard's writings and is found equally in his other works, ones which he didn't mention in *Peregrinations* and which have been given little consideration. It seems to us that it is worth bearing testimony to some of these other works, in particular those linked with cinema and in which we shared, as companions in some of his peregrinations.

AESTHETICS, POLITICS, ETHICS

This triad was revealed in all its essentials to the students of philosophy at the University of Nanterre who followed the course Lyotard taught, in the university year 1967–8, on Discourse and Figure. The successive episodes of this course led up to May '68. This was an occasion to see the ex-militant of Socialism or Barbarism reappear, commenting, with the force of an extreme pertinence, on the figural, surging up in the order of rules.

THE FILM WORK[2] (1969–70)

May '68 transformed relations at the university, as well as the work that was done there. This was indicated by Lyotard's institution of a closed seminar, dedicated to an in-depth analysis of the Freudian approach to the dream. Material from this seminar would turn up in 'The Dream-Work Does Not Think' (an article, and then a section of *Discourse, Figure*), which is a non-canonical approach to this central aspect of psychoanalysis. This precise return to the operations of the dream-work as described by Freud, particularly along with some images borrowed from the photography and cinema of the era used as models, suggested a novel approach to the filmic fact: to understand the film-work from the dream-work and vice versa, by taking into account the new filmic modalities of electronic cinema.[3] Thus, Freud analyses condensation on the model of photographic superimposition, up to the point of viewing the creation of the dream's dramatis personae on the model of the composite photography of Francis Galton. What then, for example, would be the mechanism of condensation/displacement in the case of electronic images combining heterogeneous elements through the modality of an embedded form? That remained to be seen.

L'AUTRE SCÈNE (1969–72)

'That remained to be seen': which meant to experiment, especially as video – the Latin name given to electronic cinema – was itself in the process of changing. The group constituted within the seminar then closed, and opened onto *Le Travail du film* [The Film Work], which took up this hypothesis in quite a singular experiment. Access to the Research Studio of the ORTF was negotiated, and obtained from its director Pierre Schaeffer, in exemption of its usual production rules. The scenario of the experiment was the project of a critical approach to the functioning of an advertisement, chosen by Lyotard, for the Gillette razorblade: '*cette lame est amoureuse de votre peau*' ['*this blade is in love with your skin*']. The video filming sessions included experiments with formal operations, conducted within the limits of instrumental and institutional possibilities. They were a singular learning process in several ways, not the least of which proved to be due to the severe technical-industrial prohibition of the 'good image': particularly, in the present case, that of a beautiful woman's face. On the other hand, there was also a battle for independent control of the work. The experiment resulted in a film in two versions, celluloid and video: *L'Autre scène* [*The Other Scene*] (1969 for the silent version, 1972 for the sound version), signed by Dominique Avron, Claudine Eizykman, Guy Fihman and Jean-François Lyotard.

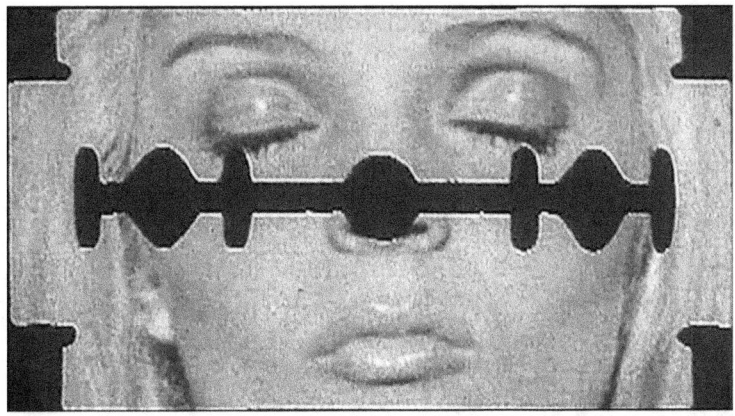

Still from *L'Autre Scène*

ACINEMA (1973)

L'Autre scène: this film, atypical in every respect, soon produced a further effect. Dominique Noguez, who was then preparing a special edition of the *Revue d'esthétique* dedicated to 'Cinéma: Théorie, Lectures' [Cinema: Theory, Readings], solicited an article from Lyotard, who only accepted on the condition that an article by each of the co-directors of *L'Autre scène* was also published: Dominique Avron's 'Remarques sur le travail du son dans la production cinématographique standardisée' ['Remarks on the Work of Sound in Standardised Cinematographic Production'], Claudine Eizykman's 'Que sans discours apparaissent les films' ['How Films Appear Without Discourse'], and Guy Fihman's 'D'où viennent les images claires?' ['Where Do Clear Images Come From?']. As is indicated in the original publication, these articles accompany Lyotard's 'Acinema'.

THE FILMIC CRITIQUE OF IDEOLOGIES (1973–4)

L'Autre scène would be the start of a vast filmic critique of ideologies, a project disproportionate to any practical realisation. There were nevertheless two other works realised in film: *France-Soir* (1973) by Guy Fihman, which exhibits, over a trimester, the immobile movement of the page layout of a daily newspaper, and Lyotard's *Mao Gillette* (1974), a personal filmic essay displaying the proximity, not to say identity, of the mechanisms of the cult of personality and of advertising. In order to make this film, Lyotard carefully selected certain documents, pieces chosen from his personal files, that he

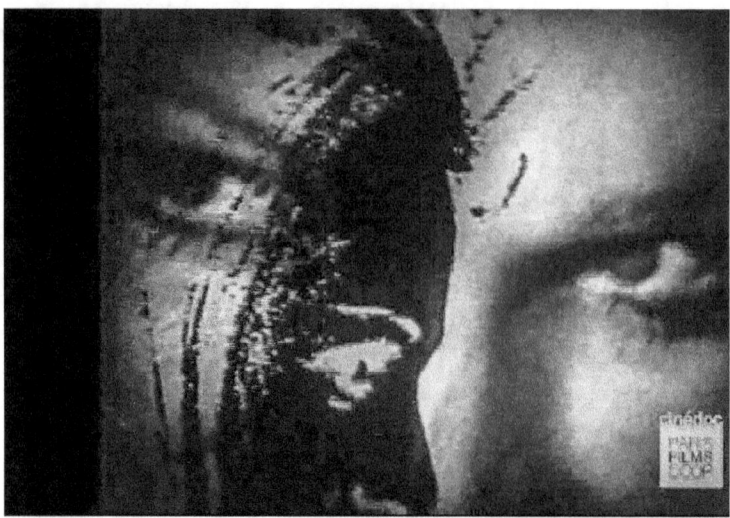

Still from *Mao Gillette*

wanted to be mixed up with plans for *L'Autre scène*. The assemblage of these two heterogeneous series necessitated filming with an animation stand with virtual image, to which one of the authors (Guy Fihman) provided his strictly limited assistance to a mediation/translation between Lyotard's aestheticophilosophical demands and the technical imperatives of the cameras, animation stand, and virtual image.

EXPRMTL 5 – KNOKKE-LE-ZOUT (1974–5)

For the fifth, and last, International Festival of Experimental Film, its director and founder Jacques Ledoux, aided by René Micha – after the successes and the scandals of the last one in 1967 – introduced video, theatre and music: the non-cinematic arts. They invited an impressive number of universities, critics, representatives of cultural institutions, and artists, who were invited each day to discuss the themes of the experimental films, plays and concerts which they could attend. Ledoux and Micha's project aimed to make experimental cinema known to and appreciated by an intellectual and artistic public. Particularly in France, experimental cinema was subject to a strong rejection, as much on the part of certain cinema journals as on the part of institutions. Several participants, specialists of avant-garde literature, displayed a virulent opposition to the experimental films, of which Lyotard was one of the rare defenders. What was at stake then was the place of cinema and the technological arts which had not yet gained the status of subjects of reflection in universities; they would only become such in the following decade. This situation revealed France's significant delay in these areas. Lyotard, however, understood.

TRIBUNE SANS TRIBUN (1978)

This work is exemplary of the concomitant triad of aesthetics, ethics and politics. Solicited by public television for an opinion [*tribune*] for a series reserved for intellectuals, Lyotard successfully performed the project and the programme of his title: a podium without a speaker [*une tribune sans tribun*].[4] It's his text, it's his voice, they're his intonations, it's his face, it's his look, it's his hair. But with a subtle game he concocted, a game of desynchronisation of the sound and the image, of duplication, of inversion – with this *dispositif* he managed to avoid this televisual intervention becoming a spectacle. It's one of the rare examples of film in which suspense is aroused and sustained by a critical argument concerning the relations of power, media, and those who speak, the intellectuals.

COLLEGE AND COOPERATIVE (1979)

At the end of the 1970s, Dioptre, a gallery in Geneva, invited us – Jean-François Lyotard, Claudine Eizykman and Guy Fihman – to present a selection of our films. Return trip by train, installation, presentation and projections: Lyotard experimented then with the mode of existence of independent-experimental filmmakers, of their cooperative form of organisation. And when he contributed to the organisation of the Collège international de philosophie, thinking all the while of one of his last interventions, he said that this institution is to philosophers what the cooperative is to independent-experimental filmmakers.

THE IDEA OF THE SWEET (1979–80)

A partire dal Dolce (*Starting from the Sweet*): this is the Italian title that its author Gianfranco Baruchello – painter, plastic artist, maker of film and video – gave to an experimental video recording, around twenty hours long, with different personalities, starting from the idea of the sweet (French *doux*, Italian *dolce*). Lyotard agreed to participate, and an improvised dialogue with Baruchello was filmed in Fillerval and Paris. This complex discussion, lasting two-and-a-half hours, displays a form of speech that is theoretical but particular, neither academic nor conventional.

À BLANC (1980–2)

At the beginning of the 1980s, the cultural service of the Ministry of Foreign Affairs launched an institutional series on the topic 'Painters Filmmakers', of which different parts saw different fortunes. The dialogue proposed between Lyotard and Jacques Monory, on painting and cinema, was the occasion of several filmings.[5] Lyotard then hijacked the cameraman's equipment in order to make *À Blanc, à propos d'une série* [*To White: apropos of a series*], an audio-visual essay carefully analysing a group of pictures by René Guiffrey.

Let us recall that Lyotard's apprenticeship to cinema and video art – these games of electronics – dates from 1969; that in 1976 he wrote a text, 'On Five Paintings by René Guiffrey' (in MT2), and that in 1982 he produced *À Blanc*, on another series by Guiffrey, with the collaboration of the painter. This series was even more understated than that of 1976. The formats of these paintings were always square and white, inlaid with a single, interior central square, constituted by four protruding stops and composing, under these particular conditions, a form in relief. The dimensions of the pictures ranged from 30 cm to more than 2 metres around the edges. In the text from 1976, Lyotard raised the unfaithfulness of descriptions of works of art, which seemed to him perhaps due to the fact that 'they never succeed in revealing an object . . . [since this object] cannot be reproduced with clichés' (MT2 125) Nevertheless, six years later he 'reproduced' a series in film with commentaries which, far from arousing an ungrateful feeling of incompletion, made Guiffrey's painting visible, transitively and differently. Indeed, his critique of 1976 had not sufficiently explained the *dispositif* by which the effects described were produced. Because it was produced and exhibited, the filmic *dispositif* of *À Blanc* captured the effects of appearance and disappearance of the inlaid square, the reversals of values and tones up to the complete effacement of all trace of painting and the emergence of (or return to) the blank canvas, then obscure. All these changes, recorded and reproduced – but also produced – by the film, result from the *dispositif* employed in order 'to see' Guiffrey's painting. This *dispositif* involves Lyotard moving several pictures: he makes them turn and move around before stopping. It also involves the movement of the camera, notably above the series of paintings, placed on the ground, which activates deformations of perspective. Lyotard gave a mobility to each picture-support, making continuous transformations surge forth. The commentary of 1976 perhaps needs this artistic, filmic stage to express its insight. Thus with *À Blanc*, the sense of expression and the effects of film converge: to make the white fully appear and thus to complete the painting is at the same time to experimentally push the artistic activity to its limit with film.

CERISY (1982)

The colloquium at Cerisy, *Comment juger? À partir de Jean-François Lyotard* [*How to Judge? Starting from Jean-François Lyotard*], held, beyond the discussions, several artistic workshops, among which was a substantial one on film: the workshop *Acinema*, conducted by Guy Fihman in the presence of Peter Kubelka and Michael Snow. Lyotard had dedicated an article to the work of the latter – 'The Unconscious as Mise-en-scène' – which extends the thematic of filmic experimentation a long way. Peter Kubelka's *Arnulf Rainer* and Michael Snow's *Presents* were screened in a plenary session in a room of the Chateau de Cerisy which was not well adapted for such a screening. We imposed on the participants some conditions, close to those of Plato's cave: not to leave during the screening! This revealed that certain philosophers had a strong resistance to filmic experimentation.

LES IMMATÉRIAUX (1985)

Six years after *The Postmodern Condition*, the exhibition *Les Immatériaux*, of which Lyotard was the *commissaire général*, was a historical milestone: it marked the advent of the postmodern society in a series of productions. Initially, the Centre de création industrielle [Centre for Industrial Creation] (CCI) of the Georges Pompidou Centre had scheduled an exhibition on 'new materials', a project first conducted by Thierry Chaput, who then invited Lyotard to participate. Lyotard overturned the perspective of the project: from the modernity of new materials it passed to the postmodernity of immateriality, by illuminating and giving place to the dematerialisation that was then emerging. The exhibition was also formally innovative: the visitors were placed before the impossible choice of a plurality of paths (from the entrance, five directions were offered) through which some sixty-seven 'sites' were distributed. The word 'site' was new in the language of the art gallery, and so was the thing it designated: a 'putting in place' of quite variable configuration, accompanied by a particular sound that the visitor received in a headset.

The exhibition was a new stage for Lyotard, another aspect of practice after commentary and film. It realised, or 'put in scene' ['*met en scène*'], an ensemble of propositions and objects, charged with the task of presenting the emergence of a new sensibility characterised by its 'refinement' and its corollary probity, 'an ability to be responsive to slight changes' (P 8). This was rendered possible by new *dispositifs* of mobile vision, such as the woven screens which 'scanned' the space-time of the exhibition of *Immaterials*. Lyotard wrote about these screens: 'Here the picture rails are replaced by mesh veils which vary from transparency to opacity, calling for several kinds of look depending on proximity . . . The positioning of these suspended semi-screens allows the visitor to choose his course semi-freely. He is not constrained, but led' (Lyotard 1984). The woven semi-screens had the quality of making their consistency and their penetrability vary (just as the white pictures of *À Blanc* varied from obscurity to the appearance of the interior frame, from the neutral planarity to the bulbous interior square), which encouraged the vision of imperceptible changes. The woven semi-screens in the exhibition and the white pictures of René Guiffrey are not without association with the criss-crossed electronic frames of *L'Autre scène*. In the latter, a woman's moving hair (which Lyotard took care to recall in 'Acinema') bursts in blocks of texture and infinite form at the points closest to the electronic support-frames, where the figurative images smash on the surface.

CINÉ-IMMATÉRIAUX (1985)

> Composed of a regular flow of fixed snapshots, cinematic movement is by nature immaterial. Narrative cinema has particularly developed dramatic movement and the fictional power capable of immaterialising all the productions of the imagination (from the invisible man to the shrinking man). Born in order to see and know movement, the scientific usage of cinema continued to explore all manner of phenomena, spatial (from the infinitely small to the infinitely large) and temporal (from extreme slow motion to extreme acceleration). Rather than the simple crude documentary, then, scientific cinema perhaps displays a curiosity which manifests an unusual space-time. But the cinema is also apprehended for itself by artists who do not limit themselves only to photographic cinema but also practise cinema which is graphic, electronic (also called video), and even holographic . . . So many determinations and possibilities proper to cinema, which constitute some 'sites' of *Immatériaux*. (Eizykman and Fihman 1985)

Forty-five sessions gathering together films and videos – narrative cinema, scientific cinema, raw documents, artists' films – and all of the themes defined in relation to the 'sites' of the exhibition, such as: All the histories, Analogical and digital hybrids, Movement of colours, Skins on skins, Representatives of representation, Flashes of light, Immaterial crises, Machines of cinema, Detours of reason, The Eye in the camera, Paths and labyrinths, Objective Moon, Dematerialisation, To see/to name/to number, Weakness and force of cinema, Dimensions, Transitions, Adventures of perception, Movement of immobilities, Grains of light.

The *Ciné-Immatériaux* was a decisive occasion for the presentation of the passage from a revolutionary state of cinema to a formative state, by a new programme of films freed from the compartmentalisations, conceptions and exclusions – both rigid and vague – which persisted in the production, circulation and programming of films, as well as in reflections on cinema.

A programme which did not separate, but rather put in relation fictional films, experimental films, documents, documentaries, scientific films and television productions. It no longer opposed genre films and auteur films, classical forms and youthful subjects; nor did it enshrine the celebrated theoretical distinction between writing and images. Rather, it set out from the assessment that most of the notions utilised: history, technique, or even constituents, operations, are reduced to a system of mono-signification; it was a question of differentiating and of widening these determinations. A good example is history, typically limited to the plot: it was developed under the category of 'All the histories' and was extended to constituents, colours, light grains, movements, immobilities and machines, and taking into account analogical, digital and hybrid technologies. Since classics such as *A Trip to the Moon* and *Man with a Movie Camera* were included, the dimension of the smile, of the comic, of laughter, which did not seem present in *Les Immatériaux*, was there in certain films of the *Ciné-Immatériaux*.

These filmic peregrinations contributed to Lyotard's specific philosophical approach to cinema, but one also should not disregard the contribution of cinema to Lyotardian thought (see Eizykman and Fihman 2000). Until the 1960s, cinematic discourses generally made reference to the philosophy of their epoch, then principally to the human sciences, with the structuralism and semiology of cinema. Until the 1950s, in France, they did not yet exclude the films of the avant-garde. In the 1970s some rare philosophical texts on cinema appeared, such as those of Stanley Cavell in the United States. These were little read in France, where a particular and sustained disinterest in the cinematographic and videographic avant-garde was manifest, with the exception of the respective milieu which practised them. In contact with them, Lyotard wrote 'Acinema' in 1973, followed by three other studies, the last in 1996.[6]

Lyotard's manner of seeing film in this first essay was to approach it neither as research, nor as the imposition of a philosophical legitimacy vis-à-vis films, nor to find a totalising typology. Rather, it was that of approaching cinema by way of its unthought: by painting, literature and political economy, and vice versa, reconsidering these as they traverse cinema. By exposing from the outset the reduction of present movements in the cinema, 'Acinema' rendered justice to the films of the avant-garde: it openly exposed the exclusions of categories, of thoughts, of visions which were, according to Lyotard, causes of confusion, of the petrification of actions and reflections, and the indices of terror.

Another aspect of Lyotard's approach to cinema was his appetence for cinematic practice as object and as *dispositif* of thought-vision, which he discovered with electronic cinema [video] in 1969. His curiosity towards this technological art was piqued, stimulated. The investigations that he pursued alone or with others ['*en équipe*'] until the 1980s included the multiply innovative international exhibition *Les Immatériaux* in 1985. This aspect, conferred by his practical sensibility, was inseparable from his reflection and distinguished his contribution to cinema.

Translated by Ashley Woodward

NOTES

1. TN: This text was first published under the title 'Aperçus sur la pratique postmoderne de Jean-François Lyotard' ['Glimpses of the Postmodern Practice of Jean-François Lyotard'] in Coblence and Enaudeau 2014.
2. *Le Travial du film* [*The Film Work*]: title of a special journal issue dedicated to 'Cinema and Psychoanalysis', Paris, January 1970.
3. TN: As a later passage makes clear, what is meant by 'electronic cinema' is what, in English, is more familiarly called 'video'.
4. TN: See Peter W. Milne's discussion of this title and its English translation at the beginning of his chapter in this volume.
5. TN: See Vlad Ionescu's chapter in this volume for a discussion of these.
6. TN: These are of course the four texts by Lyotard collected in this volume. The last text referred to is 'The Idea of a Sovereign Film', which we have preferred to date to its initial conference presentation (1995).

REFERENCES

Coblence, Françoise and Enaudeau, Michel (eds) (2014), *Lyotard et des arts*, Paris: Klincksieck.
Eizykman, Claudine and Fihman, Guy (1985), *Ciné-Immatériaux*, Paris: Centre Georges-Pompidou.
Eizykman, Claudine and Fihman, Guy (2000), 'L'Œil de Lyotard, de l'acinema au postmoderne', in *À partir de Jean-François Lyotard*, Arts 8, ed. Claude Amey and Jean-Paul Olive, Paris: L'Harmattan.
Lyotard, Jean-François (1984), *Les Immatériaux*, Press Release.

APPENDIX 2

Memorial Immemorial

In addition to the film projects outlined by Claudine Eizykman and Guy Fihman in Appendix 1, Lyotard notably planned one further film which was not produced. The synopsis of the projected film, titled *Memorial Immemorial* [*Mémorial immémorial*], dated 1986–7, may be found in the Lyotard Archive at the Bibliothèque Jacques Doucet.[1] Part of the synopsis was published in a special issue of the online journal *Appareil*, along with a brief introduction by Jean-Louis Déotte, who was involved with the project (Lyotard 2012; Déotte 2012). Déotte explains that the project originated with the plans of the Senator-Mayor of Caen, Jean-Marie Girault, to create a memorial museum for the Battle of Normandy. He wanted the memorial to be much more than a historical museum: a place for philosophical speculation and ethical reflection. Accordingly he sought the involvement of the Collège international de philosophie, of which Lyotard was a principal member, and Déotte was charged by Girault with researching the topic. His research eventually led to a philosophical thesis supervised by Lyotard and submitted to the University of Paris 8 in 1990. Girault's plans culminated in a Museum for Peace in Caen, inaugurated by President Mitterrand in 1988. Lyotard's project for a film was not funded and did not proceed further than the written plans. As Déotte notes, however, these plans can be seen as something like a first, rough draft of Lyotard's 1988 book *Heidegger and 'the jews'*, treating as they do similar themes. Moreover, as Déotte also points out, they are interesting in opening a further path in Lyotard's work in film, which remains to be reflected on and thematised (Déotte 2012). We present here the synopsis in translation.[2]

   Writer and director: Jean-François Lyotard
   52 minutes / 16 mm
   JBA Production / Jacques Bidou / april 1987

1. GENESIS OF THE PROJECT

The occasion of the film project *Memorial Immemorial* is the creation of a Memorial Museum of the Battle of Normandy in Caen on the initiative of the senator-mayor Mr. Girault.

The Collège international de philosophie (Jean-Louis Déotte, Bernard Stiegler, Jean-François Lyotard), in contact with the ministerial and regional directions of Culture and Communication, showed interest.

The themes Memory / Archive / Museum, New Technologies / Media, War / Law, are listed in the research priorities of the Collège with respect to real intervention.

The Bibliothèque publique d'information of the Centre Pompidou and the Service audio-visuel of the CNRS are interested in turn.

Several months of deliberation between the parties led to the current project of a 52-minute film.

2. SYNOPSIS OF THE FILM

2.1. Subject: The Battle of Normandy and its filmic memory.

2.2. Argument: the film will pose the following questions in relation to this subject.

2.2.1. What is a 'mnesic product'? That is, an object on which the memory fixes itself, or: an object producing a 'memory-effect'.

2.2.2. What is such a 'product' when it is obtained by the cinema, that is, by a medium which has as its vocation the 'reality effect' and the 'total work of art'?

2.2.3. What is a mnesic film when the past fixed on it is:

- collective (community / singularity)
- eminent (the Battle of Normandy was an eminent event which punctuated the Second World War)
- overwhelming (this war is a punctuation in a crisis which shook Europe and at least all the 'developed' countries).

2.3. Problematic: three interlinked problems.

2.3.1. What is it to remember?

There are at least three memories: memorial, objective, subjective.

And there is forgetting, in the strong sense, implicated in all recollection.

2.3.2. What is a modern battle?

A point or line of confrontation of (very diverse) fluxes of energy which have been in contradiction with each other for a long time (a global crisis since the end of the 1920s).

The result of this violent composition of forces is the 'new' state of societies (the 'we'). But are there not some energies which were not involved in the confrontation and which escape the result? Which are forgotten?

2.3.3. What is a mnesic film?

- The simulacra of a past (the representation of Battle).
- But the proper aim of the filmic narrative simulation is to produce the 'reality effect'.
- Doesn't the 'reality effect' delay or detain the 'memory effect'? Narrative film creates too much presence. What the event makes absent is forgotten.

2.4. Method: To articulate the three paradoxes around the axis presence / forgetting, and to inscribe them in all the registers of film:

2.4.1. Topic

Presence: the (military) front is the line of confrontation of energies and the mirror of their face-off. The film on screen is the mirror where the community identifies itself as the result of the confrontation.

Forgetting: the (civil, 'bureaucratic') 'rear' is the non-front, the insolent [*effronté*], outside the mirror and therefore outside the film. Presence and (total) war necessitate the suppression of all 'rear'. The administration of the 'rear' is its *Vernichtung* (annihilation, the SS term for extermination) and its *Verneinung* (denegation, the Freudian term for originary repression): the extermination is not known as such. (See Kafka, *The Castle*.)

What kind of film can show this hiddenness?

2.4.2. (Iconological) Thematic

Presence: The vehicles (energy as movement) and the (static) lodgings of the conflict: armoured cars, tanks, ships, aeroplanes, missiles; bunkers, walls, trenches – all under the regime of the 'move forward', the 'launch'. Blazons.

Forgetting: vehicles and lodgings of effacement: gassing trucks, train convoys, barracks, gas chambers, desks – all under the regime of 'withdrawal' 'throw away',[3] 'to put to rest', 'disappear'. Black holes.

2.4.3. Rhythmic

Presence: speed (with the slowness in the speed: the approach of the conflict. The fleets coming together in the Channel), explosion, action.

Forgetting: slowness (with the speed in the slowness: *bremze laufschritt*, in *Shoah* pages 132 and 135: rushing towards the chambers), implosion, thoughtfulness.

2.5. Stakes

– to show that at the 'rear' of the stakes of the War and the Battle, what is at stake is to annihilate 'the rear' as slowness, thoughtfulness, 'lost' time.

– the main traits of the Judaic tradition: alliance, promise, incredulity, 'passibility' to the event, reading and perlaboration of the event, anamnesis, desert as absence of frontier (front), itinerancy as absence of strategy – it's this element of its own tradition of life and thought that the Final Solution wanted to make forgotten in Europe. *Triumph of the Will.*

– Nazism was defeated on the front of war; it won on the non-front of the 'rear'. All the values cited (in the Judaic tradition, as paradigms of the 'rear') were destroyed in the post-war society, which is ours (cf. Syberberg, *Hitler: A Film from Germany*). Triumph of the values of will, auto-affirmation, techno-scientific control, 'useful' memory.

– The success of cinema participates in this triumph. The film as medium makes 'forget'; it memorises the useful (information and utilisable feelings). Is it possible to make a film medium which shows this forgetting, this denegation?

2.6. Genre

– Say: critique. Film of montage: neither fiction (pleasure), nor documentary (information), nor 'historical film' (pedagogy).

– To subordinate the visual and sonic documents to the clarification of problems (cf. 2.3.). Neither 'chatty' nor 'hermetic' (cf. 2.7.).

Principle: some spectators (of very diverse kinds) cannot discern that an ensemble of (current) questions hang on the signification of the Battle of Normandy and on the modalities of its memory (cf. 2.3., 2.4.). The accent placed on the 'Forgetting' must open the field of this interrogation. Each must be turned to its reflection.

2.7. Audience

General public, international.

The possibility of distribution by satellite and/or cable is to be pursued. The population of the regions of Normandy and Brittany will be key.

The public of England, Germany, Canada, the US, etc. Old soldiers of the engaged forces (Germany, Canada, France, GB, USA, etc.).

Scholars, students, teachers: Europe and North America.

Historians, archivists and documenters, cinema professionals, politicians.

3. OUTLINE OF THE SCENE ORGANISATION [DÉCOUPAGE]

Five moments, on average ten minutes each.

3.1. The memorial constructs the figure of heroism (heroism of the will). In the Battle, the energies of conflict, rising up and concluding. The epic genre, the rhetoric of the eulogy imposes the auto-identification of a community with itself, by mobilising all the passions (including for the 'good death').

3.2. The cinema as equivalent of the Battle: it mobilises genres and quantities in view of 'realising' a total work of art. It is a mirror designed to focus auto-identification and autolegitimation. The spectator leaves 'strengthened'.

3.3. Second mode of memory: scientific history. The Battle taken as object of knowledge (and no longer of identification): the economic, social and political 'causes' and 'effects'. The mere chances (weather on the Channel at dawn on the 6th of June).

3.4. The third memory: the 'slice of life', the minor history, the epic non-hero: tragi-comic, tragic. The drama of everyday life.

3.5. The denial, the forgetting, the immemorial: the 'rear' as black hole. Meditative. Here: the extermination hidden beneath the conflict.

4. PRINCIPLE OF THE RHYTHM

4.1. In the course of the 52 minutes, to go from the major mode towards the minor mode.

4.2. Analogous sound: to go from the *Heroica*, or *Ninth Symphony* (Beethoven), or *Hymnen* (Stockhausen) to the *Hatikva* (the song that the Czech Jews sang while entering the gas chambers). From sacrificial eloquence to the mutism of the 'disaster' (obviously with some counter-points and some rests: moment 2, for example).

4.3. Analogous image-movement: to go from the dense-rapid to the slow-sparse (but also with some differences: moment 3 must be 'derhythmed' because its aim is explicative; moment 2 will be 'contra rhythm' according to its reflexive-critical aim).

4.4. Analogous iconology: to go from the conveyance of the conflict of the All with itself to the conveyance of the administration of the Nothing (cf. 2.4.2.).

4.5. Analogous style: to go from the immense memory-medium (Abel Gance's *Napoléon*) to the impossible memory-medium (Lanzmann's *Shoah*).

4.6. Analogous tone of voice: from eloquent to thoughtful.

4.7. The major rhythms must not repeat one another, but shift (syncopations, 'dead' time, etc.), in order to give rhythm to the whole.

5. PRODUCTION

5.1. Writer and director: Jean-François Lyotard

Assistants:

I.   Jean-Louis Déotte (sociopolitics, iconography)
II. Sylvie Dreyfus (filmic documentation)
III. Michel Enaudeau (coordination, written documentation)
VI. Bernard Stiegler (techno-scientific documentation)

A council of historians: Second World War, contemporary economies and societies, history of the Third Reich.

5.2. Plan of work

Start of archival research: July to December 1987
Envisioning and drawing up of definitive text: December 1987
Filming and editing: January – March 1988
Mixing: April 1988

Translated by Ashley Woodward

NOTES

1. The reference in the archive index is: JFL 447. – « Memorial Immemorial » (synopsis), 1986–1987, ms autogr. et dactyl, 148ff.
2. These notes were composed by Jean-Louis Déotte from Jean-François Lyotard's manuscript notes. Déotte writes: 'This text was published once in the proceedings of a Franco-German philosophical colloquium which took place at Wolfenbüttel in the Herzog August Library from 24–29 October 1987. There is no date on the edition, but I am inclined to think 1988. I certify the text as I have re-transcribed it from Lyotard's manuscript and I presented it as is during the colloquium.
   The texts of this colloquium were collected by Ulrich Johannes Schneider of the Institut für Philosophie de Berlin and distributed by the Collège international de philosophie in Paris, in 100 copies' (note in Lyotard 2012).
3. In English in the original.

REFERENCES

Déotte, Jean-Louis (2012), 'Présentation du project de film de Jean-François Lyotard: *Le Memorial immemorial* (1987)', *Appareil* 10 (2012), 'Lyotard et la surface d'inscription numérique' [Lyotard and the Surface of Digital Inscription], https://appareil.revues.org/1501 (accessed 30 March 2017).
Lyotard, Jean-François (2012), 'Memorial immemorial', *Appareil* 10.

APPENDIX 3

Filmography

Written and directed by Jean-François Lyotard:

- With Dominique Avron, Claudine Eizykman and Guy Fihman, *L'Autre scène* (1969 (silent version)/1972) 6 mins.
- *Mao Gillette* (1974) 3 mins.
- *Tribune sans tribun* (1978) 15 mins.
- *À blanc* (1982) 15 mins – on René Guiffrey.

Planned but not produced:

- *Mémorial immémorial* (1987)

Featuring Lyotard:

- Gianfranco Baruchello (dir.), *A partire dal Dolce* (1979-80) 22mins /143 mins.
- David Carr-Brown (dir.), *Premier tournage* (1982) 31 mins – with Jacques Monory.
- David Carr-Brown (dir.), *Peintres cinéastes* (1982) 32 mins – with Jacques Monory.
- Gérard Courant (dir.), *Le portrait de Jean-François Lyotard* (*Cinématon* #465) (1985) 4 mins.
- Paule Zajdermann (dir.), *Octave au pays des Immatériaux* (1985) 36 mins.
- Janine Quint (dir.), *Lyotard / signature* (no date – 1990s) 30 mins.

APPENDIX 4

Bibliography

LYOTARD ON FILM

Lyotard, Jean-François, 'L'acinema', in *Des dispositifs pulsionnels*, Paris: Union Générale, 1973. Reprinted in *Des dispositifs pulsionnels*, Paris: Galilée, 1994. English translation: 'Acinema', trans. Paisley Livingston, *Wide Angle* 2:3 (1978), pp. 53–9. Reprinted in *The Lyotard Reader*, ed. Andrew Benjamin, London: Blackwell, 1989. Modified by Peter W. Milne and Ashley Woodward, this volume.

Lyotard, Jean-François, 'Notes sur la fonction critique de l'oeuvre', in *Dérive à partir de Marx et Freud*, Paris: Union Générale, 1973. English translation: 'Notes on the Critical Function of the Work of Art', trans. Susan Hanson, in *Driftworks*, ed. Roger McKeon, New York: Semiotext(e), 1984.

Lyotard, Jean-François, 'The Unconscious as Mise-en-scène', trans. Joseph Maier, in *Performance in Postmodern Culture*, ed. Michel Benamou and Charles Caramello, Milwaukee: Center for Twentieth Century Studies, University of Wisconsin-Milwaukee, 1977.

Lyotard, Jean-François, 'Tribune sans tribun', *Education 2000*, 1978. English translation: 'A Podium without a Podium: Television according to J.-F. Lyotard', in *Political Writings*, trans. Bill Readings and Kevin Paul Geiman, Minneapolis: University of Minnesota Press, 1993.

Lyotard, Jean-François, 'Deux métamorphoses du séduisant au cinéma', in *La séduction*, ed. Maurice Olender and Jacques Sojcher, Paris: Aubier, 1980. English translation: 'Two Metamorphoses of the Seductive in Cinema', trans. Peter W. Milne and Ashley Woodward, this volume.

Lyotard, Jean-François, 'Idée d'un film souverain', in *Misère de la philosophie*, Paris: Galilée, 2000, pp. 209–21. English translation: 'The Idea of a Sovereign Film', trans. Peter W. Milne and Ashley Woodward, this volume.

Lyotard, Jean-François and Pomarède, Alain, 'Jean-François Lyotard/Entretien', *Art Présent* 8 (1979).

WRITINGS ON LYOTARD AND FILM

Bertetto, Paolo, 'Il figurale e il cinema', *Aut Aut* 338 (2008). Special issue, 'L'acinema di Lyotard', ed. Antonio Costa and Raoul Kirchmayr.
Bignell, Jonathan, *Postmodern Media Culture*, Edinburgh: Edinburgh University Press, 2000.
Cantone, Damiano, 'Un accordo nel disaccordo. Proposta per un confronto tra le estetiche di Deleuze e Lyotard', *Aut Aut* 338 (2008).
Chateau, Dominique, 'Il figurale e l'allucinazione filmica', *Aut Aut* 338 (2008).
Costa, Antonio, 'Da 'L'autre scène' a 'L'acinéma': lavoro del film e teoria del cinema', *Aut Aut* 338 (2008).
Déotte, Jean-Louis, *L'Époque des appareils*, Paris: Lignes-Léo Scheer, 2004.
Déotte, Jean-Louis, 'L'acinéma de J.-F. Lyotard', *Appareil* 6 (2010), https://appareil.revues.org/973 (accessed 30 March 2017).
Durafour, Jean-Michel, *Jean-François Lyotard: questions au cinéma. Ce que le cinéma se figure*, Paris: PUF, 2009.
Eizykman, Claudine, *La Jouissance-cinéma*, Paris: Union Générale d'Éditions, 1975.
Eizykman, Claudine and Fihman, Guy, 'L'Œil de Lyotard: De l'acinéma au postmoderne', in *À partir de Jean-François Lyotard*, ed. Claude Amey and Jean-Paul Olive, Paris: L'Harmattan, 2000.
Eizykman, Claudine and Fihman, Guy, 'Aperçus sur la pratique postmodern de Jean-François Lyotard', in *Lyotard et des arts*, ed. Françoise Coblence and Michel Enaudeau, Paris: Klincksieck, 2014.
Eleftheriotis, Dimitris, *Cinematic Journeys: Film and Movement*, Edinburgh: Edinburgh University Press, 2010.
Fornara, Paola, 'L'approdo al 'cinématograph' dell'ultimo Lyotard', *Materiali di Estetica* 1 (2014), pp. 110–18.
French, Sarah, '"If they don't see happiness in the picture at least they'll see the black": Chris Marker's *Sans Soleil* and the Lyotardian Sublime', *Image & Narrative* 11:1 (2010), pp. 64–81.
Geller, Theresa L., '"The Film-Work Does Not Think": Refiguring Fantasy for Feminist Film Theory', in *Gender After Lyotard*, ed. M. Grebowicz, Albany: SUNY Press, 2007.
Grundmann, Ron, 'Between Adorno and Lyotard: Michael Haneke's Aesthetic of Fragmentation', in *A Companion to Michael Haneke*, Chichester: Blackwell, 2010.

Hainge, Greg (2007), 'Le Corps concret: Of Bodily and Filmic Material Excess in Philippe *Grandrieux's* Cinema', *Australian Journal of French Studies* 44:2, pp. 153–71.

Hansson, Karl, 'Screening the Figural in Film and New Art Media', *Nordic Journal of Aesthetics* 16:29–30 (2004), pp. 22–9.

James, David E., *Allegories of Cinema: American Film in the Sixties*, Princeton: Princeton University Press, 1989.

Jones, Graham, '"Look how I forget you, look how I have forgotten you!": *Hiroshima Mon Amour* and the Lyotardian Sublime', in *Sensorium: Aesthetics, Art, Life*, ed. Barbara Bolt, Felicity Colman, Graham Jones and Ashley Woodward, Newcastle: Cambridge Scholars Publishing, 2007.

Jones, Graham, *Lyotard Reframed*, London and New York: I.B. Tauris, 2013.

Kirchmayr, Raoul, 'Estetica pulsionale. Merleau-Ponty con Lyotard', *Aut Aut* 338 (2008).

Knox, Simone, 'Eye Candy for the Blind: Re-introducing Lyotard's Acinema into Discourses on Excess, Motion, and Spectacle in Contemporary Hollywood', *New Review of Film and Television Studies* 11:3 (2013), pp. 1–16.

Krauss, Rosalind E., *The Optical Unconscious*, Cambridge, MA: MIT Press, 1994.

MacCormack, Patricia, *Cinesexuality*, London and New York: Routledge, 2008.

Magli, Patrizia, 'I paradossi della materia tra "presenza" e "immaterialità"', *Aut Aut* 338 (2008).

Mee, Sharon Jane, 'A Terrifying Spectatorship: Jean-François Lyotard's Dispositif and the Expenditure of Intensities in Steven Kastrissios's *The Horseman*', *Philament* 21 (2016), pp. 19–44.

Metz, Christian, *The Imaginary Signifier: Psychoanalysis and Cinema*, Indiana University Press, Bloomington, 1982.

Migliore, Tiziana, '"Questo è il mio corpo." Operatività del segno tra Jean-François Lyotard e Louis Marin', *Aut Aut* 338 (2008).

Murray, Timothy, *Like a Film: Ideological Fantasy on Screen, Camera and Canvas*, London: Routledge, 1993.

Obodiac, Erin, 'Autoaffection and Lyotard's Cinematic Sublime', in *Traversals of Affect: On Jean-François Lyotard*, ed. Julie Gaillard, Claire Nouvet and Mark Stoholski, London and New York: Bloomsbury, 2016.

Olivier, Bert, 'Extra-ordinary Cinema', *South African Journal of Art History* 24 (2009), pp. 20–33.

Parente, André and Victa de Carvahlo, 'Cinema as *dispositif*: Between Cinema and Contemporary Art', *Cinémas: revue d'études cinématographiques / Cinémas: Journal of Film Studies* 19:1 (2008), pp. 37–55.

Rodowick, D. N., *The Difficulty of Difference: Psychoanalysis, Sexual Difference and Film Theory*, New York and London: Routledge, 1991.

Rodowick, D. N., *Reading the Figural, or, Philosophy After the New Media*, Durham NC: Duke University Press, 2001.

Rose, Jacqueline, 'The Cinematic Apparatus – Problems in Current Theory', in *Sexuality in the Field of Vision*, London and New York: Verso, 1986.

Sarikartal, Eminé, 'Discours du figural', *Appareil* 6 (2010), https://appareil.revues.org/355 (accessed 30 March 2017).

Trahair, Lisa, 'Figural Vision: Freud, Lyotard, and Early Cinematic Comedy', *Screen* 46:2 (2005), pp. 175–94.

Trahair, Lisa, *The Comedy of Philosophy: Sense and Nonsense in Early Cinematic Slapstick*, Albany: SUNY Press, 2008.

Trahair, Lisa, 'Jean-François Lyotard', in *Film, Theory and Philosophy: The Key Thinkers*, ed. Felicity Colman, Chesham: Acumen, 2009.

Turim, Maureen, 'The Place of Visual Illusions', in *The Cinematic Apparatus*, ed. Teresa De Lauretis and Stephen Heath, London: Macmillan, 1979.

Turim, Maureen, 'Desire in Art and Politics: The Theories of Jean-François Lyotard', *Camera Obscura* 4 (1984), pp. 3–12.

Woodward, Ashley, 'A Sacrificial Economy of the Image: Lyotard on Cinema', *Angelaki: Journal of the Theoretical Humanities* 19:4 (2014), pp. 141–54. Reprinted in *Cinema and Sacrifice*, ed. Costica Bradatan and Camil Constantin Ungureanu, London and New York: Routledge, 2015.

Notes on Contributors

Kiff Bamford is Senior Lecturer in the School of Art, Architecture and Design, Leeds Beckett University. He is preoccupied with the writings of French philosopher Jean-François Lyotard and the history and documentation of Performance Art. The issue of writing about, or in response to, art underpins both these concerns. He is author of *Lyotard and the figural in Performance, Art and Writing* (Bloomsbury, 2012), and *Jean-François Lyotard: A Critical Life* (Reaktion, 2017).

Keith Crome is Principal Lecturer in Philosophy, Manchester Metropolitan University. He is author of *Lyotard and Greek Thought: Sophistry* (Palgrave Macmillan, 2004), and co-author and co-editor, with James Williams, of *The Lyotard Reader and Guide* (Edinburgh University Press, 2006). He researches contemporary French philosophy, in particular work related to Lyotard and Foucault; phenomenology, and in particular Merleau-Ponty; and European political philosophy from the nineteenth and twentieth centuries.

Jean-Michel Durafour is Maître de conferences in Cinema and Visual Studies, University Paris-Est. He previously taught at the Université Lille 3 Charles-de-Gaulle and the École normale supérieure. He is author of *Jean-François Lyotard: questions au cinema* (PUF, 2009), as well as a number of other books, including studies of Brian de Palma and Howard Hawks.

Claudine Eizykman is Professor Emeritus of Cinema at the University of Paris 8, where she is a member of the EA Aesthetics, Sciences and Technologies of Cinema. She is a filmmaker, and president of the film co-op Cinédoc Paris.

Guy Fihman is Professor Emeritus of Cinema at the University of Paris 8, where he is a member of the EA Aesthetics, Sciences and Technologies of Cinema. He is a filmmaker, and a member of the film co-op Cinédoc Paris.

Julie Gaillard is Fellow at the Berlin Institute for Cultural Inquiry. She was an organiser of the conference *Traversals of Affect: On Jean-François Lyotard* at Emory in 2013, and an editor of the book arising from it (Bloomsbury, 2016). Her areas of research interest include literature and philosophy; psychoanalytic theory; the construction of thought and the notion of episteme.

Jon Hackett is Programme Director of Film and Screen Media, St Mary's University. He is currently writing a monograph for Bloomsbury, *Scary Monsters: Masculinity, Monstrosity and Popular Music Culture*, with Dr Mark Duffett of the University of Chester. He has published on popular music, film-philosophy and early cinema, as well as on the American novelist Thomas Pynchon.

Vlad Ionescu is a researcher in the Faculty of Architecture and Arts at Hasselt University. He is one of the principal translators of the six-volume edition of Lyotard's *Collected Writings on Contemporary Art and Artists* (Leuven University Press, 2009–13). His work has been published in *Deleuze Studies, Cultural Politics, The Journal of Art Historiography, ARS, Art History Supplement* and various edited volumes.

Graham Jones is Lecturer in Creative Writing, Literary Studies and Media and Communications at Federation University. He is the author of *Lyotard Reframed* (I.B. Tauris, 2013), and co-editor of *Deleuze's Philosophical Lineage* (Edinburgh University Press, 2009) and *Sensorium: Aesthetics, Art, Life* (Cambridge Scholars, 2007). He was the founding convenor of the Australasian Society for Continental Philosophy. His research focuses on French poststructuralist philosophy, popular culture, and film.

Peter W. Milne is Associate Professor of Aesthetics, Seoul National University. He has published numerous articles on Lyotard and on contemporary European philosophy, and is an editor and one of the principal translators of the six-volume edition of Lyotard's *Collected Writings on Contemporary Art and Artists* (Leuven University Press, 2009–13). He is also an editor of the 2013 special edition of *Cultural Politics* dedicated to Lyotard's aesthetics, *Rewriting Lyotard: Figuration, Presentation, Resistance*.

Lisa Trahair is Senior Lecturer in Film Studies at the University of New South Wales. She is author of *The Comedy of Philosophy: Sense and Nonsense in Early Cinematic Slapstick* (SUNY, 2007) and is currently working on a monograph entitled *Understanding Cinematic Thinking* (Edinburgh University Press) with Gregory Flaxman and Robert Sinnerbrink. She is co-editor of special issues of *Angelaki: Journal for the Theoretical Humanities, Screening the Past* and *SubStance* devoted to belief in cinema and issues pertaining to cinematic thinking.

Susana Viegas is an FCT postdoctoral research fellow at the Ifilnova FCSH – Universidade Nova de Lisboa and Deakin University. She is developing a project on moving images, cinematic ethics and Deleuze's philosophy of time. She is co-editor of *Cinema: Journal of Philosophy and the Moving Image* (cjpmi.ifilnova. pt) and *Aniki: Portuguese Journal of the Moving Image* (aim.org.pt/aniki).

James Williams is Honorary Professor of Philosophy at the Alfred Deakin Institute for Citizenship and Globalisation, Deakin University. He has published widely on contemporary continental philosophy, particularly Deleuze and Lyotard. His many books include *Lyotard: Towards a Postmodern Philosophy* (Polity, 1998), *Lyotard and the Political* (Routledge, 2000), and *Gilles Deleuze's* Difference and Repetition*: A Critical Introduction and Guide* (Edinburgh University Press, 2nd edn, 2013). His latest book is *A Process Philosophy of Signs* (Edinburgh University Press, 2016).

Ashley Woodward is Lecturer in Philosophy at the University of Dundee. He is the author of *Nihilism in Postmodernity: Lyotard, Baudrillard, Vattimo* (Davies group, 2010), *Understanding Nietzscheanism* (Acumen, 2011), and *Lyotard and the Inhuman Condition: Reflections on Nihilism, Information, and Art* (Edinburgh University Press, 2016). He is an editor of *Parrhesia: A Journal of Critical Philosophy* and of the translation series *Groundworks* (Rowman & Littlefield International).

Index

À Blanc, 20, 138, 147n2, 202–3, 204
Abramović, Marina, 152–4, 157, 161n
affect(s), 6, 8, 12, 36, 38, 47, 49, 75, 84, 99, 110, 111, 112, 113, 144, 147, 155, 159, 164, 170, 172, 174, 175, 177n, 183, 184, 185, 187, 188–9
Anna O, 184, 187, 188, 189
Apocalypse Now, 7, 14, 23, 55, 58–60, 89, 95, 97–9, 108, 110, 127
Artist is Present, The, 152–4, 156, 157, 158
Autre scène, L', 19, 198–200, 204
Avildsen, John G., 6
Avron, Dominique, 19, 42n, 125, 198, 199

Baruchello, Gianfranco, 6, 14, 41, 148n, 201–2
Bataille, Georges, 7, 58–9, 62, 69, 97–8, 108, 111, 113, 114
Baudry, Jean-Louis, 124–5
Bazin, André, 14, 17, 63, 66, 111, 113, 115n

Bosetti, Roméo, 180–92
Brecht, Bertolt, 60, 96–7, 109, 114n
Breuer, Joseph, 183–91, 192n

Carr-Brown, David, 140
Cassavetes, John, 27–8
Cavell, Stanley, 11, 205
Coppola, Francis Ford, 7, 14, 23, 55, 58, 59, 60, 87, 89, 95, 108

Dame vraiment bien, Une, 189–90
Deleuze, Gilles, 3, 6, 8, 10, 11, 13, 15, 16, 16n, 17, 23–4, 29n, 63, 66, 112, 113, 151, 155, 156
Déotte, Jean-Louis, 29n, 207, 208, 213, 213n
Derrida, Jacques, 157, 159, 162n
Diderot, Denis, 140–2, 144, 146, 147n
Differend, 10, 29n, 93, 114
Dispositif, 12, 39, 40, 42, 55, 77, 79, 82, 86n, 124–6, 152, 174, 175, 201, 202, 204, 206

Durafour, Jean-Michel, 3, 8, 10, 86n, 112, 114n, 125
Duras, Marguerite, 69

Eggeling, Viking, 6, 14, 21, 41, 65
Eizykman, Claudine, 3, 4, 7, 19, 20, 42n, 125, 198, 199, 201, 207

Faces, 27–8
figural, 8, 10, 11, 17, 18, 20, 21, 22, 24, 26, 28, 29n, 119, 120, 123, 125, 126, 129, 130, 131, 134, 137, 143, 148n, 156, 157, 172, 177, 178n, 197
Fihman, Guy, 3, 4, 7, 19, 20, 42n, 125, 198, 199, 200, 201, 203, 207
Focillon, Henri, 25
Freud, Sigmund, 6, 19, 26, 34, 36, 39, 44–53, 67–8, 74, 75, 76, 79, 83, 84, 121–2, 124, 140, 154–6, 163, 166, 171–4, 182–6, 188–9, 191, 192n, 198

Ghost Dance, 157–8
Gorgias, 55–6, 59, 87, 88, 90, 92, 93, 96, 107
Guiffrey, René, 20, 136, 137, 138–9, 147, 147n, 202–3, 204

Hitler: A Film from Germany, 23, 61, 95, 96, 97, 109, 210
Homme aimanté, L', 181–3, 189
Hyperrealism, 14, 27, 58–9, 97–9, 106–10, 111

Immatériaux, Les, 22, 203–6
Inception, 119, 127–31, 134

Je t'aime, je t'aime, 5–6, 105–6
Joe, 6, 37, 112, 127
jouissance, 13, 15, 34–6, 40–2, 80–2, 156, 168, 176, 181

Kant, Immanuel, 6, 7, 12, 66–7, 99, 112, 138, 140, 161n
Klossowski, Pierre, 35, 40–1, 79, 181
Kubelka, Peter, 203

Lacan, Jacques, 39, 46, 73–85, 121–3, 163, 166–9, 171–3, 176, 178n
Lost Highway, 167–9, 174, 176–7
Lynch, David, 163–77, 177n, 178n

McGowan, Todd, 166–9, 171, 175
McMullen, Ken, 157–8
Mao Gillette, 19, 199–200
Marks, Laura, 151
Marx, Karl, 6, 100, 140
Matter, 8, 25–8, 29n, 99–100, 137, 145
Méliès, Georges, 21, 122
Memorial, Immemorial, 8, 207
Merleau-Ponty, Maurice, 7, 17, 20, 21, 24, 68, 133
Metamorphosis of Mr Samsa, The, 119, 131–4
Metz, Christian, 36, 125
Miller, Jacques-Alain, 121–4

Monory, Jacques, 14, 20, 58, 136, 137, 139–40, 147, 202
Mulvey, Laura, 123

neo-realism, 62–70, 111–13
Nietzsche, Friedrich, 6, 7, 46, 52, 53, 91, 155, 170
Night of the Hunter, The, 69
nihilism, 15, 33–4, 91–3, 99, 100, 170–1

Ozu, Yasujirō, 15, 23, 62, 63, 64, 111, 112

Plato, 25, 55, 56, 57, 87, 88, 91, 93, 94, 124, 203

Rancière, Jacques, 10, 12
real, the, 8, 28, 38, 68–70, 78, 104, 108, 111–14, 167–9, 171, 172
Région centrale, La, 6, 15, 51–4, 85, 155, 185–7
Resnais, Alain, 5, 105
Richter, Hans, 6, 14, 21, 41, 65

Schrader, Paul, 66–7, 112
Snow, Michael, 6, 15, 22, 51–4, 65, 85, 155, 185–6, 191, 203
stasis/stases, 12, 15, 66–7, 112–13
Stewart, Mark Allyn, 165–6, 170–1
Strauss, Richard, 43–4, 48, 53
suture, 120–4, 129
Syberberg, Hans-Jürgen, 7, 23, 55, 60–1, 87, 89, 95–7, 109, 110, 210

Tic, Le, 190
Tribune sans tribun, 19, 102–4, 201

Warhol, Andy, 21, 58, 59, 65, 98, 153
Welles, Orson, 15, 23, 63, 64, 111–12, 139
Wittgenstein, Ludwig, 6, 7, 10, 87, 88, 92

Žižek, Slavoj, 13, 123, 166–9, 171, 175, 176